W9-BJD-750

The MacArthur New Testament Commentary

1 Timothy

John MacArthur, Jr.

Moody Press/Chicago

Scripture quotations marked (KJV) are taken from the King James Version.

ISBN: 0-8024-0756-0

9 10

Printed in the United States of America

To Jim Rickard, my loyal friend,
who always finds a way to invade
the routines of life with adventure.
Thanks for including me.

New Testament Commentary Series by Dr. John F. MacArthur, Jr.

Matthew 1-7
Matthew 8-15
Matthew 16-23
Matthew 24-28
Acts 1-12
Acts 13-28
Romans 1-8
Romans 9-16
First Corinthians
Galatians
Ephesians
Colossians and Philemon
First Timothy
Second Timothy
Titus
Hebrews
James
Revelation 1-11

Contents

Preface

It continues to be a rewarding divine communion for me to preach expositionally through the New Testament. My goal is always to have deep fellowship with the Lord in the understanding of His Word and out of that experience to explain to His people what a passage means. In the words of Nehemiah 8:8, I strive "to give the sense" of it so they may truly hear God speak and, in so doing, may respond to Him.

Obviously, God's people need to understand Him, which demands knowing His Word of truth (2 Tim. 2:15) and allowing that Word to dwell in us richly (Col. 3:16). The dominant thrust of my ministry, therefore, is to help make God's living Word alive to His people. It is a refreshing adventure.

This New Testament commentary series reflects this objective of explaining and applying Scripture. Some commentaries are primarily linguistic, others are mostly theological, and some are mainly homiletical. This one is basically explanatory, or expository. It is not linguistically technical, but deals with linguistics when this seems helpful to proper interpretation. It is not theologically expansive, but focuses on the major doctrines in each text and on how they relate to the whole of Scripture. It is not primarily homiletical, though each unit of thought is generally treated as one chapter, with a clear outline and logical flow of thought. Most truths are illustrated and applied with other Scripture. After establishing the context of a passage, I have tried to follow closely the writer's development and reasoning.

My prayer is that each reader will fully understand what the Holy Spirit is saying through this part of His Word, so that His revelation may lodge in the minds of believers and bring greater obedience and faithfulness—to the glory of our great God.

Introduction to the Pastoral Epistles

First Timothy, along with 2 Timothy and Titus, belongs to the group of Paul's writings known as the Pastoral Epistles. They are so named because they were addressed to two of Paul's dear sons in the faith, Timothy and Titus, who had pastoral duties. Timothy was in charge of the church at Ephesus, and Titus of those on the island of Crete. Along with Philemon, they are the only letters of Paul addressed to an individual.

The Pastoral Epistles yield valuable insights into the heart of the beloved apostle. They show a different side of him than do his other epistles, revealing his personal relationships with his intimate friends and associates. As the last of his letters to be written, they alone inform us of the later years of his ministry, following his release from his first Roman imprisonment recorded in Acts. They carry his life through to its triumphant conclusion, which he declares in 2 Timothy 4:7: "I have fought the good fight, I have finished the course, I have kept the faith."

The Pastoral Epistles are also important because of the wealth of information they contain concerning practical matters of church life and organization. In fact, Paul states that his purpose in writing 1 Timothy was that Timothy "may know how one ought to conduct himself in the household of God, which is the church of the living God, the pillar and support of the truth" (1 Tim. 3:15). Public worship, the selection and qualifications of church leaders, the pastor's personal life and public ministry, how to confront sin in the church, the role of women, the care of widows, and how to handle money are among the matters discussed. Besides the wealth of practical information they contain, the Pastoral Epistles, as will be discussed below, also teach important doctrinal truths about the Scriptures, salvation, and the Savior.

AUTHORSHIP

Until the rise of destructive higher criticism in the nineteenth century, the Pauline authorship of the Pastoral Epistles was not questioned in the church (except by obvious heretics such as Marcion). In fact, the testimony from the early church that Paul wrote the Pastoral Epistles is as strong as that for any of his inspired writings, except for Romans and 1 Corinthians. There are references to them in the writings of several second-century church fathers, including Ignatius, Polycarp, and Clement of Rome. The Muratorian Canon, a list of canonical books from the late second century, includes them. In the third century, such writers as Origen, Clement of Alexandria, and Tertullian quote passages from these epistles and attribute them to Paul. Finally, the church historian Eusebius, writing early in the fourth century, includes the Pastoral Epistles with the genuine Pauline Epistles. (For a detailed listing of the historical evidence for the Pastoral Epistles' genuineness, see William Hendricksen, *New Testament Commentary: Exposition of the Pastoral Epistles* [Grand Rapids: Baker, 1981], 29–33; Homer A. Kent, Jr., *The Pastoral Epistles*, rev. ed. [Winona Lake, Ind.: BMH, 1982], 24–33.)

In spite of the clear testimony of the epistles themselves (cf. 1 Tim. 1:1; 2 Tim. 1:1; Titus 1:1) and the evidence from the early church, many modern critical scholars deny that Paul wrote the Pastoral Epistles. Instead, they propose that a devoted follower of Paul composed them in the second century, possibly using some genuine fragments of Paul's writings. As proof they offer five lines of evidence.

First, they argue that the historical references in the Pastoral Epistles cannot be fitted into the chronology of Paul's life given in Acts. That is true, and it is acknowledged by those who defend Pauline authorship. However, for it to be a valid argument against the genuineness of the Pastoral Epistles, critics would have to prove that Paul was never released from the imprisonment in Rome recorded at the end of Acts. Since Acts does not record Paul's execution, that is obviously an argument from silence. The view that Paul was released from his first Roman imprisonment finds support from the rest of the New Testament and from tradition.

The narrative of Acts makes clear that there was no valid charge brought against Paul. Both the Roman Proconsul Festus (Acts 25:14–21) and Herod Agrippa (Acts 26:32) acknowledged that fact. In light of that "it is a fair assumption that the normal course of Roman justice would have resulted in his release" (Donald Guthrie, *New Testament Introduction* [Downers Grove, Ill.: InterVarsity, 1990], 623). In the epistles that he wrote during his first imprisonment, Paul expressed his confident hope that he would be released (Phil. 1:19, 25–26; 2:24; Philem. 22). That is in sharp contrast to his expectation of imminent execution in 2 Timothy 4:6. Further, many in the early church believed that Paul visited Spain (cf. Rom. 15:28). For example, Clement of Rome, writing to the Corinthians about thirty years after the apostle's death, notes that "after preaching both in the east and in the west, [Paul] gained the illustrious reputation due to his faith, having taught righteousness to the whole world, and came to the extreme limit of the west, and suffered martyrdom under the prefects" (*The First Epistle of Clement to the Corinthians* V, vol. 1 of *The Ante-Nicene Fathers* [reprint; Grand Rapids: Eerdmans, 1973], 6). The "extreme limit of the west" was not Rome, the center of the empire, but its western frontier in Spain (cf. Kent, *Pastoral Epistles*, 45–46). Such a visit would have been impossible had Paul not been released.

Following his release, Paul ministered for a few years before being rearrested (probably in connection with the outbreak of Nero's persecution) and eventually executed. It was during this period of freedom between his two Roman imprisonments that the events mentioned in the Pastoral Epistles took place.

Second, critics charge that the heresy mentioned in these letters was the full-blown Gnosticism of the second century. Though there are similarities between the heresy in view in the Pastoral Epistles and Gnosticism, there are also important differences. Unlike the second-century Gnostics, the false teachers in the Pastoral Epistles were still within the church. And unlike second-century Gnosticism, the heresy they taught contained Jewish elements (1 Tim. 1:7; Titus 1:10, 14; 3:9). It is true that in 1 Timothy 4:1–5 Paul combats asceticism and that the Gnostics were ascetics. Yet the Gnostics did not invent asceticism, and Paul also warns against it in Colossians 2:20–23. The Gnostics denied the resurrection of the body, and Paul mentions that error in 2 Timothy 2:18. However, from the beginning there were those who denied the physical resurrection, and Paul opposes that heresy in 1 Corinthians 15. In short, there were no features of the heresy in view in the Pastoral Epistles that were not extant in Paul's lifetime.

Another argument advanced against Pauline authorship is that the church organizational structure of the Pastoral Epistles is too well developed for the first-century church. Critics charge that the Pastorals adopt a second-century model of church organization. Timothy and Titus, they maintain, correspond to the second-century bishops, with elders and deacons below them. In contrast, church leadership in the New Testament consisted only of elders and deacons. That, they claim, dates the Pastoral Epistles after the close of the New Testament. Such an argument fails to account for Titus 1:5 and 7, where the terms *presbuteros* (elder) and *episkopos* (bishop) refer to the same individuals. It is also not true, as some argue, that Paul had no interest in church organization. Acts 14:23 records that on his first missionary journey he and Barnabas "appointed overseers and deacons" (Phil. 1:1). Arguing "against a second-century date is the writer's concentration on the qualities looked for in elders and deacons. By the second century these would surely have been well known" (D. A. Carson, Douglas J. Moo, and Leon Morris, *An Introduction to the New Testament* [Grand Rapids: Zondervan, 1992], 364).

Some argue that Paul could not have written the Pastoral Epistles because they lack the great themes of his theology. But that argument fails to consider the nature of these letters. They were written to two of Paul's closest associates who were already deeply imbued with his theology. Further, as noted above, these epistles largely deal with the practical matters of church life and organization.

The Pastoral Epistles *do* contain the essentials of Paul's theology. There is no clearer presentation of the inspiration of Scripture to be found anywhere in the Bible than in 2 Timothy 3:15–17. And Titus 3:5–7 is one of the most lucid and forceful statements of the doctrine of salvation in all of Paul's writings. The Pastoral Epistles teach the deity of the Lord Jesus Christ (Titus 2:13), His mediatorial work (1 Tim. 2:5), and His substitutionary atonement (1 Tim. 2:6). Because of that evidence (and much more that could be cited), commentator William Hendricksen aptly remarks, "One stands amazed that this argument is still being repeated" (*Pastoral Epistles*, 18).

The final and most convincing argument (to those who deny that Paul wrote the Pastoral Epistles) against Pauline authorship comes from vocabulary. Critics point out that more than one-third of the Greek words in the Pastoral Epistles are not found in Paul's other ten epistles. Of that third, more than half the words appear nowhere else in the New Testament. Those statistics, they argue, group the Pastoral Epistles together and set them apart from the rest of Paul's writings, which points to an author other than Paul.

Again, such an argument fails to consider the circumstances in which the Pastoral Epistles were written. In contrast to Paul's other writings, which (except Philemon) were addressed to churches, these letters were written to individuals. Further, their subject matter was different. Much of Paul's other inspired writing is devoted to teaching doctrine and correcting error. Obviously, Timothy and Titus did not need that type of instruction. Different circumstances demand a different vocabulary; certainly a pastor today would use a very different vocabulary when writing to a close friend than when preaching to his congregation. Summing up this point, Donald Guthrie noted the following reasons for the different vocabulary of the Pastoral Epistles:

> 1. Dissimilarity of subject matter undoubtedly accounts for many new words. Themes not previously dealt with unavoidably produce a crop of new expressions.
> 2. Variations due to advancing age must be given due weight, since style and vocabulary are often affected this way.
> 3. Enlargement of vocabulary due to change of environment may account for an increased use of classical words.
> 4. The difference in the recipients as compared with the earlier Epistles addressed to churches would account for certain differences in style in the same way that private and public correspondence inevitably differs. (*The Pastoral Epistles*, rev. ed. [Grand Rapids: Eerdmans, 1990], 240)

Critics also note that two-thirds of the words that appear in the Pastoral Epistles but not in the rest of Paul's epistles are found in the writings of the second-century Christians. From that they infer that the Pastoral Epistles, too, date from the second century. However, "most of the words shared by the Pastorals and the second-century writers are also found in other writings prior to A.D. 50. It cannot be argued that Paul would not have known them" (Carson, Moo, and Morris, *Introduction*, 361).

The dangers of deciding authorship based on vocabulary led nineteenth-century lexicographer Joseph Henry Thayer to warn of the "monumental misjudgments committed by some who have made questions of authorship turn on vocabulary alone" (*Greek-English Lexicon of the New Testament* [reprint; Grand Rapids: Zondervan, 1970], 689). As Homer Kent rightly observes, "The uniform testimony of early history must carry more weight than the variety of vocabulary" (*Pastoral Epistles*, 67; cf. Guthrie, *Pastoral Epistles*, 21). (For a thorough discussion of the vocabulary argument, see Guthrie, *Introduction*; *Pastoral Epistles* (especially the Appendix); Hendricksen, *Pastoral Epistles*; and Kent, *Pastoral Epistles*.)

None of the five arguments advanced by the critics is valid. In addition, there are serious difficulties with the view that a pseudonymous author (a "pious forger") authored the Pastoral Epistles. (For a discussion of the issue of pseudonymity, see Carson, Moo, and Morris, *Introduction*, 367ff.)

First, despite claims by the critics, the early church did not approve of "pious forgeries." Paul warned of the danger of false letters purporting to come from him (2 Thess. 2:2) and took steps to authenticate his letters (cf. 2 Thess. 3:17). The church father Tertullian wrote of a church leader who was removed from office for forging a document in Paul's name, although he did it out of love for Paul (*On Baptism* XVII, vol. 3 of *The Ante-Nicene Fathers* [Grand Rapids: Eerdmans, 1973], 677).

Nor was forging personal letters a common practice in the early church. Carson, Moo, and Morris caution that "we should not approach the New Testament epistles as though it were common for the early Christians to write letters in a name not their own. As far as our knowledge goes, there is not one such letter emanating from the Christians from anywhere near the New Testament period" (*Introduction*, 368). The pious forger hypothesis raises a number of troublesome questions: Why would he have forged *three* letters that cover much of the same ground? Why did he not invent an itinerary for Paul that would fit in with the record of Paul's life given in Acts? And how did he deceive the early church into accepting the historical details of the Pastoral Epistles if they never happened? Into what specific historical situation in the second century do the Pastoral Epistles fit? How likely is it that a devoted follower of Paul would describe his master as "a blasphemer and a persecutor and a violent aggressor . . . the foremost of all [sinners]" (1 Tim. 1:13, 15)? Would it not have been the height of hypocrisy to include warnings about deceivers (cf. 2 Tim. 3:13; Titus 1:10) when he himself was one?

The evidence is clear. Paul the apostle wrote the Pastoral Epistles, as the church (until recent times) has always maintained. (For more information on Paul, see chapter 1 of this volume.)

Date, Place, and Occasion of Writing

Following his release from his first imprisonment, Paul revisited some of the key churches in which he had ministered, including Ephesus. He then went to Macedonia, leaving Timothy behind to deal with some problems in the Ephesian church (1 Tim. 1:3). From Macedonia, Paul wrote this letter, giving Timothy further instructions to help him carry out his task. At about this time (A.D. 63–64), he wrote to Titus, who was engaged in ministry on the island of Crete. Rearrested in connection with the outbreak of Nero's persecution, Paul wrote his final letter (2 Timothy) while in prison awaiting execution (ca. A.D. 66).

Outline

I. Greeting (1:1–2)
II. Instructions concerning false doctrine (1:3–20)
  A. The false doctrine at Ephesus (1:3–11)
  B. The true doctrine of Paul (1:12–17)
  C. The exhortation to Timothy (1:18–20)
III. Instructions concerning the church (2:1–3:16)
  A. The importance of prayer (2:1–8)
  B. The role of women (2:9–15)
  C. The qualifications for leaders (3:1–13)
  D. The reason for Paul's letter (3:14–16)
IV. Instructions concerning false teachers (4:1–16)
  A. The description of false teachers (4:1–5)
  B. The description of true teachers (4:6–16)
V. Instructions concerning pastoral responsibilities (5:1–6:2)
  A. The responsibility to sinning members (5:1–2)
  B. The responsibility to widows (5:3–16)
  C. The responsibility to elders (5:17–25)
  D. The responsibility to slaves (6:1–2)
VI. Instructions concerning the man of God (6:3–21)
  A. The peril of false teaching (6:3–5)
  B. The peril of loving money (6:6–10)
  C. The character and motivation of a man of God (6:11–16)
  D. The proper handling of treasure (6:17–19)
  E. The proper handling of truth (6:20–21)

A True Child in the Faith

1

Paul, an apostle of Christ Jesus according to the commandment of God our Savior, and of Christ Jesus, who is our hope; to Timothy, my true child in the faith: Grace, mercy and peace from God the Father and Christ Jesus our Lord. (1:1–2)

The supreme joy for any parent is to see their child grow into a mature, well-developed adult. For that they pray, labor, and hope. The same is true in the spiritual realm. There is no greater joy for a spiritual parent than to beget a true child in the faith and lead him to maturity.

Paul desired, as every Christian should, to reproduce in his spiritual children his virtues of Christlikeness. He sought to lead others to Christ, then nurture them to maturity, so they would then be able to repeat the same process. He describes that process through four generations in 2 Timothy 2:2, "The things which you have heard from me in the presence of many witnesses, these entrust to faithful men, who will be able to teach others also." To so reproduce himself was a central goal in the apostle's life.

The degree to which he was used by God in producing genuine spiritual children is astonishing. While many of his companions, such as Barnabas, Silas, John Mark, Apollos, and Luke were not his spiritual offspring, many others were. Dionysius, Damaris, Gaius, Sopater, Tychicus, Trophimus, Stephanas, Clement, Epaphras, the Corinthians (1 Cor. 4:15), and many others, including probably most of those mentioned in Romans 16, were in all likelihood the fruit of the apostle's evangelistic efforts. Some he reached personally, others were saved through his public preaching. Still others were reached indirectly through those Paul himself had reached.

Of all those who were saved before Paul met them, and those who were the fruit of his labors, only two does he call "true child in the faith." One is Titus (Titus 1:4), and the other is Timothy. That unique description was reserved for these key men in the apostle's life. Of the two, Timothy most reflected Paul. Paul wrote of him,

> But I hope in the Lord Jesus to send Timothy to you shortly, so that I also may be encouraged when I learn of your condition. For I have no one else of kindred spirit who will genuinely be concerned for your welfare. For they all seek after their own interests, not those of Christ Jesus. But you know of his proven worth that he served with me in the furtherance of the gospel like a child serving his father. (Phil. 2:19–22)

> For this reason I have sent to you Timothy, who is my beloved and faithful child in the Lord, and he will remind you of my ways which are in Christ, just as I teach everywhere in every church. (1 Cor. 4:17)

Timothy was Paul's protégé, his spiritual son, the most genuine reflection of the apostle.

This letter to Timothy (as well as the second one) is first and foremost a letter from one man in the ministry to another, from the beloved mentor to his most cherished pupil. We must therefore first understand it in terms of what was happening in the lives of Paul and Timothy, and the situation at Ephesus. Only then can we apply its truths to our own day.

The Author

Paul, an apostle of Christ Jesus according to the commandment of God our Savior, and of Christ Jesus, who is our hope; (1:1)

Paul is certainly a name familiar to any student of the New Testament. Paul (Paulus in Latin) was a common name in Cilicia, in which his home city of Tarsus was located. It means "little," or "small," and may be an indication that he was small from birth. He was not a man of striking stature or marked appearance. A second-century writer described him as "a man small of stature, with a bald head and crooked legs, in a good state of body, with eyebrows meeting and nose somewhat hooked, full of friendliness; for now he appeared like a man, and now he had the face of an angel" (cited by R. N. Longenecker, "Paul, The Apostle," in Merrill C. Tenney, ed., *The Zondervan Pictorial Encyclopedia of the Bible* [Grand Rapids: Zondervan, 1977], 4:625). His demeaning opponents at Corinth said of him, "His letters are weighty and strong, but his personal presence is unimpressive, and his speech contemptible" (2 Cor. 10:10).

Whatever his physical stature may have been, his spiritual stature is unsurpassed. He was one of a kind in the history of redemption, responsible for the initial spread of the gospel message through the Gentile world.

This unique man was born into a Jewish family (Phil. 3:5), and held Roman citizenship (Acts 22:25–28). His Hebrew name was Saul, after the most prominent member of his tribe of Benjamin, King Saul. The New Testament refers to him as "Saul" until his first missionary journey (Acts 13:9), after which he is called "Paul."

He had a traditional, orthodox upbringing. He described himself as "circumcised the eighth day, of the nation of Israel, of the tribe of Benjamin, a Hebrew of Hebrews; as to the Law, a Pharisee" (Phil. 3:5). He was a fanatically committed, zealous devotee of Judaism. In Galatians 1:14, he described himself as "advancing in Judaism beyond many of my contemporaries among my countrymen, being more extremely zealous for my ancestral traditions." His fiery zeal was seen in his willing participation in Stephen's murder (Acts 8:1), and his subsequent persecution of the church (Acts 8:3; 9:1–2; 26:9–11).

He was on his way to Damascus to carry out further persecutions when his life was suddenly, dramatically changed forever. The risen, ascended, glorified Christ appeared to him and his terrified companions. All in a brief time, he was struck blind, saved, called to the ministry, and shortly afterward baptized (Acts 9:1–18). Following a period of solitary preparation in the Nabatean (Arabian) wilderness near Damascus, he returned to that city and began proclaiming the gospel. After his fearless preaching aroused the hostility of both the Jewish and Gentile leaders (Acts 9:22–25; 2 Cor. 11:32–33), he escaped and went to Jerusalem. The church in that city was naturally hesitant to accept the one who had persecuted them so violently. Eventually, through the efforts of Barnabas, Paul was accepted. He later became one of the pastors of the church at Antioch (Acts 13:1ff.). It was from that ministry that the Holy Spirit sent him to his life's work as the apostle to the Gentiles (Acts 22:14–15; 26:16–18).

The verb *apostellō*, from which the noun *apostolos* (**apostle**) derives, means "to send off on a commission to do something as one's personal representative, with credentials furnished" (Kenneth S. Wuest, *The Pastoral Epistles in the Greek New Testament*, vol. 2 of *Word Studies in the Greek New Testament* [Grand Rapids: Eerdmans, 1978], 22). We could translate *apostolos* as "envoy," or "ambassador," someone who goes on a mission bearing the credentials of the one who sent him.

An apostle in the New Testament was one sent to carry the gospel to sinners. In the broadest sense, many individuals were called apostles. Barnabas (Acts 14:14), Epaphroditus (Phil. 2:25), Andronicus and Junius (Rom. 16:7), and James the Lord's brother (Gal. 1:19) all bore the title, though they were not among the twelve chosen by our Lord. They are what 2 Corinthians 8:23 calls "messengers [apostles] of the churches."

In its more restricted and common New Testament usage, "apostle" refers to an apostle **of Christ Jesus.** Those apostles included the original twelve (with the deletion of Judas and the addition of Matthias after Judas's defection) and Paul. In contrast to the apostles of the churches, these men were commissioned by Christ Himself. They were personally chosen by Him (cf. Luke 6:13; Acts 9:15), and learned the gospel from Him, not other men (cf. Gal. 1:11–12). The apostles of Christ were witnesses of His words, deeds, and especially His resurrection (Acts 1:21–22). Paul qualified on that count since he met the risen Christ on the way to Damascus, and on three other occasions (Acts 18:9–10; 22:17–18; 23:11).

Apostles of Christ were also gifted by the Holy Spirit to receive and impart divine truth. It was to them that Jesus said, "But the Helper, the Holy Spirit, whom the Father will send in My name, He will teach you all things, and bring to your remembrance all that I said to you" (John 14:26). They also had the power to cast out demons and heal the sick, performing those signs, wonders, and miracles that constituted the "signs of a true apostle" (2 Cor. 12:12; cf. Heb. 2:3–4). According to Ephesians 2:20, they are the foundation upon which the rest of the church is built. The church from its birth studied "the apostles' doctrine" (Acts 2:42).

The word order **Christ Jesus,** instead of the more usual "Jesus Christ," is unique to Paul. "Christ Jesus" appears in only one place in the New Testament outside of Paul's writings. That reference, Acts 24:24, occurs in Luke's description of the apostle's testimony to Felix and Drusilla. While Paul also uses the word order "Jesus Christ," the other apostolic writers (Peter, James, and John) do so exclusively. A possible explanation is that the other apostles knew first the man Jesus, and only later understood that He was the divine Christ. On the other hand, Paul's first exposure to Him was as the risen, glorified Christ.

It may seem unnecessary for Paul to emphasize his apostolic authority to Timothy, who certainly didn't question it. Timothy, however, faced a difficult situation in Ephesus, and needed the full weight of Paul's apostolic authority backing him. This letter, as it was read and enforced in the church, would strengthen Timothy's hand.

The use of *epitagē* (**commandment**) instead of the more usual *thelēma* ("will") further stresses Paul's apostolic authority. Paul had a direct charge from God the Father and Jesus Christ to carry out his ministry. That mandate included the writing of this letter, which put on Timothy and the church a heavy burden to obey its injunctions. *Epitagē* refers to a royal command that is not negotiable, but mandatory. Paul, Timothy, and the congregation at Ephesus were all under orders from the Sovereign of the universe. Paul also may have chosen this stronger term because of the false teachers at Ephesus, who likely questioned his authority.

Paul's orders came from **God our Savior** and **Christ Jesus, who is our hope.** Someone has well said that Christianity is a religion of personal pronouns. We do not worship a distant, impersonal deity, but God our Savior and Christ Jesus our hope. By linking God the Father and Jesus Christ as the source of his divine commission, Paul alludes to the deity of Christ. Jesus frequently linked Himself with God the Father in the Gospels (cf. Matt. 11:27; John 5:17–18; 10:30; 17:1–5, 11, 21–22). Christ's deity may well have been under attack at Ephesus (cf. 1 Tim. 3:16).

God our Savior is a title that appears only in the Pastoral Epistles, though it has roots in the Old Testament (cf. Pss. 18:46; 25:5; 27:9; Mic. 7:7; Hab. 3:18). God is the deliverer from sin and its consequences; He is the source of salvation, and planned it from eternity (cf. 2 Thess. 2:13). The liberal notion that the God of the Old Testament is a wrathful, vengeful God whom the gentle, loving Christ placated is both false and blasphemous.

God the Father's plan for salvation was carried out by **Christ Jesus, who is our hope.** We have hope for the future because of what Christ has done in the past and is doing in the present. In Colossians 1:27 Paul says, "Christ in you, [is] the hope of glory." The apostle John wrote,

> Beloved, now we are children of God, and it has not appeared as yet what we shall be. We know that, when He appears, we shall be like Him, because we shall see Him just as He is. And everyone who has this hope fixed on Him purifies himself, just as He is pure. (1 John 3:2–3)

There were no doubt some errorists in the Ephesian assembly trying to rob believers of salvation's hope. Paul responds by stressing both aspects of Christ's work (cf. 1:11, 14–17; 2:3; 4:10) as he writes to Timothy, so Timothy can confront such attacks.

THE RECIPIENT

to Timothy, my true child in the faith (1:2a)

The name **Timothy** means "one who honors God." He was named by his mother and grandmother, Eunice and Lois, who were no doubt devout Jews before they became believers in the Lord Jesus. They taught Timothy the Scriptures from the time he was a child (2 Tim. 3:15). His father was a pagan Greek (Acts 16:1), and may well have been dead by this time. As the son of a Jewish mother and a Greek father, Timothy had credentials that gave him access to both cultures.

Timothy was Paul's disciple, friend, co-worker, and dear son spiritually. By the time 1 Timothy was written, he had been with Paul for about fifteen years as the apostle's constant companion. He remained behind in Berea with Silas after persecution forced Paul to leave for Athens (Acts 17:13–15), but later joined Paul there (cf. Acts 17:15). He was with Paul in Corinth (Acts 18:5), was sent by Paul into Macedonia (Acts 19:22), and accompanied him on his return trip to Jerusalem (Acts 20:4). He was with Paul when he wrote Romans (Rom. 16:21), 2 Corinthians (2 Cor. 1:1), Philippians (Phil. 1:1), Colossians (Col. 1:1), the Thessalonian epistles (1 Thess. 1:1; 2 Thess. 1:1), and Philemon (Philem. 1). He frequently served as Paul's troubleshooter, being sent by him to the churches at Corinth (1 Cor. 4:17), Thessalonica (1 Thess. 3:2), and Philippi (Phil. 2:19), and now Ephesus.

Gnēsios (**true**) refers to a legitimate child, one born in wedlock. It is the opposite of *nothos,* which means "bastard," or "illegitimate child." Timothy was a *gnēsios* child of Paul, while Demas was a *nothos.* Timothy's faith was genuine. The use of *teknon* (**child**) instead of *huios* ("son") speaks of Paul's giving birth to Timothy spiritually. Since **in the faith** is anarthrous (lacking the definite article) in the Greek, it could be translated "in faith." In that sense, Paul would be saying Timothy is his son in the sphere of faith. The NASB translation **in the faith** refers to the objective body of the Christian faith. Both senses are possible, and consistent with Paul's usage elsewhere.

The phrase **true child in the faith** gives insight into Timothy's character. Paul sets Timothy up as an example of what a true child in the faith is like. His authenticity is thus verified, and the Ephesian church called to follow his example. Five characteristics implied in this opening section marked Timothy as a true child in the faith. Examining them provides a brief overview of the epistle.

SAVING FAITH

It is obviously impossible to be a true child in the faith without experiencing divine salvation in Jesus Christ. Paul testifies throughout the epistle to the genuineness of Timothy's conversion. In 1:1–2, he suggests through the use of the plural pronouns that Timothy has the same God and the same Christ as he does (cf. 4:10). In 6:11, Paul calls him "you man of God," then exhorts him to "fight the good fight of faith; take hold of the eternal life to which you were called, and you made the good confession in the presence of many witnesses" (6:12). Timothy was not only called to eternal life by God, but also publicly professed his faith in Christ. Unmistakable affirmation of Timothy's salvation comes in 2 Timothy 1:5, where Paul speaks of his "sincere faith."

The circumstances of Timothy's conversion are not recorded in Scripture. It is likely connected, however, with the ministry of Paul and Barnabas in Lystra (Timothy's hometown) on the first missionary journey (Acts 14:6–23). After seeing Paul heal a lame man, the people decided he and Barnabas were gods, and attempted to sacrifice to them. Shortly afterward, however, some of Paul's Jewish opponents from nearby cities came and turned the crowds against him. They stoned Paul, dragged him out of the city, and left him for dead. Timothy, Eunice, and Lois must have been aware of those events, and may have been converted then. Timothy thus had a very dramatic introduction to Paul. When Paul revisited Lystra on his second missionary journey, he chose Timothy to minister with him.

Unfortunately, not all those associated with the church at Ephesus may have had genuine faith. Some may have questioned the deity of Christ, prompting Paul to write, "By common confession great is the mystery of godliness: He who was revealed in the flesh, was vindicated in the Spirit, beheld by angels, proclaimed among the nations, believed on in the world, taken up in glory" (3:16). No one who rejects Christ's deity can be saved. Our Lord said in John 8:24 that "unless you believe that I am He, you shall die in your sins." Salvation, according to Paul, comes from confessing Jesus as Lord and believing that God raised Him from the dead (Rom. 10:9). Evidently there were those in Ephesus not committed to those essential truths. Some, likely even among the leadership, were openly teaching false doctrine (1:3), the very thing Paul warned the Ephesian elders against (Acts 20:29–30). Such men had strayed from the truth, and had "turned aside to fruitless discussion" (1:6).

In chapter 4 Paul warns,

> But the Spirit explicitly says that in later times some will fall away from the faith, paying attention to deceitful spirits and doctrines of demons,

> by means of the hypocrisy of liars seared in their own conscience as with a branding iron, men who forbid marriage and advocate abstaining from foods, which God has created to be gratefully shared in by those who believe and know the truth. (4:1–3)

Since the "later times" began with the coming of Christ (cf. 1 Peter 1:20), some in Ephesus fell short of true saving faith, believing instead demonic lies. They listened to hypocrites, with seared and deadened consciences, teaching a false asceticism.

According to 6:20–21, some at Ephesus had fallen prey to "worldly and empty chatter and the opposing arguments of what is falsely called 'knowledge.'" As a result, they had "gone astray from the faith." They had missed the mark regarding saving faith, and were lost.

Timothy's genuine faith stood out in sharp contrast with the false faith of many at Ephesus.

CONTINUING OBEDIENCE

The New Testament teaches repeatedly that the hallmark of a true believer is a life-pattern of obedience. Our Lord said in John 14:15, "If you love Me, you will keep My commandments" (cf. vv. 21, 23). In John 8:31 He told those who had professed faith in Him, "If you abide in My word, then you are truly disciples of Mine." Paul wrote in Ephesians 2:10, "We are His workmanship, created in Christ Jesus for good works, which God prepared beforehand, that we should walk in them." Good works are not the grounds of salvation, but the evidence of it. As Martin Luther put it, "Good works do not make a good man, but a good man does good works" ("The Freedom of a Christian," in John Dillenberger, ed., *Martin Luther: Selections from His Writings* [Garden City, N.Y.: Anchor Books, 1961], 69).

The pattern of Timothy's life was obedience. When Paul returned to Lystra on his second missionary voyage, he found that Timothy was "well spoken of by the brethren who were in Lystra and Iconium" (Acts 16:2). Paul testified of Timothy's loyal devotion in 4:6: "In pointing out these things to the brethren, you will be a good servant of Christ Jesus, constantly nourished on the words of the faith and of the sound doctrine which you have been following."

Others at Ephesus did not have that pattern of continual obedience. In 1:19 Paul writes of those who, having rejected "faith and a good conscience," had "suffered shipwreck in regard to their faith." They had started on the right course, but had been lost before they reached safe harbor.

In chapter 5, Paul advises younger widows to remarry, because "some have already turned aside to follow Satan" (5:15). Such women exemplified the truth of 1 John 2:19, "They went out from us, but they were not really of us; for if they had been of us, they would have remained with us; but they went out, in order that it might be shown that they all are not of us."

In chapter 6, Timothy was told to warn those who pursued riches that

> those who want to get rich fall into temptation and a snare and many foolish and harmful desires which plunge men into ruin and destruction. For the love of money is a root of all sorts of evil, and some by longing for it have wandered away from the faith, and pierced themselves with many a pang. (6:9–10)

Timothy's unwavering obedience was truly "an example of those who believe" (4:12). He had been a persevering believer in a church riddled with defectors.

HUMBLE SERVICE

A true child in the faith is a servant. Paul described the conversion of the Thessalonians in these words, "you turned to God from idols to serve a living and true God" (1 Thess. 1:9). The Christian life is to be lived as a stewardship of service to the sovereign lordship of Jesus Christ. The disciples left everything to follow and serve Jesus. True salvation is marked by a servant's heart.

Humble service characterized Timothy's life. At Paul's urging, he willingly remained in the difficult post at Ephesus (1:3). Although in his late teens or early twenties at the time, he endured circumcision to better serve with Paul (Acts 16:3). As already noted, he served Paul for many years, through difficult circumstances. No wonder, then, that Paul called him "my fellow worker" (Rom. 16:21). There is no higher praise.

There were others at Ephesus who were not interested in humble service. Paul warned in 3:6 against making a recent convert an elder because of the danger of pride. Apparently some in the Ephesian assembly sought leadership roles only to exalt themselves (1:6–7). Those elders marked by humble, diligent service were to be rewarded (5:17). Those who proudly continued in sin were to be publicly confronted (5:19–20). The false teachers at Ephesus were characterized by conceit, not humility (6:4).

Timothy's humble service made him a fitting heir to the unselfish, sacrificial apostle himself.

SOUND DOCTRINE

A true child in the faith will adhere to sound doctrine. Jesus said to the Pharisees, "He who is of God hears the words of God; for this reason you do not hear them, because you are not of God" (John 8:47). The early church devoted itself to the apostles' teaching (Acts 2:42).

Timothy was a student and a teacher of sound doctrine. He was "constantly nourished on the words of the faith and of the sound doctrine" which he had been following (4:6). Paul exhorted Timothy to teach the truths he had learned (4:11; 6:2), confident that Timothy was doctrinally sound.

Ephesus was plagued by false teachers. Some had turned aside from the truth to fruitless discussion (1:6). They presumed to be teachers of the law, though they did not understand it (1:7). Paul disciplined two of them, Hymenaeus and Alexander (1:20). Paul describes the false teaching at Ephesus as "worldly fables fit only for old women" (4:7), "disputes about words, out of which arise envy, strife, abusive language, evil suspicions" (6:4). Its perpetrators were conceited and understood nothing (6:4).

In contrast to the false teachers, Paul was confident of Timothy's orthodoxy. He trusted Timothy to "give attention to the public reading of Scripture, to exhortation and teaching" until he arrived in Ephesus (4:13).

COURAGEOUS CONVICTION

Those who make an impact for the cause of Christ must have the courage of their convictions. Any dead fish can float downstream; it takes a live one to fight the current. Strong conviction comes from spiritual maturity and knowledge of the Word, and is an essential element in any effective ministry.

Timothy was to be a fighter. Paul put him in Ephesus to "instruct certain men not to teach strange doctrines" (1:3). He was to "fight the good fight" (1:18), and guard what had been entrusted to him (6:20).

Many in the Ephesian congregation lacked the convictions of their pastor. They were compromisers. Such men were not qualified to be elders (3:2), or deacons (3:10), since they were not above reproach. Some of the younger widows were in danger of reneging on their commitment to Christ (5:11–12). Still others in the congregation had compromised with money and "pierced themselves with many a pang" (6:10).

In contrast, Timothy maintained his convictions, even when that cost him his life. According to tradition, he was martyred in Ephesus some thirty years later for opposing the worship of the goddess Diana. He "[held] fast the beginning of [his] assurance firm until the end" (Heb. 3:14).

THE SALUTATION

Grace, mercy and peace from God the Father and Christ Jesus our Lord. (1:2b)

Grace and **peace** is the familiar Pauline greeting, appearing in all of his epistles. Only here and in 2 Tim. 1:2 does he add **mercy.** Timothy would need all three in dealing with the situation at Ephesus. **Grace** refers to God's undeserved favor, love, and forgiveness that frees sinners from the consequences of sin. **Mercy** frees us not from the consequences of sin, but from the misery that accompanies it. **Peace** is the result of grace and mercy. It refers not only to harmony with God but also to tranquillity of soul. Grace, mercy, and peace are needed throughout the Christian life, not merely at salvation.

Once again Paul links **God the Father and Christ Jesus our Lord,** thus stressing Christ's deity and equality with the Father. As already noted, part of the heresy at Ephesus involved a rejection of Christ's deity.

In these two short, seemingly perfunctory verses, Paul reveals his passion for the Ephesian church, a passion kindled during his three years of ministry there. To help Timothy combat the heresy threatening the church, he throws the full weight of his apostolic authority behind him. He also asks God to pour out on Timothy, his true child in the faith, the grace, mercy, and peace he needs to handle the situation. These verses thus serve as a fitting introduction to this important letter.

How to Treat False Prophets

2

As I urged you upon my departure for Macedonia, remain on at Ephesus, in order that you may instruct certain men not to teach strange doctrines, nor to pay attention to myths and endless genealogies, which give rise to mere speculation rather than furthering the administration of God which is by faith. But the goal of our instruction is love from a pure heart and a good conscience and a sincere faith. For some men, straying from these things, have turned aside to fruitless discussion, wanting to be teachers of the Law, even though they do not understand either what they are saying or the matters about which they make confident assertions. But we know that the Law is good, if one uses it lawfully, realizing the fact that law is not made for a righteous man, but for those who are lawless and rebellious, for the ungodly and sinners, for the unholy and profane, for those who kill their fathers or mothers, for murderers and immoral men and homosexuals and kidnappers and liars and perjurers, and whatever else is contrary to sound teaching, according to the glorious gospel of the blessed God, with which I have been entrusted. (1:3–11)

In the definitive words of John 8:44, Jesus informs us that Satan is a liar. Wherever God sows truth, His arch-enemy endeavors to sow falsehood and error. It is no surprise, then, that one of his most persistent attacks on the church has been through false doctrine. False teachers and their demonic doctrine have been at the core of the battle the church has had to fight throughout its history. Nor are they unique to the church age. The Old Testament contains repeated condemnations of the false prophets that plagued Israel (cf. Deut. 13:1–5; Jer. 14:14ff.; 23:1ff.; Lam. 2:14; Ezek. 13:1ff.; Zech. 10:2).

Our Lord reminded us often of the danger of false teachers. He warned in Matthew 7:15, "Beware of the false prophets, who come to you in sheep's clothing, but inwardly are ravenous wolves." In the Olivet Discourse, He forewarned of false prophets who would arise in the future: "And many false prophets will arise, and will mislead many. . . . For false Christs and false prophets will arise and will show great signs and wonders, so as to mislead, if possible, even the elect" (Matt. 24:11, 24).

The New Testament authors echoed our Lord's warning. Paul wrote to the Corinthians about "false apostles, deceitful workers, disguising themselves as apostles of Christ" (2 Cor. 11:13). Second Peter 2:1 says, "False prophets also arose among the people, just as there will also be false teachers among you, who will secretly introduce destructive heresies." Writing at the close of the New Testament era the apostle John noted that "many false prophets have gone out into the world" (1 John 4:1; cf. 2:18; 2 John 7).

False teachers are dangerous because, like their evil master, their appearance is deceiving. Satan "disguises himself as an angel of light" (2 Cor. 11:14). "Therefore it is not surprising if his servants also disguise themselves as servants of righteousness; whose end shall be according to their deeds" (v. 15). The subtlety, and danger, of false teachers lies in their clever twisting of Scripture for their own ends. They are hucksters, guilty of "peddling," and "adulterating" the Word of God (2 Cor. 2:17; 4:2). Their teaching, which appears to be biblical and spiritual, is far more dangerous than an open attack on the truths of Scripture. False teachers first confuse, then captivate, and finally damn unwary souls to hell.

Despite its rich history, the church at Ephesus was not spared from the onslaught of false teachers, just as Paul had predicted (Acts 20:29–30). Paul penned this letter to Timothy to tell him to make every effort to halt the influence of the false teachers and set things right in the church. The opening charge in 1:3–11 sets the scene for the rest of the epistle. Paul divulges four things that are true about false teachers: their error, their goal, their motive, and their effect.

The Error of False Teachers

As I urged you upon my departure for Macedonia, remain on at Ephesus, in order that you may instruct certain men not to teach strange doctrines, nor to pay attention to myths and endless genealogies, which give rise to mere speculation rather than furthering the administration of God which is by faith. (1:3–4)

Verses 3 and 4, though a complete thought, are not a complete sentence in the Greek. Paul starts with a clause beginning with **as,** but never completes it. The NASB resolves this by translating the infinitive *prosmeinai* as an imperative (**remain**). The Authorized Version renders it as an infinitive ("to abide") and supplies the words "so do" at the end of verse 4. In either case the meaning is the same. Timothy is to remain at Ephesus to deal with the false teachers there. Paul's concern for proper grammar is swallowed up by his passionate concern for a church dear to his heart.

Urged is from *parakaleō,* which can mean "to beg," "beseech," "entreat," or "implore." Paul pleads with Timothy to stay on at Ephesus, which may indicate that he was considering leaving. Even though he was Paul's "true child in the faith" (1:2), Timothy was not invulnerable to timidity (2 Tim. 1:7). He was somewhat intimidated by those who looked down on him because of his youth (4:12). He may have felt inadequate to handle the arguments of the false teachers. That they were evidently leaders in the church presented further difficulties for Timothy. On top of that was the threat of persecution.

The most natural understanding of verse 3 is that Paul and Timothy had been together in **Ephesus** before Paul's **departure for Macedonia.** Paul at that time began the confrontation and expulsion of the false teachers by dealing with Hymenaeus and Alexander (1:20), perhaps the ringleaders. He urged Timothy to carry it through to completion. To do that, he was to **instruct certain men not to teach strange doctrines. Instruct** is from *parangellō,* which doesn't mean to teach, but to command. It demands obedience from an inferior to an order from a superior. False teachers are not to be taken lightly, but as Paul said to Titus, their mouths "must be silenced" (Titus 1:11). They are to be commanded to stop teaching error. Timothy was to use the full weight of Paul's apostolic authority in dealing with them.

The use of **certain** implies that the false teachers were few in number. Nevertheless, they had a wide influence, not only in Ephesus, but also in the surrounding region. They were not outsiders, as in Corinth and Galatia, but most likely elders in the Ephesian church and some of the surrounding churches. Paul had told them this would happen when they met together at Miletus. He said, "and from among your own selves men will arise, speaking perverse things, to draw away the disciples after them" (Acts 20:30).

There are at least four reasons for concluding that the false teachers were elders. First, they presumed to be teachers (1:7), a role reserved for elders (3:2; 5:17). Second, Paul, not the church, excommunicated Hymenaeus and Alexander. That implies they were in positions of power and the congregation couldn't deal with them. Third, the qualifications of an elder are given in great detail in chapter 3. Giving those implies that unqualified men were serving in that office, and Timothy needed to see them replaced. Finally, Paul stresses that sinning elders are to be publicly disciplined (5:19–22).

Timothy was to command these erring elders **not to teach strange doctrines.** *Heterodidaskalein* (**to teach strange doctrines**) is a word most likely coined by Paul. It is a compound word, made up of *heteros* ("of a different kind") and *didaskalein* ("to teach"). The errorists' teaching was of a different kind than the revealed truth of apostolic teaching (cf. Acts 6:3–4). The teaching of the apostles was the standard by which all other teaching was judged.

After describing the false teachers, Paul described their error. It consisted of **myths and endless genealogies,** legends and fanciful stories manufactured by men. These "doctrines of demons" (4:1) were being passed off as God's truth. Paul ridicules them as "worldly fables fit only for old women" (4:7).

What the specific **myths** being taught were, or how exactly the false teachers were using **genealogies** is not clear. Whatever form it took, the errorists' teaching was contrary to the truth. While the exact heresy at Ephesus is unknown, some of its general features can be pieced together from 1 and 2 Timothy. From 1:7 we learn that it contained elements of Judaism, since the false teachers wished to be teachers of the law. Commentator J. N. D. Kelly suggests that the **myths and endless genealogies**

> must have had to do with allegorical or legendary interpretations of the O.T. centering on the pedigrees of the patriarchs. Much of the rabbinical Haggadah consisted of just such a fanciful rewriting of Scripture; the Book of Jubilees and Pseudo-Philo's *Liber antiquitatum biblicarum,* with its mania for family trees, are apt examples. It has also been shown that in postexilic Judaism there was a keen interest in family trees, and that these played a part in controversies between Jews and Jewish Christians. (*The Pastoral Epistles* [Peabody, Mass.: Hendrickson, 1987], 44–45)

In 4:3 we learn that the heresy involved a false asceticism. The errorists were "men who forbid marriage and advocate abstaining from foods." They hoped to obtain divine acceptance through legalistic attention to self-deprivation. Their preoccupation with myths and genealogies resulted not in edification but in "controversial questions and disputes about words, out of which arise envy, strife, abusive language, evil suspicions" (6:4). Timothy was to "solemnly charge them in the presence of God not to wrangle about words, which is useless, and leads to the ruin of the hearers" (2 Tim. 2:14). Their teaching was nothing but "worldly and empty chatter" leading to "further ungodliness" (2 Tim. 2:16). Such talk "will spread like gangrene" (2 Tim. 2:17), leading people "astray from the truth" (2 Tim. 2:18). The errorists' "foolish and ignorant speculations" would only "produce quarrels" (2 Tim. 2:23). It all stemmed from a failure to handle accurately the Word of truth (cf. 2 Tim. 2:15), and to "examine everything carefully" (1 Thess. 5:21).

The effect of false teaching is to **give rise to mere speculation.** The false teachers' endless questions and speculations contributed nothing to **furthering the administration of God which is by faith.** That phrase refers to God's saving plan. Their heresy struck a blow at the gospel of saving faith. It may be safe to conclude, therefore, that like all other false religion, it was a legalistic system of works righteousness.

All the myriad religions of the world fall into one of two categories. There is the religion of divine accomplishment, that God in Christ accomplished salvation apart from human efforts. That is the Christian gospel. The other category is that of human achievement, where men attempt to gain salvation by their own efforts in good deeds, ceremonies, or rituals. Every other religion to one extent or another fits into this category. The false teachers at Ephesus, like all other false teachers, offered a way to God which required human achievement.

Since they threaten people with eternal ruin, false teachers are not to be taken lightly. As Paul wrote to the Galatians,

> But even though we, or an angel from heaven, should preach to you a gospel contrary to that which we have preached to you, let him be accursed. As we have said before, so I say again now, if any man is preaching to you a gospel contrary to that which you received, let him be accursed. (Gal. 1:8–9)

To believe wrongly about the saving gospel is to be eternally lost. Any one who tampers with the gospel is deadly because they lure the unwary to eternal damnation.

THE GOAL OF FALSE TEACHERS

But the goal of our instruction is love from a pure heart and a good conscience and a sincere faith. For some men, straying from these things, have turned aside to fruitless discussion, (1:5–6)

Paul contrasts **the goal** of his **instruction** with that of the false teachers. He seeks to produce in the church that which God requires, **love** toward Him and those who are His. It is essential that believers "love the Lord your God with all your heart, and with all your soul, and with all your mind," and "your neighbor as yourself" (Matt. 22:37, 39). **Love,** indeed, is the mark of the Christian. Jesus said in John 13:35, "By this all men will know that you are My disciples, if you have love for one another." John added, "Beloved, let us love one another, for love is from God; and everyone who loves is born of God and knows God. The one who does not love does not know God, for God is love" (1 John 4:7–8). *Agapē* (**love**) is the love of choice, of will. It involves self-denial and self-sacrifice to benefit others. This kind of **love** flows from three sources.

The concept of a **pure heart** is a rich Old Testament theme. The psalmist asks, "Who may ascend into the hill of the Lord? And who may stand in His holy place?" (Ps. 24:3). He then answers his question, "He who has clean hands and a pure heart" (Ps. 24:4). After his sin with Bathsheba, David cried out in Psalm 51:10, "Create in me a clean heart, O God." Psalm 73:1 exclaims, "Surely God is good to Israel, to those who are pure in heart!" A heart washed by regeneration (Titus 3:5), an obedient heart (Rom. 6:17), is a pure heart.

A second prerequisite for love is a **good conscience.** *Agathos* (**good**) is that which is perfect, producing pleasure, satisfaction, and a sense of well-being. The *conscience* is the God-created self-judging faculty of man. It either affirms or accuses a person (Rom. 2:14–15). The mind knows the standard of right and wrong, and when that standard is violated, the conscience reacts to accuse, producing guilt, shame, doubt, fear, remorse, or despair (cf. Titus 1:15). Those with a pure heart (mind) will not be condemned by their conscience. To maintain a blameless conscience, one free of offense against either God or man, was Paul's goal (Acts 24:16). Peace, confidence, joy, hope, courage, and contentment are the results of a conscience that is nonaccusing, and love will flow.

Finally, love comes from **a sincere faith,** one without any pretense. The hypocritical faith of the false teachers will not produce it. Real trust and love go together. As noted in chapter 1 of this volume, Timothy was marked by such a sincere faith (2 Tim. 1:5).

False teachers have dirty hearts, uncleansed by the gospel. They have guilty condemning consciences triggered by their impure hearts. Finally, they have hypocritical, false faith. That kind of life will never produce love for God. Therefore it is no surprise that Paul adds, **straying from these things** they **have turned aside to fruitless discussion. Straying** means "to miss the mark," while **turned aside** means "to go off course." The goal of the false teachers was not to create an environment of love, but to fulfill their egos (cf. 1:7), and to fill their pockets. Consequently, their teaching was nothing but **fruitless discussion.** It certainly could not produce love, which is the fruit of the Spirit (Gal. 5:22–23).

The Motives of False Teachers

wanting to be teachers of the Law, (1:7a)

The false teachers were driven by a strong, consuming desire **to be teachers of the Law.** They were not concerned about truly learning the law, or knowing the God of the law, or serving people in love by the law. They desired the kind of prestige accorded rabbis in Judaism, only they sought that within the church. Like the Pharisees denounced by our Lord, "they do all their deeds to be noticed by men . . . and they love the place of honor at banquets, and the chief seats in the synagogues, and respectful greetings in the market places, and being called by men, Rabbi" (Matt. 23:5–7). They were proud and sought the applause of men (1 Tim. 6:4).

Theirs was the opposite of a proper motivation for ministry. James warned in James 3:1, "Let not many of you become teachers, my brethren, knowing that as such we shall incur a stricter judgment." The one who really understands the role of a teacher understands that it's not a place for proud people.

John Knox, the Scottish Reformer, understood the seriousness of preaching. When he was called forth to preach the gospel, he "burst forth in most abundant tears, and withdrew himself to his chamber. His countenance and behaviour, from that day till the day that he was compelled to present himself to the public place of preaching, did sufficiently declare the grief and trouble of his heart" (William Barclay, *The Letters to Timothy, Titus, and Philemon,* rev. ed. [Philadelphia: Westminster, 1977], 50). The thought of preaching the gospel was so sobering that Knox was overwhelmed.

D. Martyn Lloyd-Jones, the great twentieth-century British preacher, wrote that teaching the Word is such an awesome task that a godly man "shrinks from it. Nothing but this overwhelming sense of being called, and of compulsion, should ever lead anyone to preach" (*Preachers and Preaching* [Grand Rapids: Zondervan, 1972], 107). John Stott added,

> I cannot help wondering if this may not be why there are so few preachers whom God is using today. There are plenty of popular preachers, but not many powerful ones, who preach in the power of the Spirit. Is it because the cost of such preaching is too great? It seems that the only preaching God honours, through which His wisdom and power are expressed, is the preaching of a man who is willing in himself to be both a weakling and a fool. God not only chooses weak and foolish people to save, but weak and foolish preachers through whom to save them, or at least preachers who are content to be weak and seem foolish in the eyes of the world. We are not always willing to pay this price. We are constantly tempted to covet a reputation as men of learning or men of influence; to seek honour in academic circles and compromise our old-fashioned message in order to do so; and to cultivate personal charm or forcefulness so as to sway the people committed to our care. (*The Preacher's Portrait,* Grand Rapids: Eerdmans, 1979], 122)

It requires humility, and the compulsion of God's call, to be a servant of God. The Ephesian false teachers knew neither. They sought leadership roles for the sake of their own satisfaction. Seeking the prestige of a rabbinic role, they imposed on the congregation a false, legalistic heresy, offering salvation by works. In sharp contrast to godly, humble leaders like Paul and Timothy, they, like Diotrephes (3 John 9), sought the preeminence, personal power, and prosperity.

The Effect of False Teachers

even though they do not understand either what they are saying or the matters about which they make confident assertions. But we know that the Law is good, if one uses it lawfully, realizing the fact that law is not made for a righteous man, but for those who are lawless and rebellious, for the ungodly and sinners, for the unholy and profane, for those who kill their fathers or mothers, for murderers and immoral men and homosexuals and kidnappers and liars and perjurers, and whatever else is contrary to sound teaching, according to the glorious gospel of the blessed God, with which I have been entrusted. (1:7*b*–11)

Although the false teachers wished to be teachers of the law, such was an impossibility. Paul writes that **they do not understand either what they are saying or the matters about which they make confident assertions.** The present active participle *noountes* (**understand**) indicates they were in a continual state of not understanding. They were like all unconverted people, who by the absence of the Holy Spirit and His discernment and anointing, cannot know the things of God, for they are spiritually appraised while such men are spiritually dead (cf. 1 Cor. 2:14). Worse still, they were making *confident assertions,* as if what they said was absolute truth. It is bad enough to be ignorant, but they were dogmatic about their ignorance. Unfortunately, their spiritual children plague the church to this day. The church today, like the Ephesians, faces proud, ignorant, dogmatic purveyors of false teaching.

Lest anyone get the wrong idea, Paul hastens to add that **we know that the Law is good.** While he condemned those desiring to be teachers of the law, Paul did not intend to condemn the law itself. He is careful not to throw the baby out with the dirty bath water. *Kalos* (**good**) could be translated "useful." The law is **good** or useful because it reflects God's will. As the psalmist put it, "The law of the Lord is perfect" (Ps. 19:7). Paul wrote in Romans 7:12 that "the Law is holy, and the commandment is holy and righteous and good."

The **Law** is good when it is applied **lawfully.** There is a proper understanding and use of the law, but the false teachers were misusing it. Deluded by their pride into thinking they could please God through their own efforts, they used the law as a means of salvation. That is a role the law could never fill (cf. Rom. 3:20, 28; Gal. 2:16; 3:11). **Law** in general, and the Mosaic Law in particular, **is not made for a righteous man.** Those who think they are righteous will never be saved (cf. Luke 5:32), since they fail to understand the true use of the law. The law was made **for those who are lawless and rebellious, for the ungodly and sinners, for the unholy and profane.** The purpose of the law is to show willing sinners their sin (cf. Rom. 3:19), and need of a savior (Gal. 3:24). The law is morally right and good, but the law alone is not good news. The law forces man to recognize the bad news that all are guilty of violating God's standards. It thus condemns everyone and sentences them to hell (Rom. 3:19–20).

Paul then illustrates the type of people for whom the law was made. Taking his cue from the Decalogue, he lists sins against both God and men. The first three couplets deal with sins from the first part of the Ten Commandments, those dealing with our relationship to God. Each couplet contains both a negative element and the effect it produces. *Anomia* (**lawless**) describes those with no commitment to any law or standard. That leads to the effect of being **rebellious.** To be **ungodly** is to be without regard for anything sacred. Such people are **sinners;** they live without regard for God's law because they have no regard for God. An **unholy** person is indifferent to what is right. He is indifferent to God and his duty to Him. That indifference leads him to be **profane,** to trample on what is sacred. Lawlessness produces rebellion, ungodliness sinners, unholiness, and profanity. The law was made for just such disobedient, impure, and irreverent people. If they would heed it, it would show them their sin and need of salvation.

The rest of the sins in Paul's list come from the second half of the Ten Commandments, those dealing with our relationship to other people. He probably selected the specific sins in this list because they characterized the false teachers at Ephesus. **Those who kill their fathers or mothers** are in obvious violation of the fifth commandment to "honor your father and your mother" (Ex. 20:12). That commandment is broadened in Exodus 21:15 and 17 to include striking or cursing parents. It forbids everything from dishonor to murder. **Murderers** are in violation of the sixth commandment, "You shall not murder" (Ex. 20:13). **Immoral men and homosexuals** (*arsenokoitais,* literally "males in the marriage bed") violate the seventh commandment, which forbids sexual activity outside of marriage. The eighth commandment forbids stealing. In light of that, Paul mentions **kidnappers,** since in his day theft of children was commonplace. Kidnapping was a capital offense in the Old Testament (Ex. 21:16; Deut. 24:7). The ninth commandment, "You shall not bear false witness against your neighbor" (Ex. 20:16), condemns **liars and perjurers.**

Then to make sure nothing is omitted, Paul adds, **whatever else is contrary to sound teaching. Sound** is from *hugiainō,* from which we get our English word "hygiene." It refers to that which is healthy and wholesome. Paul advocates teaching that produces spiritual life, growth, and health.

To use the law lawfully is to use it **according to the glorious gospel of the blessed God.** The law, since it shows men their sin, is a necessary part of the gospel. If there were no bad news that men were lost sinners, there could be no good news of Christ's redemption. The gospel is **glorious** because it reveals God's glory, His attributes. One of those attributes is holiness, which involves hatred of sin. Another is justice, which demands punishment when His law is violated. Any gospel that ignores the law and sin is not the true gospel, since it does not reflect God's attributes. **The blessed God** is both blessed in Himself (cf. 6:15), and the source of blessing for His people (Eph. 1:3). It was the true gospel **with which** Paul was **entrusted** (Gal. 2:7).

All believers have a responsibility to be on the alert for false teachers. What do we watch for? First, look at their understanding of Scripture, and ask if their teaching is biblically sound. Do they place extrabiblical teachings on a par with the Bible? Do they handle accurately the Word of truth (2 Tim. 2:15)?

Second, examine their goals. Do they seek to love, honor, and glorify God? Or do they pursue self-love, material wealth, or personal happiness? Does their message speak of purity of heart, a good conscience, and nonhypocritical faith?

Third, examine their motives. Are they humble and selfless? Or do they seek the preeminence?

Finally, examine the effect of their teaching. Do their followers understand clearly the gospel of Jesus Christ? Do they define the gospel properly? Do they use the law properly, as part of the gospel message, or do they promote works righteousness?

Those who pass the above checks should be welcomed as brothers in Christ, even if we differ with them at some points of interpretation or doctrine. Those who do not are to be rejected, no matter what experiences they may have had, or what else they may teach. Constant vigilance is our defense against those who would enslave us to a false gospel.

A Personal Testimony of God's Saving Grace

3

I thank Christ Jesus our Lord, who has strengthened me, because He considered me faithful, putting me into service; even though I was formerly a blasphemer and a persecutor and a violent aggressor. And yet I was shown mercy, because I acted ignorantly in unbelief; and the grace of our Lord was more than abundant, with the faith and love which are found in Christ Jesus. It is a trustworthy statement, deserving full acceptance, that Christ Jesus came into the world to save sinners, among whom I am foremost of all. And yet for this reason I found mercy, in order that in me as the foremost, Jesus Christ might demonstrate His perfect patience, as an example for those who would believe in Him for eternal life. Now to the King eternal, immortal, invisible, the only God, be honor and glory forever and ever. Amen. (1:12–17)

The good news of the Christian gospel is that God has the power to transform lives. History abounds with stories of dramatic conversions that testify to that fact.

One such story is about a nineteenth-century South African named Afrikaner, a chief of the Hottentot tribe. He was a hardened, vicious warrior. He and his men were the terror of South Africa. He was so dangerous that the governor of Cape Town offered a large reward for him—dead or alive. Into the scene stepped Robert Moffat, a young Scottish missionary. Believing that God had called him to preach the gospel to the Hottentots, he sought them out. The first person converted under Moffat's ministry was Afrikaner. His was a remarkable testimony to God's saving grace.

Billy Sunday was a hard-drinking professional baseball player in the early days of the sport. Walking down the street one day in Chicago with several of his teammates, he came across a man preaching on a street corner. They stopped to mock the preacher, but something he said struck a responsive chord in Billy Sunday's heart. He embraced Jesus Christ as his savior and went on to become a noted evangelist.

The list is endless. It includes Martin Luther, a former Roman Catholic monk, John Newton, a former slave trader, and Charles Colson, a former White House aide to President Richard Nixon. It even includes former skeptics such as Lew Wallace, Frank Morison, and C. S. Lewis. In my own church I have seen alcoholics, drug addicts, murderers, adulterers, thieves, fornicators, homosexuals, and even a former motorcycle gang leader give their lives to Christ.

The Bible records the conversions of the maniac at Gadara, the despised tax collector and traitor to his people Matthew, blind Bartimaeus and his friend, the adulterous Samaritan woman, Zacchaeus, the Roman centurion at the crucifixion, Cornelius, the Ethiopian eunuch, the Philippian jailer, and Lydia, among others. But of all the conversions ever recorded none was more remarkable than that of Saul of Tarsus. This bitter enemy of the cause of Christ, in his own words the foremost of all sinners, became the greatest evangelist and theologian the world has ever seen. Acts 9, 22, 26, Galatians 1 and 2, Philippians 3, and 1 Timothy 1 all describe aspects of his conversion. Paul never lost the wonder that God could and did redeem someone like him. He viewed himself as the supreme example of God's saving grace.

Some commentators have contended that Paul's testimony in this passage is a digression from his flow of thought in 1 Timothy. That is not the case, however. Paul's purpose in writing this letter was to charge Timothy with the formidable task of correcting the church at Ephesus. A major part of that task involved dealing with the false teachers described in 1:3–10. Since they were presenting a false gospel, Paul gives his testimony to the true one, which he mentioned in 1:11. In contrast to the errorists' false view of the law as a means of salvation (1:8–10), Paul shows that a proper use of the law brings conviction of sin and the need of grace. The apostle's testimony in 1:12–17 is thus an integral part of the epistle. It contrasts the glory of the true gospel with the emptiness of false doctrine.

In giving his testimony, Paul celebrated the significance of God's grace. In so doing he extolled six elements of grace: the source of grace, the need for grace, the power of grace, the extent of grace, the purpose of grace, and the response to grace.

The Source of Grace

I thank Christ Jesus our Lord, who has strengthened me, because He considered me faithful, putting me into service; (1:12)

Grace may be defined as God's loving forgiveness, by which He grants exemption from judgment, and the promise of temporal and eternal blessing to guilty and condemned sinners freely, without any worthiness on their part, and based on nothing they have done or failed to do. Paul directs his thanks to **Christ Jesus our Lord** because He is the source of that grace (cf. 1:14). The word order in the Greek text emphasizes Paul's gratitude. It literally reads "Grateful am I." Paul was grateful continually to **Christ Jesus,** the Messiah, the earthly Son of God with the heavenly glory. **Our** includes Timothy, too, as a subject of the **Lord.**

The Bible repeatedly affirms that Jesus Christ, along with God the Father, is alone the source of all grace. John wrote, "For the Law was given through Moses; grace and truth were realized through Jesus Christ" (John 1:17). Romans 3:24 tells us we were "justified as a gift by His grace through the redemption which is in Christ Jesus."

Paul was conscious of the work of grace in his own life. In 1 Corinthians 15:9–10 he wrote,

> For I am the least of the apostles, who am not fit to be called an apostle, because I persecuted the church of God. But by the grace of God I am what I am, and His grace toward me did not prove vain; but I labored even more than all of them, yet not I, but the grace of God with me.

To the Ephesians he wrote, "To me, the very least of all saints, this grace was given, to preach to the Gentiles the unfathomable riches of Christ" (Eph. 3:8).

Paul expresses thankfulness for four aspects of God's grace in his life. First, for electing grace. Paul was ever conscious of God's choice of him, both for salvation, and apostleship. In Acts 22:14 and 26:16 he mentions it when giving his testimony. In Romans 1:5 he speaks of God's electing grace in relation to himself; in Titus 2:11 and Ephesians 2:8–9 to all believers.

Second, for enabling grace. Through God's grace, Paul was **strengthened.** God not only graciously elected him to salvation but also graciously gave him the strength he did not have or deserve, but needed to live out that salvation (cf. 2 Cor. 9:8). The Lord strengthened Paul during the darkest hour of his life. He was imprisoned a second time, facing execution, and deserted by all his companions (2 Tim. 4:16), yet he could still testify that "the Lord stood with me and strengthened me" (2 Tim. 4:17). He lived his whole life in the strength the Lord provided. "I can do all things," he wrote in Philippians 4:13, "through Him who strengthens me." Believers do not merely receive grace at salvation, they live from then on in the sphere of grace (cf. Romans 5:2).

Third, for entrusting grace. God **considered** him **faithful,** or trustworthy, and it was grace that made Paul so. In 1 Corinthians 7:25 he described himself as "one who by the mercy of the Lord is trustworthy." Through God's grace, Paul was a faithful steward of the ministry entrusted to him (cf. 1 Cor. 4:1–2).

Fourth, for the employing grace that put him **into service.** *Diakonia* (**service**) refers to lowly, humble service (cf. Col. 1:23–25). By using that term, Paul shows that he is not boasting of his faithfulness or trustworthiness. William Barclay relates a story that illustrates selfless service:

> [The Greek writer] Plutarch tells us that when a Spartan won a victory in the games, his reward was that he might stand beside his king in battle. A Spartan wrestler at the Olympic games was offered a very considerable bribe to abandon the struggle; but he refused. Finally, after a terrific effort, he won his victory. Someone said to him: "Well, Spartan, what have you got out of this costly victory you have won?" He answered: "I have won the privilege of standing in front of my king in battle." (*The Letters to Timothy, Titus, and Philemon* [Philadelphia: Westminster, 1975], 42–43)

Like the Spartan, Paul sought no honor for himself. His humble spirit was reflected in his statement that "I bear on my body the brand-marks of Jesus" (Gal. 6:17), and in his desire to "know Him, and the power of His resurrection and the fellowship of His sufferings, being conformed to His death" (Phil. 3:10). The words of Jesus in 2 Corinthians 12:9, "My grace is sufficient for you," were proven true again and again in Paul's life.

THE NEED FOR GRACE

even though I was formerly a blasphemer and a persecutor and a violent aggressor. (1:13a)

The grace of God was especially vivid in Paul's mind because of his past. As a great sinner he needed great grace. Before his dramatic encounter with the risen Christ on the Damascus Road, Paul **was formerly a blasphemer and a persecutor and a violent aggressor. A blasphemer** is one who slanders God, who overtly speaks evil of Him. Not only had Paul been a blasphemer, he had compelled others to blaspheme. Giving his testimony before King Agrippa in Acts 26:11, Paul related how he "tried to force [Christians] to blaspheme." His attack was directed ultimately not against the church, but Jesus Christ (cf. Acts 9:4–5; 22:7–8; 26:14–15).

Paul had shattered the Decalogue, smashing its commandments on the rock of his own pride. As **a blasphemer,** Paul violated the first half of the Ten Commandments, which speak of man's relationship to God. As a **persecutor and a violent aggressor,** he violated the second half, which speak of man's relationship to man. Paul was a relentless, driven, ferocious **persecutor** of the church. Acts 8:3 and 9:1 relate the havoc he created, even entering houses to arrest believers. Not only did he approve of Stephen's death (Acts 8:1), but many others as well (Acts 26:10). A **violent aggressor** is a person with no normal concern for human kindness. In our vernacular we might call such a person a bully. *Hubristēs* (**violent aggressor**) denotes the person driven by violence and contempt for others to mistreat them. To see them humiliated and suffering brings him pleasure. We might even call a **violent aggressor** a sadist. The word appears in the list of sins in Romans 1:30, and our Lord used the verb form to describe the mistreatment He would suffer during His arrest and trial (Luke 18:32).

Given Paul's violent past, it is no wonder that Ananias (Acts 9:13) and the disciples (Acts 9:26) were slow to accept him. Remembering what he had been delivered from helped Paul to maintain a humble, grateful attitude.

The Power of Grace

And yet I was shown mercy, because I acted ignorantly in unbelief; (1:13b)

Although Paul's need for grace was great, the power of grace was greater. Paul was living proof of the truth he expressed in Romans 5:20, "where sin increased, grace abounded all the more." In spite of his sinful past, he **was shown mercy.** The aorist passive verb *ēleēthēn* (**I was shown mercy**) might be translated "I was mercied." Paul's wretchedness was met with God's compassion. He could say with the hymn writer,

And from my smitten heart with tears
Two wonders I confess,
The wonders of redeeming love
And my unworthiness.
(Elizabeth C. Clephane,
"Beneath the Cross of Jesus")

Mercy differs from grace in that grace removes guilt, while **mercy** takes away the misery caused by sin. Paul received the undeserved relief of misery that accompanies saving grace.

How could so vile a sinner as Paul receive **mercy? Because,** he writes, **I acted ignorantly in unbelief.** He was no hardened apostate, rejecting the full light of God's revelation. He was not like the Pharisees who understood Christ's teaching and power, but rejected Him. Nor was he to be classed with those who "have once been enlightened and have tasted of the heavenly gift and have been made partakers of the Holy Spirit, and have tasted the good word of God and the powers of the age to come, and then have fallen away" (Heb. 6:4–6). He did not understand the ramifications of his actions. Sinning willfully after having the truth can result in permanent judgment (Heb. 10:26–27).

Both the Old and New Testaments speak of unwitting or unintentional sins. Numbers 15:22–29 says

> But when you unwittingly fail and do not observe all these commandments, which the Lord has spoken to Moses, even all that the Lord has commanded you through Moses, from the day when the Lord gave commandment and onward throughout your generations, then it shall be, if it is done unintentionally, without the knowledge of the congregation, that all the congregation shall offer one bull for a burnt offering, as a soothing aroma to the Lord, with its grain offering, and its libation, according to the ordinance, and one male goat for a sin offering. Then the priest shall make atonement for all the congregation of the sons of Israel, and they shall be forgiven; for it was an error, and they have brought their offering, an offering by fire to the Lord, and their sin offering before the Lord, for their error. So all the congregation of the sons of Israel will be forgiven, with the alien who sojourns among them, for it happened to all the people through error. Also if one person sins unintentionally, then he shall offer a one year old female goat for a sin offering. And the priest shall make atonement before the Lord for the person who goes astray when he sins unintentionally, making atonement for him that he may be forgiven. You shall have one law for him who does anything unintentionally, for him who is native among the sons of Israel and for the alien who sojourns among them.

On the other hand,

> the person who does anything defiantly, whether he is native or an alien, that one is blaspheming the Lord; and that person shall be cut off from among his people. Because he has despised the word of the Lord and has broken His commandment, that person shall be completely cut off; his guilt shall be on him. (Num. 15:30–31)

Those who sinned deliberately and willfully were beyond the hope of atonement because they were unrepentant. Those who sinned unintentionally and came in repentance and faith were covered by the atonement made on the Day of Atonement.

In the New Testament, Jesus prayed for those who had crucified Him, "Father, forgive them; for they do not know what they are doing" (Luke 23:34). Peter affirmed that truth in Acts 3:17: "And now, brethren, I know that you acted in ignorance."

Paul was responsible for his sin. He was the foremost of sinners (1:15), but he received forgiveness because he "did not prove disobedient to the heavenly vision" (Acts 26:19). When faced with the truth, he believed it (cf. Rom. 7:9; Phil. 3:7–9). The grace of God is powerful enough to redeem the worst sinner who is willing to repent.

THE MEASURE OF GRACE

and the grace of our Lord was more than abundant, with the faith and love which are found in Christ Jesus. (1:14)

Grace appears only here in the passage, yet it permeates Paul's thought in 1:12–17. Abundant sin gives way to the **more than abundant** grace supplied by **our Lord. More than abundant** is from *huperpleonazō,* a compound word made up of the normal word for **abundant,** *pleonazō* with the preposition *huper* added. Paul loved to add *huper* to words to intensify them. He gives us insight into the surpassing measure of God's grace, which is greater than man's sin (Rom. 5:20), and sufficient to meet all our needs (2 Cor. 9:8).

With superabundant grace comes **the faith and love which are** also **found in Christ Jesus.** Saving faith is not a meritorious work whereby we earn divine grace. Rather, it is a gift of God's grace: "For by grace you have been saved through faith; and that not of yourselves, it is the gift of God" (Eph. 2:8). Electing grace grants us the ability to believe in Jesus Christ and trust God for salvation. **Faith and love** are frequently linked with salvation in the New Testament (cf. Eph. 1:15; 3:17; Col. 1:4; 1 Thess. 1:3; 3:6; 5:8; 2 Thess. 1:3; Philem. 5), since they are part of the salvation package. A true Christian is marked by continuing faith (Col. 1:23) and love (1 John 3:14). God's grace is so abundant that it includes not only salvation, but the faith and love that accompany it.

The Purpose of Grace

It is a trustworthy statement, deserving full acceptance, that Christ Jesus came into the world to save sinners, among whom I am foremost of all. And yet for this reason I found mercy, in order that in me as the foremost, Jesus Christ might demonstrate His perfect patience, as an example for those who would believe in Him for eternal life. (1:15–16)

The phrase **it is a trustworthy statement** is unique to the Pastoral Epistles, appearing five times (cf. 3:1; 4:9; 2 Tim. 2:11; Titus 3:8). These statements were familiar, recognized summaries of key doctrines. That they were common in the church by the time of the writing of the Pastoral Epistles indicates that a well-articulated theology had developed. Paul indeed quotes them as if they were common knowledge. This one and the one in 1 Timothy 4:9 have the phrase **deserving full acceptance** appended for added emphasis.

The trustworthy statement in 1:15 acts as a condensed articulation of the gospel. In only eight Greek words is found a marvelous summation of the gospel message. Each word is chosen carefully. **Christ Jesus** is the word order preferred by Paul in the Pastoral Epistles. He uses it twenty-five times compared to six uses of "Jesus Christ." Bound up in those two words is all that He is. **Christ** is the anointed King who came to redeem, and became the earthly **Jesus** at the Incarnation. That He **came into the world** implies not only His incarnation but His preexistence. Note carefully that it does not say that He came into existence, or that He was created. He existed somewhere else before coming into the world. This phraseology is used frequently by John, who often speaks of Christ's coming into the world (cf. John 1:9; 3:19; 6:14; 11:27; 12:46; 16:28; 18:37).

The **world** refers to the world of humanity, blind, lost, and condemned to hell because of its hostility to God (cf. 1 John 5:19). It is into that world of sinners, of darkness and unbelief, that Jesus came. John 3:17 says, "God did not send the Son into the world to judge the world, but that the world should be saved through Him" (cf. John 12:46–47).

Christ's purpose in coming into this fallen world was **to save sinners.** Before his birth the angel told Joseph "it is He who will save

His people from their sins" (Matt. 1:21). In Luke 19:10 our Lord stated the purpose of His coming into the world: "For the Son of Man has come to seek and to save that which was lost." To **save** is to deliver from death and darkness, from sin, hell, and judgment. **Sinners** was a term used by the Jews to describe Gentiles (cf. Gal. 2:15), but our Lord used it to refer to all of fallen mankind (cf. Matt. 9:13). It denotes man's constant violation of God's law; men are sinners by nature.

In the realm of **sinners,** Paul saw himself as **foremost of all** (cf. 1 Cor. 15:9; Eph. 3:8). Many in our day would hasten to correct Paul's self-image and restore his self-esteem. But that was a healthy self-view for Paul because it was accurate. It's hard to imagine anyone worse than a blasphemer of God and persecutor of His church. Such a view of himself also served to keep Paul humble and grateful.

It was **for this reason** that **Paul** found mercy. God didn't save him merely to get him out of hell or into heaven. Nor did He save him to preach the gospel or write the epistles; God could have had others do that. The purpose of salvation, whether Paul's or ours, is to display God's grace, power, and patience and produce a true worshiper of God (John 4:21–24). It is for His glory primarily, our benefit is secondary.

It was through saving Paul that **Jesus Christ** could most clearly **demonstrate His perfect patience.** *Makrothumia* (**patience**) means to be patient with people. Paul's point is that if the Lord was patient with the worst of sinners, no one is beyond the reach of His grace. **As an example for those who would believe in Him for eternal life,** Paul was living proof that God can save any sinner. He was the *hupotupōsis,* the model, type, or pattern. Those who fear that God cannot save them would do well to consider the case of Paul.

THE RESPONSE TO GRACE

Now to the King eternal, immortal, invisible, the only God, be honor and glory forever and ever. Amen. (1:17)

Having begun the passage with thanksgiving, Paul now closes it with a doxology. **Eternal** literally means "of the ages." It refers to the two ages in Jewish thought, the present age, and the age to come. God had no beginning and will have no end. He exists outside of time, though He acts in it. He is **immortal,** imperishable, and incorruptible. He will never know death, decay, or loss of strength. Because God is **invisible,** He can be known only by His self-revelation. That He is **the only God** is a fundamental truth of Scripture (cf. Deut. 4:35, 39; 6:4; Isa. 43:10; 44:6; 45:5–6, 21–22; 46:9; 1 Cor. 8:4, 6; 1 Tim. 2:5). He alone is worthy of all **honor and glory forever and ever.** The doxology closes with the emphatic **Amen,** meaning "let it be said."

In contrast to the false gospel of the errorists, Paul emphasizes the true gospel and his participation in it by God's grace. That grace is available to the worst sinner who comes to the Lord Jesus Christ in humble faith and repentance.

Fighting the Noble War

4

This command I entrust to you, Timothy, my son, in accordance with the prophecies previously made concerning you, that by them you may fight the good fight, keeping faith and a good conscience, (1:18–19a)

Our Lord Jesus Christ has called His followers to an abundant life of love, peace, joy, and communion with Him. Gospel presentations and tracts stress those truths in their appeal to unbelievers. There is another side to the Christian life, however, one that doesn't often find its way into our evangelism. The Christian life is also a warfare, as believers enter a lifelong fight against the evil world system, Satan, and their own sinful human flesh.

Sadly, much of the contemporary church seems to have missed that reality. Many have heard only the gospel of easy believism and cheap grace. They have an inadequate concept of the spiritual struggle involved in loving the Lord Jesus Christ. Such people often magnify the petty temporal annoyances of everyday life until they seem like trials of epic proportions. Frankly, that is as absurd as a soldier in the midst of a raging firefight complaining about the dirt on his uniform.

Paul was very much aware of the reality of spiritual warfare. Not only did he battle his flesh (as he shows in Rom. 7:14–25), but he also had to continually engage the world in conflict (cf. Gal. 6:14). And he was relentlessly assaulted by Satan, as his mention of the "messenger of Satan" sent to beat him (2 Cor. 12:7) indicates. Satanic opposition also kept him from visiting the Thessalonians (1 Thess. 2:17–18). As he summarizes the introduction to this letter in 1:18–19, he calls Timothy to fight the good or noble fight against Satan. Like all those in the ministry, Timothy was called to an unceasing spiritual warfare. That fight demands equipped, trained, and devoted soldiers. Paul wrote this letter to help Timothy gear up for the current battles.

Paul had left him in Ephesus to oppose the enemies encroaching on the Ephesian church. False leaders in positions of power and authority were teaching heresy about the Person and work of Jesus Christ (cf. 1:4–7; 4:1–3). These false teachers were also living impure lives (cf. 1:4–5, 19–20; 5:19–20). Timothy was set in the forefront of the battle, and Paul wanted him to acquit himself well.

To understand the full scope of Timothy's battle, we need to step back and look at the big picture. Spiritual conflict is, at its highest level, a war between God and Satan. It is fought also on the angelic level, between Satan's wicked demons and God's elect holy angels. On the human level, it is a battle between godly and ungodly men.

Originally, there was no such war. The Bible knows of no eternal dualism between good and evil, as in Zoroastrianism (the religion of ancient Persia). Genesis 1:31 records that at the end of the sixth day, "God saw all that He had made, and behold, it was very good." Everything in God's creation submitted to His sovereign rule; there was no conflict or rebellion. There was no Satan, no adversary, no rebel, no deceiver. Then came a disastrous event that ignited the cosmic war. Ezekiel describes it:

> Again the word of the Lord came to me saying, "Son of man, take up a lamentation over the king of Tyre, and say to him, 'Thus says the Lord God, "You had the seal of perfection, full of wisdom and perfect in beauty. You were in Eden, the garden of God; every precious stone was your covering: The ruby, the topaz, and the diamond; the beryl, the onyx, and the jasper; the lapis lazuli, the turquoise, and the emerald; and the gold, the workmanship of your settings and sockets, was in you. On the day that you were created they were prepared. You were the anointed cherub who covers, and I placed you there. You were on the holy mountain of God; you walked in the midst of the stones of fire. You were blameless in your ways from the day you were created, until unrighteousness was found in you. By the abundance of your trade you were internally filled with violence, and you sinned; therefore I have

> cast you as profane from the mountain of God. And I have destroyed you, O covering cherub, from the midst of the stones of fire. Your heart was lifted up because of your beauty; you corrupted your wisdom by reason of your splendor. I cast you to the ground; I put you before kings, that they may see you. By the multitude of your iniquities, in the unrighteousness of your trade, you profaned your sanctuaries. Therefore I have brought fire from the midst of you; it has consumed you, and I have turned you to ashes on the earth in the eyes of all who see you. All who know you among the peoples are appalled at you; you have become terrified, and you will be no more."'" (Ezek. 28:11–19)

Beginning in chapter 26, Ezekiel has been giving prophecies against the city of Tyre. In Ezekiel 28:1–19, he indicts the human ruler of Tyre. He then goes beyond him to speak of the supernatural power behind the human ruler. Verses 1–10 focus on the human leader of Tyre, but verses 11–19 contain descriptions that could not apply to any human. The leader of Tyre did not have "the seal of perfection" (v. 12), nor was he in "Eden, the garden of God" (v. 13). No mere human could be called "the anointed cherub who covers" (v. 14), and of no man except Adam could it be said, "You were blameless in your ways from the day you were created, until unrighteousness was found in you" (v. 15). Verses 11–19, then, describe Lucifer.

Before his fall, which obviously took place after the creation of the Garden of Eden, Satan was the "anointed cherub who covers" (v. 14). He was the highest ranking angelic being, concerned particularly with the glory of God. He was "on the holy mountain of God," and "walked in the midst of the stones of fire." That speaks of his dwelling in the immediate presence of God. How such a being, blameless since his creation, existing in a perfectly holy environment, could sin remains a mystery. That he did sin is a fact, however. All Ezekiel says of him is that "unrighteousness was found in you" (v. 15). He was then cast from his station among the holy ones in God's presence (v. 16), although he is still allowed access to that presence (Job 1:6; Rev. 12:10). It was then that he became Satan, the adversary; Apollyon, the destroyer; Devil, the slanderer.

As already noted, it is difficult for our finite minds to understand how a perfect being in a perfect environment could fall into sin. Ezekiel describes Lucifer's motivation in verse 17: "Your heart was lifted up because of your beauty; you corrupted your wisdom by reason of your splendor." Satan somehow became enamored with his beauty and splendor, and his response was the sin of pride, which led to rebellion.

Isaiah 14:12–14 confirms that it was indeed pride that caused Satan's downfall:

> How you have fallen from heaven, O star of the morning, son of the dawn! You have been cut down to the earth, you who have weakened the nations! But you said in your heart, "I will ascend to heaven; I will raise my throne above the stars of God, and I will sit on the mount of assembly in the recesses of the north. I will ascend above the heights of the clouds; I will make myself like the Most High."

As Ezekiel described Satan as the greater power behind the ruler of Tyre, so Isaiah shows him to be the power behind the king of Babylon. He calls him "star of the morning," emphasizing the glory Satan possessed before his fall (cf. Rev. 22:16 where a similar phrase is used to describe Christ). Isaiah's exclamation "How you have fallen from heaven" is reminiscent of our Lord's words in Luke 10:18, "I was watching Satan fall from heaven like lightning."

Satan's pride is revealed in the five statements in verses 13 and 14 that begin, "I will." He was not content with being the highest-ranking created being, dwelling constantly in God's presence. He became jealous of God, and sought equality with Him. That sin, a projection of his pride, was the same one he soon tempted Eve to commit (Gen. 3:5). When Satan, in his pride, tried to "ascend above the heights of the clouds," and make himself "like the Most High," the long war with God began.

Satan was not alone in his rebellion. Revelation 12:3–4 reveals that hosts of other angels joined him:

> And another sign appeared in heaven: and behold, a great red dragon having seven heads and ten horns, and on his heads were seven diadems. And his tail swept away a third of the stars of heaven, and threw them to the earth. And the dragon stood before the woman who was about to give birth, so that when she gave birth he might devour her child.

The dragon is none other than Satan, and the stars of heaven symbolize the angels (cf. Job 38:7). When Satan fell, he took one third of the angels with him. These fallen angels, or demons, aid Satan in his warfare against God. While some God has permanently bound (Jude 6), and others He has temporarily bound until the Tribulation (cf. Rev. 9:3ff.), the others move through the world to do Satan's bidding and their own evil.

The specific target of Satan and his demonic hosts is Christ and His redemptive work and final glory. In Revelation 12:5, we read of the woman, symbolizing Israel, giving birth to the Messiah, who was to rule the nations with a rod of iron. In verse 4, we see Satan attempting to destroy the child. Throughout history, that has been the special focus of his attack. In Genesis 6, we learn of his attempt to produce a race of half-breed demon-men that would be unredeemable. He often tried to corrupt Israel with sin or mixed marriages so there would be no possibility of a godly seed. He even tried to accomplish the genocide of the Jews, but God used Mordecai to save them (see Esther). He tried to kill Jesus through Herod's slaughter of the infants, and by having Him thrown off a cliff at Nazareth (Luke 4:29). He tried to get Him to fall to his temptations. Finally, he had Him crucified, only to have his own head crushed and his power forever shattered by Christ's resurrection.

Satan and his angels, in battling God and His purposes, also wage war against God's elect angels, led by Michael. That warfare has a past (Jude 9; Dan. 9), present, and future (Rev. 12:7) aspect. Although hidden from our view, their battle is no less real (cf. Dan. 10:12–13).

Satan also attacks the people of God. In Revelation 12:17, we read of his future attack on Israel in the Tribulation. Right now he attacks the church, both personally, and through fallen angels and evil men (cf. Eph. 6:12). He has limited interest in individual believers; even his attacks on them are ultimately attacks on God and attempts to thwart His plans. How we fare in the battle, then, reflects on God. If we are defeated, Satan has in that sense been effective. When we are victorious, his attack against God is beaten off. In light of that, Paul urged Timothy to "suffer hardship with me, as a good soldier of Christ Jesus" (2 Tim. 2:3).

If we would be victorious, we must understand how Satan attacks the church today. Then, like Paul, we will not be "ignorant of his schemes" (2 Cor. 2:11). First, Satan attacks the church by blinding the minds of unbelievers to the gospel (2 Cor. 4:3–4), thereby keeping them away from the truth and the church. He accomplishes that through ignorance, false religion, pride, lust, and the wickedness that results from his control over the world system.

Second, Satan attempts to devastate those who are already believers to cripple them and destroy the credibility of their witness. Jesus warned Peter, "Simon, Simon, behold, Satan has demanded permission to sift you like wheat" (Luke 22:31). Satan wanted to destroy Peter's faith, to shake him and make what was genuine in him blow away in the wind. If he had succeeded, Peter would have been useless to God. Peter remembered our Lord's warning, and in 1 Peter 5:8 exhorted us to "be of sober spirit, be on the alert. Your adversary, the devil, prowls about like a roaring lion, seeking someone to devour." Satan attacks believers, trying to destroy their faith and trust in God, thereby rendering them ineffective for the battle.

Third, Satan attacks the church by attacking marriage and the family. Paul commanded husbands and wives not to deprive each other of sexual relations so Satan would have no opportunity to tempt them (1 Cor. 7:5). Strong marriages and families are a prerequisite to a healthy church and witness. By attacking those institutions, Satan weakens the church. The recent upsurge in divorce and other family problems among Christians indicates he is having success in that area.

Fourth, Satan attacks the church through her leaders. Paul tells Timothy in 1 Timothy 3 that leaders must be well qualified for their positions. Otherwise, they may "fall into reproach and the snare of the devil" (1 Tim. 3:7). There is no one in the church Satan would rather destroy than leaders. This, too, is an area where Satan has had much success in recent years. Leader after leader has been devastated by Satan's attacks, whether through sexual sin, pride, materialism, or authoritarianism. The results for the church are tragic. When the shepherds are destroyed, the flock will scatter.

Finally, Satan attacks the church through false religious systems. Liberal Christianity, the cults, world religions, and humanism are a constant menace. The leaders of those movements, like their evil master, can transform themselves into angels of light (2 Cor. 11:14–15). The things taught in the name of biblical truth are sometimes frightening (cf. Acts 20:28–32; 1 Tim. 4:1–7; Titus 1:10–11; 2 Peter 2:1–3, etc.). The church faces a constant barrage of error, all of it ultimately spawned by Satan—"doctrines of demons" (1 Tim. 4:1).

How can the church defend itself against such assaults of the wicked one? Paul gives the answer in 2 Corinthians 10:4–5:

> For the weapons of our warfare are not of the flesh, but divinely powerful for the destruction of fortresses. We are destroying speculations and every lofty thing raised up against the knowledge of God, and we are taking every thought captive to the obedience of Christ.

Ephesians 6:13–18 lays out the necessary armor:

> Therefore, take up the full armor of God, that you may be able to resist in the evil day, and having done everything, to stand firm. Stand firm therefore, having girded your loins with truth, and having put on the breastplate of righteousness, and having shod your feet with the preparation of the gospel of peace; in addition to all, taking up the shield of faith with which you will be able to extinguish all the flaming missiles of the evil one. And take the helmet of salvation, and the sword of the Spirit, which is the word of God. With all prayer and petition pray at all times in the Spirit, and with this in view, be on the alert with all perseverance and petition for all the saints.

Our weapons for fighting the spiritual battle are God's Word and prayer "at all times." Apart from that, all our intellect, ability, skill, and ingenuity are useless. As Martin Luther wrote in the hymn "A Mighty Fortress is Our God,"

> Did we in our own strength confide,
> Our striving would be losing.

We successfully fight the noble war by living in obedience to Scripture. Then we can sing in triumph,

> And tho this world, with devils filled
> Should threaten to undo us,
> We will not fear, for God hath willed
> His truth to triumph through us:
> The Prince of Darkness grim,
> We tremble not for him;
> His rage we can endure,
> For lo, his doom is sure;
> One little word shall fell him.
> (Martin Luther,
> "A Mighty Fortress Is Our God")

To take up the Scripture and fight the spiritual war effectively, Timothy needed to understand his responsibility beyond himself and within himself.

THE RESPONSIBILITY BEYOND HIMSELF

This command I entrust to you, Timothy, my son, in accordance with the prophecies previously made concerning you, that by them you may fight the good fight, (1:18)

Timothy was not in the battle alone. He was commissioned by Paul, and his call to the ministry was confirmed by revelation from God concerning him. His service as a soldier for Christ was thus set in the context of the authority and affirmation of the church. He was responsible and accountable to the church and the Head of the church for his role in the battle.

To carry out his responsibility to the Lord and the church, Timothy had first a **command** to obey. *Parangelian* (**command**) is used for a military order. As such it is not a suggestion, and is not open for discussion. It is a mandate to be carried out obediently. In 5:21 Paul charged Timothy and made him accountable to God the Father, Jesus Christ, and the elect angels. In 6:13–14 he again made Timothy accountable to God for his actions. That staggering accountability led Paul to "solemnly charge" Timothy "in the presence of God and of Christ Jesus, who is to judge the living and the dead, and by His appearing and His kingdom: preach the word; be ready in season and out of season; reprove, rebuke, exhort, with great patience and instruction" (2 Tim. 4:1–2). He will answer to God and to Christ for his ministry (cf. Heb. 13:17; James 3:1). Timothy had a duty to God in the church, something our self-indulgent culture knows little about. We talk much of freedom, success, joy, and peace, but little of duty. Yet we are duty-bound to obey the Commander (2 Tim. 2:4) and fulfill our ministries (2 Tim. 4:5). Those things are not optional.

Our Lord stressed the importance of duty in Luke 17:7–10:

> But which of you, having a slave plowing or tending sheep, will say to him when he has come in from the field, "Come immediately and sit down to eat"? But will he not say to him, "Prepare something for me to eat, and properly clothe yourself and serve me until I have eaten and drunk; and afterward you will eat and drink"? He does not thank the slave because he did the things which were commanded, does he? So you too, when you do all the things which are commanded you, say, "We are unworthy slaves; we have done only that which we ought to have done."

Paul understood clearly the concept of duty. Giving his testimony before King Agrippa he said, "I did not prove disobedient to the heavenly vision" (Acts 26:19). To the Corinthians he wrote, "For if I preach the gospel, I have nothing to boast of, for I am under compulsion; for woe is me if I do not preach the gospel. For if I do this voluntarily, I have a reward; but if against my will, I have a stewardship entrusted to me" (1 Cor. 9:16–17). Paul recognized that he was under a divine obligation to use his gifts and fulfill his calling. In Acts 20:24 he told the Ephesian elders, "But I do not consider my life of any account as dear to myself, in order that I may finish my course, and the ministry which I received from the Lord Jesus, to testify solemnly of the gospel of the grace of God."

Every servant of the Lord is duty-bound to carry out his ministry. Moses (Ex. 4:10–16), Isaiah (Isa. 6:8–11), Jeremiah (Jer. 20:9), Ezekiel (Ezek. 2:7–8), and Jonah (Jonah 1:1–2) all were given a charge to fulfill. In 2 Timothy 4:1–2 Paul commanded Timothy to preach the Word "in season and out of season." In our society, with its emphasis on entertainment, anti-authoritarian attitude, critic mentality, and psychological orientation, our message will often be rejected. That, however, does not excuse us from our duty (cf. Jer. 7:27; Ezek. 2:4–5; 3:7; 33:30–32).

Second, Timothy was entrusted with a commission to fulfill. *Paratithēmi* (**entrust**) refers to committing something of value to another. It is used, for example, to speak of putting a deposit in a bank. Paul had given Timothy a valuable deposit, God's truth (cf. 2 Tim. 2:2), which was the "treasure" he was to guard diligently (6:20; 2 Tim. 1:14). Paul himself had been entrusted with that deposit (cf. 1:11), and that same deposit of truth has been handed down through the centuries to us. We must preserve it and hand it down intact to the next generation.

Third, Timothy had a confirmation to live up to. Timothy's calling had been confirmed through **prophecies.** Prophets in the New Testament era spoke the revelation of God's will to the early church. Prophecy is the gift of proclaiming God's Word. In one sense, anyone who preaches or teaches God's Word is a prophet. Unlike present-day teachers and preachers, however, New Testament prophets occasionally received direct revelation from God. While doctrine was the province of the apostles (cf. Acts 2:42), prophets seem to be the instruments God used to speak of practical issues (cf. Acts 21:10–11). (For a thorough discussion of the gift of prophecy, see my books *Charismatic Chaos* [Grand Rapids: Zondervan, 1992], 54–84 [especially pp. 69–70]; and *Reckless Faith* [Wheaton, Ill.: Crossway, 1994], 177ff.)

Proagō (**previously made**) literally means "leading the way to." It implies that a series of prophecies had been made **concerning** Timothy in connection with him having received his spiritual gift (4:14). The **prophecies,** then, were those that specifically and supernaturally called Timothy into the ministry. Paul's command to Timothy was not his own, but was confirmed by God through the ministry of some prophets.

Pastors and elders are no longer called to the ministry in such a dramatic fashion. As we will see in 3:1, the call to ministry rises from inside through desire, rather than outside from revelation. That desire is then to be confirmed by the church. The church, by observing a man's life and service, can confirm whether he gives evidence of being called by God to the ministry. That confirmation by the church should keep us going when the battle is fierce. Having been commissioned by God through divine revelation, or, as now, by the confirmation of God's people, a leader can't quit. The call of God in his life should encourage Timothy and all other preachers to **fight the good fight. Good** is from *kalos,* meaning intrinsically good—noble, excellent, or virtuous. There is the duty to God and the church of Jesus Christ to motivate the embattled preacher—and the knowledge that it is the noblest warfare in all the universe. What better thing to live and die for than the great war between God and Satan—a war for the souls of men and women and the glory of God and our Savior the Lord Jesus Christ?

William Barclay relates the dramatic story of the great Scottish Reformer John Knox's call to the ministry:

> [John Knox] had been teaching in St. Andrews. His teaching was supposed to be private but many came to it, for he was obviously a man with a message. So the people urged him "that he would take the preaching place upon him. But he utterly refused, alleging that he would not run where God had not called him. . . . Whereupon they privily among themselves advising, having with them in council Sir David Lindsay of the Mount, they concluded that they would give a charge to the said John, and that publicly by the mouth of their preacher."
>
> So Sunday came and Knox was in Church and John Rough was preaching. "The said John Rough, preacher, directed his words to the said John Knox, saying: 'Brother, ye shall not be offended, albeit that I speak unto you that which I have in charge, even from all those that are here present, which is this: In the name of God, and of his Son Jesus Christ, and in the name of these that presently call you by my mouth, I charge you that you refuse not this holy vocation, but . . . that you take upon you the public office and charge of preaching, even as you look to avoid God's displeasure, and desire that he shall multiply his graces with you.' And in the end he said to those that were present: 'Was not this your charge to me? And do ye not approve this vocation?' They answered: 'It was: and we approve it.' Whereat the said John, abashed, burst forth in most abundant tears, and withdrew himself to his chamber. His countenance and behaviour, from that day till the day that he was compelled to present himself to the public place of preaching, did sufficiently declare the grief and trouble of his heart; for no man saw any sign of mirth in him, neither yet had he pleasure to accompany any man, many days together."
>
> John Knox was chosen; he did not want to answer the call; but he had to, for the choice had been made by God. Years afterwards, the Regent Morton uttered his famous epitaph by Knox's graveside: "In respect that he bore God's message, to whom he must make account for the same, he (albeit he was weak and an unworthy creature, and a fearful man) feared not the faces of men." The consciousness of being chosen gave him courage. (*The Letters to Timothy, Titus, and Philemon* [Philadelphia: Westminster, 1975], 49–50)

Like Timothy and John Knox, those called by God must accept the duty to fulfill their ministries.

THE RESPONSIBILITY WITHIN HIMSELF

keeping faith and a good conscience (1:19a)

Paul links **faith and a good conscience** repeatedly in this letter (cf. 1:5; 3:9). The **faith** is a reference to the Christian faith, the gospel, the Word of God. **Keeping** the **faith** means holding fast to that revealed truth. Timothy's first responsibility to the Lord was to remain loyal to the objective body of revealed Scripture. Unlike those who turned away from the faith (1:6; 6:10, 21), Timothy was to remain unwaveringly devoted to the Word of God. In fact, he was to guard it (6:20), nourish himself on it (4:6), and preach it (4:13; 2 Tim. 4:2).

A good conscience is the result of a pure life. Like Paul (cf. Acts 24:16), Timothy was to maintain a blameless conscience. Conscience is a God-given device in every human mind that reacts to that person's behavior. It either accuses or excuses (Rom. 2:14–15). It produces feelings of well-being, peace, contentment, and calm when behavior is good. When behavior is evil, it activates guilt, shame, remorse, fear, doubt, insecurity, and despair. Its purpose is to warn the person of the fact that he is sinning. What a blessing to have such a warning device. It is to the soul what pain is to the body. Pain warns that something threatens the body's well-being. Guilt warns that something threatens the well-being of the soul. Paul was always anxious to have a clean, clear, pure, good conscience (cf. 2 Cor. 1:12) and desired the same for Timothy. He calls for holiness in this charge to Timothy.

Doctrinal purity must be accompanied by purity of life. There is an inseparable link between truth and morality, between right belief and right behavior. Consequently, theological error has its roots in moral rather than intellectual soil (cf. Matt. 7:15–20). People often teach wrong doctrine to accommodate their sin. That truth is borne out by the immorality that so often characterizes false teachers (cf. 2 Peter 2). It is not surprising, then, that Paul also emphasizes godliness in 1 Timothy (cf. 2:10; 4:7–8; 6:6). Sound doctrine and godly living are the twin towers guarding the purity of the church: "Pay close attention to yourself and to your teaching; persevere in these things; for as you do this you will insure salvation both for yourself and for those who hear you" (4:16).

By remembering his responsibility beyond himself to the Lord and to the church to keep himself pure, Timothy would be able to fight the spiritual battle he faced. He would serve valiantly as a "good soldier of Christ Jesus" (2 Tim. 2:3).

Delivered to Satan

5

which some have rejected and suffered shipwreck in regard to their faith. Among these are Hymenaeus and Alexander, whom I have delivered over to Satan, so that they may be taught not to blaspheme. (1:19b–20)

It is a part of the church's ministry, as it is a ministry of God Himself, to deliver certain people to Satan. Our Lord taught in Matthew 18 that those who continue in sin are to be put out of the church. Such people who are excommunicated are delivered to Satan. That is precisely what Paul called for in the Corinthian church (1 Cor. 5:4–5) and what he did to two of the false teachers in leadership at Ephesus, and what by implication he invites Timothy and us to continue to do.

To deliver someone to Satan indicates that they had not before been fully in his power. In 1 John 5:19 we learn that "the whole world lies in the power of the evil one." Unbelievers walk "according to the prince of the power of the air, of the spirit that is now working in the sons of disobedience" (Eph. 2:2). Those who are to be delivered to Satan must, therefore, have been in some way under the umbrella of protection provided by the church. Even unbelievers receive a certain amount of protection from their association with the community of redeemed people.

The history of Israel testifies to that truth. There were in Israel those who were not personally redeemed. Paul reminds us in Romans 9:6 that "they are not all Israel who are descended from Israel." Yet those unredeemed Jews still experienced the abundant blessings God poured out on the nation. They received a share of the inheritance in the Promised Land, and a measure of God's protection from their enemies. The benefits of the priesthood and the sacrificial system were theirs.

The same is true in the church. There are unbelievers who are blessed by virtue of their association with believers. In 1 Corinthians 7:14 Paul wrote, "For the unbelieving husband is sanctified through his wife, and the unbelieving wife is sanctified through her believing husband; for otherwise your children are unclean, but now they are holy." Nonbelievers in a Christian's family are beneficiaries of God's blessing on the Christian.

So there is in the shelter of God's people protection from the full force of Satan's fury. Unbelieving Jews were better off than unbelieving Gentiles outside the covenant community. Unbelievers who associate themselves with the church today are better off than those outside the church. They benefit from God's grace and goodness to his children. Delivering someone to Satan removes the insulation and protection afforded by the believing community. They are out from under God's hand of blessing and they are fully under Satan's control.

There are times when, in the sovereign plan of God, believers are turned over to Satan for positive purposes. There are several illustrations of that in the Scriptures.

Job was a man who seemingly had it all, wealth, family, wisdom, honor, and personal godliness. Job 1:1–5 introduces us to him:

> There was a man in the land of Uz, whose name was Job, and that man was blameless, upright, fearing God, and turning away from evil. And seven sons and three daughters were born to him. His possessions also were 7,000 sheep, 3,000 camels, 500 yoke of oxen, 500 female donkeys, and very many servants; and that man was the greatest of all the men of the east. And his sons used to go and hold a feast in the house of each one on his day, and they would send and invite their three sisters to eat and drink with them. And it came about, when the days of feasting had completed their cycle, that Job would send and consecrate them, rising up early in the morning and offering burnt offerings according to the number of them all; for Job said, "Perhaps my sons have sinned and cursed God in their hearts." Thus Job did continually.

Then an event took place unknown to Job that was to turn his world upside down:

> Now there was a day when the sons of God came to present themselves before the Lord, and Satan also came among them. And the Lord said to Satan, "From where do you come?" Then Satan answered the Lord and said, "From roaming about on the earth and walking around on it." And the Lord said to Satan, "Have you considered My servant Job? For there is no one like him on the earth, a blameless and upright man, fearing God and turning away from evil." Then Satan answered the Lord, "Does Job fear God for nothing? Hast Thou not made a hedge about him and his house and all that he has, on every side? Thou hast blessed the work of his hands, and his possessions have increased in the land. But put forth Thy hand now and touch all that he has; he will surely curse Thee to Thy face." Then the Lord said to Satan, "Behold, all that he has is in your power, only do not put forth your hand on him." So Satan departed from the presence of the Lord. (Job 1:6–12)

Satan, as usual, sought to tear down God's work. He implied that God's children serve Him out of selfish motives, because of the benefits He grants them. To prove the falsity of that accusation, God turned Job over to Satan:

> Now it happened on the day when his sons and his daughters were eating and drinking wine in their oldest brother's house, that a messenger came to Job and said, "The oxen were plowing and the donkeys feeding beside them, and the Sabeans attacked and took them. They also slew the servants with the edge of the sword, and I alone have escaped to tell you." While he was still speaking, another also came and said, "The fire of God fell from heaven and burned up the sheep and the servants and consumed them, and I alone have escaped to tell you." While he was still speaking, another also came and said, "The Chaldeans formed three bands and made a raid on the camels and took them and slew the servants with the edge of the sword; and I alone have escaped to tell you." While he was still speaking, another also came and said, "Your sons and your daughters were eating and drinking wine in their oldest brother's house, and behold, a great wind came from across the wilderness and struck the four corners of the house, and it fell on the young people and they died; and I alone have escaped to tell you."
>
> Then Job arose and tore his robe and shaved his head, and he fell to the ground and worshiped. And he said, "Naked I came from my mother's womb, and naked I shall return there. The Lord gave and the Lord has taken away. Blessed be the name of the Lord." Through all this Job did not sin nor did he blame God. (Job 1:13–22)

Job's reaction vindicated God, and proved Satan wrong. He showed that true saving faith is permanent and does not depend on positive circumstances. Job's love for God was not selfish, based on the benefits he had received. Job loved God with an unbreakable love for who He is, not for what He had given him. God used Job to make a point with Satan. The purpose of the book of Job is not so much to teach us how to handle suffering as to show the strength of the faith of a godly man. Through all his suffering, his physical ailments, his wife and close friends turning against him, and his bewilderment as to why all this was happening to him, Job never lost his trust in God and thus showed his godliness. His attitude is best summed up in his words in Job 13:15: "Though He slay me, I will hope in Him." He never did find out the reason for his suffering because God never told Him. When in reply to his questions God appeared to him and declared His sovereign right to do as He pleased (Job 38–39), Job humbly accepted that:

> Then Job answered the Lord, and said, "I know that Thou canst do all things, and that no purpose of Thine can be thwarted. 'Who is this that hides counsel without knowledge?' "Therefore I have declared that which I did not understand, things too wonderful for me, which I did not know." 'Hear, now, and I will speak; I will ask Thee, and do Thou instruct me.' "I have heard of Thee by the hearing of the ear; but now my eye sees Thee; Therefore I retract, and I repent in dust and ashes." (Job 42:1–6)

Job was delivered to Satan to learn to glorify God, and to give God honor. A true child of God can be delivered to Satan to bring greater glory to Him.

In Matthew 4:1–11 we read the account of One who is far more upright than Job, the Lord Jesus Christ.

> Then Jesus was led up by the Spirit into the wilderness to be tempted by the devil. And after He had fasted forty days and forty nights, He then became hungry. And the tempter came and said to Him, "If You are the Son of God, command that these stones become bread." But He answered and said, "It is written, 'Man shall not live on bread alone, but on every word that proceeds out of the mouth of God.'" Then the devil took Him into the holy city; and he had Him stand on the pinnacle of the temple, and said to Him, "If You are the Son of God throw Yourself down; for it is written, 'He will give His angels charge concerning You'; and 'On their hands they will bear You up, lest You strike Your foot against a stone.'" Jesus said to him, "On the other hand, it is written, 'You shall not put the Lord your God to the test.'" Again, the devil took Him to a very high mountain, and showed Him all the kingdoms of the world, and their glory; and he said to Him, "All

> these things will I give You, if You fall down and worship me." Then Jesus said to him, "Begone, Satan! For it is written, 'You shall worship the Lord your God, and serve Him only.'" Then the devil left Him; and behold, angels came and began to minister to Him.

As God put Job into the hands of Satan, so also did He turn His Son over to Satan. He did so to prove Jesus' character, that He would stand true as the perfect and obedient God-man. Despite being weakened by forty days of fasting and isolation, Jesus successfully resisted all of Satan's temptations to rebel against His father. He, like Job, was handed over to Satan to bring God glory.

Second Corinthians 12:1–10 reveals another example of how God's faithful people are sometimes handed over to Satan:

> Boasting is necessary, though it is not profitable; but I will go on to visions and revelations of the Lord. I know a man in Christ who fourteen years ago—whether in the body I do not know, or out of the body I do not know, God knows—such a man was caught up to the third heaven. And I know how such a man—whether in the body or apart from the body I do not know, God knows—was caught up into Paradise, and heard inexpressible words, which a man is not permitted to speak. On behalf of such a man will I boast; but on my own behalf I will not boast, except in regard to my weaknesses. For if I do wish to boast I shall not be foolish, for I shall be speaking the truth; but I refrain from this, so that no one may credit me with more than he sees in me or hears from me. And because of the surpassing greatness of the revelations, for this reason, to keep me from exalting myself, there was given me a thorn in the flesh, a messenger of Satan to buffet me—to keep me from exalting myself! Concerning this I entreated the Lord three times that it might depart from me. And He has said to me, "My grace is sufficient for you, for power is perfected in weakness." Most gladly, therefore, I will rather boast about my weaknesses, that the power of Christ may dwell in me. Therefore I am well content with weaknesses, with insults, with distresses, with persecutions, with difficulties, for Christ's sake; for when I am weak, then I am strong.

Few men had as much to boast about as the apostle Paul. It was largely through his efforts that Christianity spread throughout the Greco-Roman world. He had the unique privilege of seeing the resurrected Christ on at least three occasions. He also was inspired by the Holy Spirit to write much of the New Testament. He even had an experience so dramatic and startling that he didn't know exactly what had happened, and was forbidden to tell what he saw. Some today have falsely claimed to have gone to heaven and returned, but Paul actually did it.

To help Paul carry out his resolve not to boast, God allowed him to be tormented by a "messenger of Satan." The Lord allowed Satan to use that individual to afflict Paul. God's purpose was to keep Paul humble and dependent on His grace, and to allow His strength to be made manifest.

The story of Peter in Luke 22:31–33 gives further evidence that God sometimes allows believers to fall into Satan's grasp. Our Lord warned him: "Simon, Simon, behold, Satan has demanded permission to sift you like wheat; but I have prayed for you, that your faith may not fail; and you, when once you have turned again, strengthen your brothers." Satan desired Peter, like he desires every believer, to defect so that he could win a victory over God. If he could have caused Peter's faith to blow away like chaff in the wind, he would have destroyed someone important in God's plan. Peter was a leading figure in the early years of the church, hence he was a prime target for Satan. Jesus' prayer indicates there were divine limits on what Satan could do to Peter, as there were with Job and Paul. God's purpose in allowing Satan to sift Peter was again to prove the strength of saving faith and show Satan that he could not take any believer out of the Lord's hand. Having learned the futility of relying on his own strength (v. 33), Peter could warn others of the danger of pride.

A final positive illustration of people who are turned over to Satan is found in the book of Revelation. Revelation 7:9–15 describes believers in the Tribulation:

> After these things I looked, and behold, a great multitude, which no one could count, from every nation and all tribes and peoples and tongues, standing before the throne and before the Lamb, clothed in white robes, and palm branches were in their hands; and they cry out with a loud voice, saying, "Salvation to our God who sits on the throne, and to the Lamb." And all the angels were standing around the throne and around the elders and the four living creatures; and they fell on their faces before the throne and worshiped God, saying, "Amen, blessing and glory and wisdom and thanksgiving and honor and power and might, be to our God forever and ever. Amen." And one of the elders answered, saying to me, "These who are clothed in the white robes, who are they, and from where have they come?" And I said to him, "My lord, you know." And he said to me, "These are the ones who come out of the great tribulation, and they have washed their robes and made them white in the blood of the Lamb. For this reason, they are before the throne of God; and they serve Him day and night in His temple; and He who sits on the throne shall spread His tabernacle over them."

An entire generation of believers, exposed to Satan's wrath during the Tribulation, will learn to praise God as no other generation has. God will lift those believers to a higher level of praise because they have suffered much and their deliverance is great. They will be richly rewarded by God (cf. 2 Cor. 4:17; Rev. 2:8–10).

As the above illustrations show, God's people can be handed over to Satan for positive purposes. It may be to show the genuineness of saving faith, to keep them humble and dependent on God, to enable them to strengthen others, or to offer praise to God. In each case God receives the glory.

There is another category of people delivered to Satan, however. They are handed over to Satan not for positive purposes, but for judgment. The Scriptures also give illustrations of those people.

Saul was seemingly the embodiment of all anyone could ask for in a king. He had an imposing physical appearance (1 Sam. 9:2; 10:23), was a forceful leader (11:7), was humble (10:22), and was patient with those who opposed him (10:27; 11:12–13). Yet those qualities were deceiving (16:7). Despite the privilege of being God's anointed king, with the Spirit's enablement, Saul's heart was not fully devoted to the Lord. He usurped the role of the priests and offered a sacrifice (13:8–9). Then he flagrantly disobeyed God's instructions to destroy completely the Amalekites (15:2–28). As a result, the Lord rejected him and his heirs from being king over Israel and anointed David in his place (16:12). The Spirit of God came upon David (16:13), and left Saul (16:14), signifying the transfer of the kingship. In His place came an evil spirit (16:14–16) to torment Saul.

Saul, who had begun so well, now slid rapidly downhill. He became insanely jealous of David. He tried to murder him, forcing him to flee for his life. Saul then relentlessly pursued David through the Judean wilderness. He even murdered a group of priests who had aided David (1 Sam. 22:9–19). His rash and foolish vow almost caused him to execute his son Jonathan (14:24–30, 37–45). Finally, bereft of God's counsel and facing a massive invasion by the Philistines, he sought help from a medium (1 Sam. 28:4ff.). That was his final act of rebellion against God; the next day he was killed in battle.

Saul's life exhibits the tragic consequences of being handed over to Satan for judgment. He had been part of the covenant people, God's anointed ruler. He had known the presence of the Spirit in his role as king. Pride and impatience led to disobedience, and God abandoned him to Satan, not for His glory, but for judgment.

Judas Iscariot had privileges Saul never dreamed of. He walked with Jesus during the three years of His earthly ministry. He heard our Lord's teaching and saw His miracles. Considering all Judas's privileges, John 13:27 is one of the most tragic verses in the Bible. The scene is the night before Christ's crucifixion, as He and the disciples are sharing a last Passover meal together: "And after the morsel, Satan then entered into [Judas]." Judas had been part of the community of the apostles, blessed and protected by the presence of God's Son. Now God handed him over to Satan, and he went out and betrayed Jesus to His enemies. Later, overcome with remorse, he committed suicide. Judas, like Saul, was cast out of the place of protection and blessing because of his sin and perished in hell.

The Corinthian church was plagued by many problems, not least of which was their toleration of an incestuous affair (1 Cor. 5:1–2). Since they failed in their obligation to put the offender out of the church, Paul did so:

> For I, on my part, though absent in body but present in spirit, have already judged him who has so committed this, as though I were present. In the name of our Lord Jesus, when you are assembled, and I with you in spirit, with the power of our Lord Jesus, I have decided to deliver such a one to Satan for the destruction of his flesh, that his spirit may be saved in the day of the Lord Jesus (1 Cor. 5:3–5).

The phrase "deliver such a one to Satan" is the only use of that terminology apart from 1 Timothy 1:20. Paul put the sinning member out of the church (cf. Matt. 18:15–17; 2 Thess. 3:6, 14). The purpose was "for the destruction of his flesh." That could refer to physical illness, death, destruction of a marriage, the breakup of a family, loss of a job, or a myriad of other afflictions. Satan's power over this particular individual in Corinth was limited, however, as it was with Job, Paul, Peter, and Christ. Although his flesh might be destroyed, since this was a true, but sinful believer, his spirit would be saved. Satan can destroy a Christian's effectiveness, but not his eternal life.

As noted in the previous chapter, Paul reminds Timothy of his accountability to the church and the Lord as he fights the spiritual war. Here Paul speaks of Timothy's responsibility to deal with those teachers purveying error. He is to follow Paul's example and deliver them to Satan.

Some of these errorists were troubling Ephesus and the surrounding region. They are the ones who were teaching heresy (1:3, 6–7). They also had failed to pursue practical godliness. **Rejected** is from *apōtheō,* which means "to thrust away," or "refuse." The false teachers had no devotion to maintaining a pure conscience. They had little interest in living for holiness. Bad theology has its roots in bad morals. Those who teach error do so in order to substitute a system that accommodates their sin.

A good conscience is the rudder that steers the Christian life. Because they rejected the pangs of conscience and the truth, it is no wonder that the errorists **suffered shipwreck in regard to their faith.** Professing to be Christians and teachers of God's law (1:7), they were devoid of the truth. It is possible for a believer to have his faith "upset" (2 Tim. 2:18). Maybe that is another way to express the disaster of shipwrecked faith. It is all too common for Christians to wreck their usefulness, virtue, and sanctification by believing error.

Paul mentions two of the false teachers by name. Nothing further is known about either **Hymenaeus** or **Alexander. Hymenaeus** is mentioned again in 2 Timothy 2:17 with another false teacher, Philetus. A man named **Alexander** is mentioned as an opponent of the Christian faith in 2 Timothy 4:14–15. However since Alexander was a common name, there is no reason to assume both passages refer to the same individual. Both men **Paul delivered over to Satan,** that is he put them out of the church. They were removed from the protection and insulation of God's people and put into Satan's grasp.

Paul's purpose in delivering them to Satan was **that they may be taught not to blaspheme. Taught** is from *paideuō,* a word that refers to training through physical punishment. It is used in Luke 23:16, 22 to speak of Pilate's scourging of Christ, and in 1 Corinthians 11:32 of those who suffered illness or death for abusing the communion service.

The physical consequences of their sin were to teach them not to **blaspheme.** To **blaspheme** is to slander God (cf. James 2:7). Misrepresenting divine truth from God, as well as speaking evil against Him, is blasphemy. Even Christians can be guilty of it (cf. Col. 3:8). When believers or unbelievers are delivered to Satan because of blasphemy, God desires that they learn the consequences of their acts. But remedial chastening is reserved only for believers (cf. Heb. 12:5–11).

How can one avoid being delivered to Satan for chastening? By receiving the truth and the righteousness of God in Christ, and then keeping faith and a good conscience. Believers will also be strengthened if they suffer for God's glory. In either case, the antidote for being delivered to Satan is the pursuit of a holy life.

Evangelistic Praying

6

First of all, then, I urge that entreaties and prayers, petitions and thanksgivings, be made on behalf of all men, for kings and all who are in authority, in order that we may lead a tranquil and quiet life in all godliness and dignity. This is good and acceptable in the sight of God our Savior, who desires all men to be saved and to come to the knowledge of the truth. For there is one God, and one mediator also between God and men, the man Christ Jesus, who gave Himself as a ransom for all, the testimony borne at the proper time. And for this I was appointed a preacher and an apostle (I am telling the truth, I am not lying) as a teacher of the Gentiles in faith and truth. Therefore I want the men in every place to pray, lifting up holy hands, without wrath and dissension. (2:1–8)

Some years ago I read a book on prayer written by a respected Christian author. In that book he argued that nothing in the Word of God calls us to pray for the lost. He maintained that the only prayer commanded regarding evangelism was that of Matthew 9:37–38: "The harvest is plentiful, but the workers are few. Therefore beseech the Lord of the harvest to send out workers into His harvest." His thesis was that we do not pray for the salvation of the lost, but rather for laborers to reach them.

Such a view reveals a tragic disregard for the clear commandments of Scripture. Here Paul calls for evangelistic praying **first of all,** setting this sort of prayer high on the list of priorities in his instructions to Timothy. Fervent evangelistic prayer is not only our spiritual duty, but is also an exercise of spiritual commitment that takes much time and energy. As such it is rather easily set aside. Charles Spurgeon warned,

> One thing more, *the soul-winner must be a master of the art of prayer.* You cannot bring souls to God if you go not to God yourself. You must get your battle-axe, and your weapons of war, from the armoury of sacred communication with Christ. If you are much alone with Jesus, you will catch His Spirit; you will be fired with the flame that burned in His breast, and consumed His life. You will weep with the tears that fell upon Jerusalem when He saw it perishing; and if you cannot speak so eloquently as He did, yet shall there be about what you say somewhat of the same power which in Him thrilled the hearts and awoke the consciences of men. My dear hearers, especially you members of the church, I am always so anxious lest any of you should begin to lie upon your oars, and take things easy in the matters of God's kingdom. There are some of you—I bless you, and I bless God at the remembrance of you—who are in season, and out of season, in earnest for winning souls, and you are the truly wise; but I fear there are others whose hands are slack, who are satisfied to let me preach, but do not themselves preach; who take these seats, and occupy these pews, and hope the cause goes well, but that is all they do. (*The Soul Winner* [Grand Rapids: Eerdmans, 1989], 246–47; italics in original)

What Christian does not pray for the salvation of friends and loved ones who do not know the Lord? The issue in this passage, however, is broader than praying for those close to us. It calls us to prayer for the lost in general; **on behalf of all men.** It raises the issue of whether God answers such prayers, and what part they play in God's salvation purpose.

The Bible gives several examples of prayer for those outside salvation. In Numbers 14:19 Moses prayed, "Pardon, I pray, the iniquity of this people according to the greatness of Thy lovingkindness, just as Thou also hast forgiven this people, from Egypt even until now." He cried out to God for the forgiveness of the sinning Israelites.

Samuel the prophet also prayed for Israel's salvation. In 1 Samuel 7:3–5 we read,

> Then Samuel spoke to all the house of Israel, saying, "If you return to the Lord with all your heart, remove the foreign gods and the Ashtaroth from among you and direct your hearts to the Lord and serve Him alone; and He will deliver you from the hand of the Philistines." So the sons of Israel removed the Baals and the Ashtaroth and served the Lord alone. Then Samuel said, "Gather all Israel to Mizpah, and I will pray to the Lord for you."

Later in 1 Samuel, after rebuking them for their sin in demanding a king, he said "Moreover, as for me, far be it from me that I should sin against the Lord by ceasing to pray for you; but I will instruct you in the good and right way" (1 Sam. 12:23).

The book of Jeremiah gives an interesting insight into Jeremiah's prayer life. In Jeremiah 7:12–16 we read of God's judgment on Israel's sin, and His instructions for Jeremiah to *stop* praying for the salvation of the people:

> "But go now to My place which was in Shiloh, where I made My name dwell at the first, and see what I did to it because of the wickedness of My people Israel. And now, because you have done all these things," declares the Lord, "and I spoke to you, rising up early and speaking, but you did not hear, and I called you but you did not answer, therefore, I will do to the house which is called by My name, in which you trust, and to the place which I gave you and your fathers, as I did to Shiloh. And I will cast you out of My sight, as I have cast out all your brothers, all the offspring of Ephraim. As for you, do not pray for this people, and do not lift up cry or prayer for them, and do not intercede with Me; for I do not hear you."

Jeremiah had habitually interceded for his people, and only the command of the Lord could stop him (cf. Jer. 14:10–11).

Daniel prayed for God's forgiveness of his people:

> So now, our God, listen to the prayer of Thy servant and to his supplications, and for Thy sake, O Lord, let Thy face shine on Thy desolate sanctuary. O my God, incline Thine ear and hear! Open Thine eyes and see our desolations and the city which is called by Thy name; for we are not presenting our supplications before Thee on account of any merits of our own, but on account of Thy great compassion. O Lord, hear! O Lord, forgive! O Lord, listen and take action! For Thine own sake, O my God, do not delay, because Thy city and Thy people are called by Thy name (Dan. 9:17–19).

The New Testament relates the testimony of Stephen. While being stoned to death, he prayed what amounted to a prayer for his executioners' salvation: "And they went on stoning Stephen as he called upon the Lord and said, 'Lord Jesus, receive my spirit!' And falling on his knees, he cried out with a loud voice, 'Lord, do not hold this sin against them!' And having said this, he fell asleep" (Acts 7:59–60).

Paul had a deep desire for the salvation of his fellow Israelites. He expressed that desire in Romans 9:1–4:

> I am telling the truth in Christ, I am not lying, my conscience bearing me witness in the Holy Spirit, that I have great sorrow and unceasing grief in my heart. For I could wish that I myself were accursed, separated from Christ for the sake of my brethren, my kinsmen according to the flesh, who are Israelites.

That deep concern could not help but find expression in his prayer life: "Brethren, my heart's desire and my prayer to God for them is for their salvation" (Rom. 10:1).

The Bible, then, clearly expresses the appropriateness and propriety of praying for the lost. In addition to the examples noted above, evangelistic praying is the express teaching of 1 Timothy 2:1–8. These verses are polemical in nature; they confront a problem in the Ephesian church. Since Paul here commands prayer for the lost, we conclude that such praying had slipped from the priority it should have been at Ephesus. There were two strands of false teaching prevalent there that would account for such neglect.

First, 1:7–11 shows there was a Judaizing element at Ephesus. The Judaizers were claiming that salvation was solely for law-keeping Jews or Gentile proselytes who kept the Mosaic ceremonies. The classic example of similar narrowmindedness is Jonah. His flight was not motivated by fear of the Ninevites; he fled because he did not want salvation blessings extended to the Gentiles (cf. Jonah 4:1–11). Such exclusivism would obviously severely restrict evangelistic praying.

Second, a form of intellectual religious elitism, later called Gnosticism, was being taught at Ephesus. Its proponents argued that salvation was only for the elite, who were able to ascend to the high levels of mystical secret knowledge. They, too, would have no motive to pray for the lost.

A common theme in both those heretical teachings was the denial of the universality of the gospel. Paul counters that teaching by showing the need to pray for all men, since the scope of the gospel call is universal. The goal of the church, like Israel before it, is to reach the world with the saving truth of God. Israel failed to be the faithful nation by which God could reach the world, and the responsibility has been passed to the church. (Romans 11:1ff. explains that Israel's failure is not the end. The Jews will again be restored to faithfulness and used as an evangel to the world.) Paul writes out of concern that the exclusivity that caused Israel to fail in her mission not cripple the church. History shows that the church has, in fact, become content with itself and often neglectful of sinners.

Paul had left Timothy in Ephesus to set the church there in order. After his introductory remarks in chapter 1, Paul outlined the specific duties Timothy needed to fulfill. **First of all,** the church must understand the importance of its evangelistic mission and the role of prayer in fulfilling it. That Paul uses **urge** instead of "command" shows that he speaks from the passion of his heart. **Then** links this passage with 1:18. The first step in Timothy's carrying out Paul's charge to him was to deal with the anti-evangelistic exclusivism in the Ephesian assembly.

That Paul begins his teachings on church order with this topic sheds light on the primary focus for the church. If the primary aim of the church were fellowship, knowledge of the Word, or the holiness of the saints, all those goals could perfectly be accomplished by taking us to heaven. The central function of the church on earth is to reach the lost. Paul knew that the Ephesians would never do that as long as they maintained their selfish exclusivism. To carry out their mission in the world they must be made to understand the breadth of the gospel call. And the first feature in understanding that is to come to grips with evangelistic praying. To assist them to do that, Paul gives five elements of evangelistic prayer: its nature, scope, benefit, reasons, and attitude.

The Nature of Evangelistic Prayer

First of all, then, I urge that entreaties and prayers, petitions and thanksgivings, (2:1a)

While the first three terms Paul uses are virtually synonymous, there are some subtle shades of meaning that enrich our concept of prayer. **Entreaties** is from *deēsis,* the root meaning of which is "to lack," "to be deprived," or "to be without something." This kind of prayer arises from the sense of need. Knowing what is lacking, we plead with God to supply it. As we look out on the masses of lost humanity, the enormity of the need should drive us to our knees in evangelistic prayer.

The seventeenth-century English Puritan Richard Baxter wrote,

> Oh, if you have the hearts of Christians or of men in you, let them yearn towards your poor ignorant, ungodly neighbours. Alas, there is but a step betwixt them and death and hell; many hundred diseases are waiting ready to seize on them, and if they die unregenerate, they are lost forever. Have you hearts of rock, that cannot pity men in such a case as this? If you believe not the Word of God, and the danger of sinners, why are you Christians yourselves? If you do believe it, why do you not bestir yourself to the helping of others? Do you not care who is damned, so you be saved? If so, you have sufficient cause to pity yourselves, for it is a frame of spirit utterly inconsistent with grace. . . . Dost thou live close by them, or meet them in the streets, or labour with them, or travel with them, or sit and talk with them, and say nothing to them of their souls, or the life to come? If their houses were on fire, thou wouldst run and help them; and wilt thou not help them when their souls are almost at the fire of hell? (Cited in I. D. E. Thomas, *A Puritan Golden Treasury* [Edinburgh: Banner of Truth, 1977], 92–93)

Proseuchē (**prayers**) is a general word for prayer. Unlike **entreaties,** in Scripture it is used only in reference to God. It thus carries with it a unique element of worship and reverence. Prayer for the lost is ultimately directed at God as an act of worship, because the salvation of sinners causes them to give glory to Him. In 2 Corinthians 4:15, Paul reveals that all his efforts at reaching the ungodly were to spread saving grace to more and more people so they could give thanks to God, which would abound to His glory.

Enteuxis (**petitions**) appears only here and in 4:5 in the New Testament. It comes from a root word meaning "to fall in with someone," or get involved with them. The verb from which *enteuxis* derives is used to speak of both Christ's and the Spirit's intercession for us (Rom. 8:26; Heb. 7:25). They identify with our needs, and become involved in our struggles. *Enteuxis,* then, is a word not only of advocacy, but also of empathy, sympathy, compassion, and involvement. Evangelistic prayer is not cold, detached, or impersonal, like a public defender assigned to represent a defendant. Understanding the depths of their misery and pain, and their coming doom, we cry to God for the salvation of sinners.

Thanksgivings are a fourth element in evangelistic prayers. They call for us to pray with a spirit of gratitude to God that the gospel offer has been extended, that we have the privilege of reaching the lost with that gospel, and that some respond with faith and repentance. Thanksgiving is the only element of prayer that will continue forever.

These four nuances enrich our prayers as we pray effectively for the lost. If they are missing, we need to examine our hearts. Do we fully realize the desperate condition the lost are in? Do we really want to see God glorified by the salvation of souls? Do we sympathize with the compelling reality of their lostness, both for time and eternity? Are we thankful the gospel message is extended to all and for our privilege of sharing it? If those components are lacking in our hearts we will be indifferent. If we are indifferent, it is because we are not obedient to these urgings.

THE SCOPE OF EVANGELISTIC PRAYER

be made on behalf of all men, for kings and all who are in authority (2:1b–2a)

Our prayers are all too often narrowly confined to personal needs and wants and rarely extend beyond those of our immediate circle of friends and family. In sharp contrast, however, Paul calls for evangelistic prayer **on behalf of all men.** There is no place for selfishness or exclusivity. We are not to try to limit either the gospel call or our evangelistic prayers to the elect only. After all, we have no means of knowing who are elect *until* they respond to the gospel call. Moreover, we are told that God desires all to be saved (2:4). He takes no pleasure in the death of the wicked, but rather delights when sinners turn from their evil ways and live (Ezek. 33:11). So prayer for the salvation of the lost is perfectly consistent with the heart of God. He has commanded all men to repent (Acts 17:30). We must pray that they will do so and embrace the salvation offered to all (Titus 2:11).

Preaching to unbelieving Jews, Peter said in Acts 3:26, "For you first, God raised up His Servant, and sent Him to bless you by turning *every one of you* from your wicked ways" (emphasis added). God's purpose in raising up Jesus was to declare that everyone should turn from his or her sins. There was no exclusivism; no one was left out. The gospel call was not restricted to the elect alone. Many are called who are not chosen (Matt. 22:14).

Out of the universal group of **all men,** Paul specifically singles out some who might otherwise be neglected in evangelistic prayer, **kings and all who are in authority.** Because ancient (and modern) rulers are so often tyrannical, and even disrespectful of the Lord and His people, they are targets of bitterness and animosity. They are also remote, not part of the everyday lives of believers. Hence there is a tendency to be indifferent toward them.

Such neglect is a serious sin because of the authority and responsibility leaders have. The injunction here calls for the Ephesian assembly to pray for the emperor, who at that time was the cruel and vicious blasphemer, Nero. Although he was a vile, debauched persecutor of the faith, they were still to pray for his redemption. The request for **kings and all who are in authority** is not limited to just a petition that they would be wise and just, but that they would repent of their sins and believe the gospel for the sake of their eternal souls.

Paul does not command us to pray for the removal from office of evil rulers, or those with whom we disagree politically. Believers are to be loyal and submissive to their government (Rom. 13:1–5; 1 Peter 2:17). If the church today took the time and energy it spends on political maneuvering and lobbying and poured them into intercessory prayer, we might see a profound impact on our nation. We have all too often forgotten that "the weapons of our warfare are not of the flesh, but divinely powerful for the destruction of fortresses" (2 Cor. 10:4). The key to changing a nation is the salvation of sinners, and that calls for faithful prayer.

While the contemporary church may have forgotten that lesson, the early church knew it well. The late second- and early third-century theologian Tertullian wrote,

> Without ceasing, for all our emperors we offer prayer. We pray for life prolonged; for security to the empire; for protection to the imperial house; for brave armies, a faithful senate, a virtuous people, the world at rest, whatever, as man or Caesar, an emperor would wish. These things I cannot ask from any but the God from whom I know I shall obtain them, both because He alone bestows them and because I have claims upon Him for their gift, as being a servant of His, rendering homage to Him alone. . . .
>
> Do you, then, who think that we care nothing for the welfare of Caesar, look into God's revelations, examine our sacred books, which we do not keep in hiding, and which many accidents put into the hands of those who are not of us. Learn from them that a large benevolence is enjoined upon us, even so far as to supplicate God for our enemies, and to beseech blessings on our persecutors. Who, then, are greater enemies and persecutors of Christians, than the very parties with treason against whom we are charged? Nay, even in terms, and most clearly, the Scripture says, "Pray for kings, and rulers, and powers, that all may be peace with you."
>
> We know that a mighty shock impending over the whole earth —in fact, the very end of all things threatening dreadful woes—is only retarded by the continued existence of the Roman empire. We have no desire, then, to be overtaken by these dire events; and in praying that their coming may be delayed, we are lending our aid to Rome's duration. (*Apology,* XXX, XXXI, XXXII; *The Ante-Nicene Fathers* [reprint; Grand Rapids: Eerdmans, 1973], 3:42–43)

With that sentiment the second-century apologist Theophilus of Antioch agreed:

> I will rather honor the king [than your gods], not, indeed, worshipping him, but praying for him. But God, the living and true God, I worship, knowing that the king is made by Him. . . . Honour the king, be subject to him, and pray for him with loyal mind; for if you do this, you do the will of God. (*Theophilus to Autolycus,* I.xi; *The Ante-Nicene Fathers* [reprint; Grand Rapids: Eerdmans, 1971], 2:92)

> Moreover, concerning subjection to authorities and powers, and prayer for them, the divine word gives us instructions, in order that "we may lead a quiet and peaceable life." And it teaches us to render all things to all, "honour to whom honour, fear to whom fear, tribute to whom tribute; to owe no man anything, but to love all." (*Theophilus to Autolycus,* III.xiv; *The Ante-Nicene Fathers* [reprint; Grand Rapids: Eerdmans, 1971], 2:115)

From those examples we learn that the ancient church, often in the worst eras of persecution, prayed for Christless rulers. If we would influence our society the way earlier Christians did theirs, we must follow their example.

The Benefit of Evangelistic Prayer

in order that we may lead a tranquil and quiet life in all godliness and dignity. (2:2b)

Prayer for those in authority will create societal conditions favorable for the church's evangelistic efforts. First of all, when believers are committed to praying for all their leaders it removes any thought of rebellion or resistance against them. It makes the people of Christ into peacemakers, not reactionaries. As Paul wrote to Titus,

> Remind them to be subject to rulers, to authorities, to be obedient, to be ready for every good deed, to malign no one, to be uncontentious, gentle, showing every consideration for all men. For we also once were foolish ourselves, disobedient, deceived, enslaved to various lusts and pleasures, spending our life in malice and envy, hateful, hating one another. (Titus 3:1–3)

There Paul again calls the believers to tranquillity and submissiveness to the pagan or apostate governments over them. He urges us to be subject, eager to do good, never to slander or contend, to be meek and considerate, because we understand that they are sinners like we used to be, incapable of righteousness.

Also, when the church prays unceasingly for the lost, especially their troublesome leaders, people begin to see the church as virtuous, peaceloving, compassionate, and transcendent. Seeing that the church seeks their welfare, they will realize that it poses no threat to society, but is a welcome friend. And as more and more come to saving faith, through the prayers of Christians, the favorable conditions for the church could increase.

The church that is obedient to this mandate will **lead a tranquil and quiet life.** *Ēremos* (**tranquil**) and *hēsuchios* (**quiet**) are rare adjectives. The former, appearing only here in the New Testament, refers to the absence of outside disturbances. The latter, appearing only here and in 1 Peter 3:4, refers to the absence of internal disturbances. When the church manifests its love and goodness toward all and pours itself into compassionate, concerned prayer for the lost, it will lessen the hostility that may exist and the saints may enjoy freedom from both internal and external disturbances. The church, while uncompromising in commitment to the truth, is not to be the agitator and disrupter of the national life. That is the clear teaching of Scripture. If we are persecuted, it must be for Christ's sake, for the sake of righteous living (cf. 1 Peter 2:13–23).

In 1 Thessalonians 4:11, Paul commanded the Thessalonian believers "to make it your ambition to lead a quiet life and attend to your own business and work with your hands." Christians are to be known for their quiet demeanor, not for making disturbances. Unbelievers should see us as quiet, loyal, diligent, virtuous people. In his second letter to the Thessalonians, Paul repeated that command: "For we hear that some among you are leading an undisciplined life, doing no work at all, but acting like busybodies. Now such persons we command and exhort in the Lord Jesus Christ to work in quiet fashion and eat their own bread" (2 Thess. 3:11–12). Although we may hate the evil world system that is the enemy of God, we are not to see those in it as our personal enemies. They are captives of the real enemy (cf. 2 Tim. 2:24–26). They are not our enemies, they are our mission field.

To promote a **tranquil and quiet life,** believers must pursue **godliness and dignity. Godliness** translates *eusebeia,* a common word in the Pastoral Epistles (cf. 3:16; 4:7, 8; 6:3, 5, 6, 11; 2 Tim. 3:5; Titus 1:1). It carries the idea of reverence toward God. Believers should live for the majesty, holiness, love, and glory of God.

Semnotēs (**dignity**) is used only here, in 3:4, and Titus 2:7. It could be translated "moral earnestness." **Godliness** can refer to a proper attitude; **dignity** to proper behavior. Thus believers are to be marked by a commitment to morality; holy motives must result in holy behavior. Both contribute to the tranquillity and quietness of our lives.

That is not to say, however, that the Christian life will be free of problems. "Indeed," Paul writes in 2 Timothy 3:12, "all who desire to live godly in Christ Jesus will be persecuted." As noted in chapter 4 of this volume, the Christian life is a war against Satan and the forces of evil. Paul himself was beaten and imprisoned for his faith. His point in this passage, however, is that if we incur animosity and suffer persecution, it is to be for our godly attitude and behavior. We must not provoke those responses by being a disruptive force in society.

It is true that James 1:2–12 teaches that trials bring about spiritual maturity. Even if He chooses as part of those trials to bring persecution into our lives, it must be for Christ's sake, and because of our faithfulness to the Word of God (cf. Acts 5:27–29. When persecution comes, our attitude must be that of our Lord (Luke 23:34), or Stephen (Acts 7:60), who prayed for those taking their lives. As our Lord summed it up in Matthew 5:43–44, "You have heard that it was said, 'You shall love your neighbor, and hate your enemy.' But I say to you, love your enemies, and pray for those who persecute you."

Why? "In order that you may be sons of your Father who is in heaven; for He causes His sun to rise on the evil and the good, and sends rain on the righteous and the unrighteous" (v. 45). Goodness and mercy to one's enemies reflect the heart of God. And that truth goes to the heart of Paul's message in 1 Timothy 2.

The Reason for Evangelistic Prayer

This is good and acceptable in the sight of God our Savior, who desires all men to be saved and to come to the knowledge of the truth. For there is one God, and one mediator also between God and men, the man Christ Jesus, who gave Himself as a ransom for all, the testimony borne at the proper time. And for this I was appointed a preacher and an apostle (I am telling the truth, I am not lying) as a teacher of the Gentiles in faith and truth. (2:3–7)

This powerful and dramatic passage answers the question "Why pray for the lost?" It is one of the most definitive statements in all of Scripture of the saving purpose of God. It contains several reasons for evangelistic prayer.

EVANGELISTIC PRAYER IS MORALLY RIGHT

This points back to the commandment to pray for the lost in verses 1–2. *Kalon* (**good**) refers to what is intrinsically, morally good.

God defines prayer for the lost as the noble and spiritually proper thing to do, and our consciences agree. The lost suffer the agony of sin, shame, and meaninglessness in this life, and the eternal hell of unrelenting agony in the life to come. Knowing that, it is the most excellent task to pray for their salvation.

Some might argue that Jesus said in John 17:9, "I do not ask on behalf of the world." But there Christ was praying as Great High Priest for God's elect. Because He is sovereign, omniscient Deity, His prayer was specific in a way ours cannot be. It was a prayer exclusively for the salvation of those whom He loved and chose before the foundation of the world to be partakers of every spiritual blessing (Eph. 1:3–4). "The world" was specifically excluded from the saving design of this prayer.

Our prayers, however, are not the prayers of a high priest; we pray as ambassadors of Christ, whose task it is to beseech men and women on His behalf to be reconciled to God (2 Cor. 5:20). We are therefore commanded to offer our **entreaties and prayers, petitions and thanksgivings . . . on behalf of all men.** Our earnest desire ought to be for the salvation of all sinners (cf. Rom. 9:3; 10:1). We are not to try to limit evangelism to the elect only.

There are two reasons for this. First, God's decree of election is secret. We do not know who the elect are and have no way of knowing *until* they respond to the gospel. Second, the scope of God's evangelistic purposes is broader than election. "Many are called, but few are chosen" (Matt. 22:14). Even Jesus' high priestly prayer *does* embrace the world in this important regard. Our Lord prayed for unity among the elect so that the truth of the gospel would be made clear to the world: "that the world may believe that Thou didst send Me. . . . that the world may know that Thou didst send Me" (John 17:21, 23). God's call to all sinners is a bona fide and sincere invitation to salvation: "'As I live!' declares the Lord God, 'I take no pleasure in the death of the wicked, but rather that the wicked turn from his way and live. Turn back, turn back from your evil ways! Why then will you die, O house of Israel?'" (Ezek. 33:11).

EVANGELISTIC PRAYER IS CONSISTENT WITH GOD'S DESIRE

Obviously, in some inscrutable sense, God's *desire* for the world's salvation is different from His eternal saving *purpose.* We can understand this to some degree from a human perspective; after all, our purposes frequently differ from our desires. We may *desire,* for example, to spend a day at leisure, yet a higher *purpose* compels us to go to work instead. Similarly, God's saving purposes transcend His desires. (There is a crucial difference, of course: We might be compelled by circumstances beyond our control to choose what we do not desire. But God's choices are determined by nothing other than His own sovereign, eternal purpose).

God genuinely **desires all men to be saved and to come to the knowledge of the truth.** Yet in "the eternal purpose which He carried out in Christ Jesus our Lord" (Eph. 3:11), He chose only the elect "out of the world" (John 17:6), and passed over the rest, leaving them to the damning consequences of their sin (cf. Rom. 1:18–32). The culpability for their damnation rests entirely on them because of their sin and rejection of God. God is not to blame for their unbelief.

Since **God desires all men to be saved,** we are not required to ascertain that a person is elect before praying for that person's salvation. God alone knows who all the elect are (2 Tim. 2:19). We may pray **on behalf of all men** with full assurance that such prayers are **good and acceptable in the sight of God our Savior.** After all, "the Lord is gracious and merciful; slow to anger and great in lovingkindness. The Lord is good to all, and His mercies are over all His works" (Ps. 145:8–9).

Apodektos (**acceptable**), is from *apodechomai,* which means "to receive gladly," "to accept with satisfaction," or "to heartily welcome." The Lord eagerly accepts prayer for the lost because it is consistent with His desire for their salvation.

Such prayer is also consistent with His nature as **Savior.** The phrase **God our Savior** appears five other times in the Pastoral Epistles (1:1; 4:10; Titus 1:3; 2:10; 3:4), as well as in Jude 25. God is not only creator, sustainer, king, and judge, but also savior. His saving character is manifested through His Son, Jesus Christ (2:5–6; 2 Tim. 1:10; Titus 1:4; 2:13; 3:6). God is the "Savior of all men" in a temporal sense, but "especially of believers" in an eternal sense (1 Tim. 4:10b).

That truth of God's saving nature is also taught in the Old Testament (cf. 2 Sam. 22:3; Ps. 106:21; Isa. 43:3, 11). The idea that the God of the Old Testament is a vengeful, wrathful ogre mollified by the gentle, loving, New Testament Christ is not at all accurate.

When God **desires all men to be saved,** He is being consistent with who He is. In Isaiah 45:22 God said, "Turn to Me, and be saved, all the ends of the earth." Isaiah 55:1 invites "every one who thirsts" to "come to the waters" of salvation. Again, in Ezekiel 18:23, 32 God states very clearly that He does not desire that the wicked should perish, but that they would sincerely repent (cf. Ezek. 33:11). In the New Testament, Peter writes, "The Lord is not slow about His promise, as some count slowness, but is patient toward you, not wishing for any to perish but for all to come to repentance" (2 Peter 3:9).

No true biblical theology can teach that God takes pleasure in the damnation of the wicked. Yet though it does not please Him, God will receive glory even in the damnation of unbelievers (cf. Rom. 9:22–23). How His electing grace and predestined purpose can stand beside

His love for the world and desire that the gospel be preached to all people, still holding them responsible for their own rejection and condemnation, is a mystery of the divine mind. The Scriptures teach God's love for the world, His displeasure in judging sinners, His desire for all to hear the gospel and be saved. They also teach that every sinner is incapable yet responsible to believe and will be damned if he does not. Crowning the Scripture's teaching on this matter is the great truth that God has elected who will believe and saved them before the world began. What mystery!

> Oh, the depth of the riches both of the wisdom and knowledge of God! How unsearchable are His judgments and unfathomable His ways! For who has known the mind of the Lord, or who became His counselor? Or who has first given to Him that it might be paid back to him again? For from Him and through Him and to Him are all things. To Him be the glory forever. Amen. (Rom. 11:33–36)

To come to the knowledge of the truth is to be saved. *Epignōsis* (**knowledge**) is used three other times in the Pastoral Epistles (2 Tim. 2:25; 3:7; Titus 1:1). In all four occurrences, it refers to the true knowledge that brings about salvation. Far from desiring their damnation, God desires the lost to come to a saving knowledge of the truth.

Some have argued that this passage teaches universalism. If God desires the salvation of **all men,** they argue, then all will be saved, or God won't get what He wants. Others argue that what God wills comes to pass, because **all men** means all classes of men, not every individual. Neither of those positions is necessary, however. We must distinguish between God's will of decree (His eternal purpose), and His will expressed as desire. **Desire** is not from *boulomai,* which would be more likely to express God's will of decree, but from *thelō,* which can refer to God's will of desire. This is precisely the distinction theologians often make between God's secret will and His revealed will.

God desires many things that He does not decree. It was never God's *desire* that sin exist, yet the undeniable existence of sin proves that even sin fulfills His eternal purposes (Isa. 46:10)—though in no sense is He the author of sin (James 1:13).

Jesus lamented over Jerusalem, "O Jerusalem, Jerusalem, who kills the prophets and stones those who are sent to her! How often I wanted to gather your children together, the way a hen gathers her chicks under her wings, and you were unwilling" (Matt. 23:37). John Murray and Ned B. Stonehouse wrote, "We have found that God himself expresses an ardent desire for the fulfillment of certain things which he has not decreed in his inscrutable counsel to come to pass" (*The Free*

Offer of the Gospel [Phillipsburg, N.J.: Presb. & Ref., 1979], 26). God desires all men to be saved. It is their willful rejection of Him that sends them to hell. The biblical truths of election and predestination do not cancel man's moral responsibility.

EVANGELISTIC PRAYER REFLECTS THE UNIQUENESS OF GOD

One of the most fundamental teachings of Scripture is that **there is one God** (cf. Deut. 4:35, 39; 6:4; Isa. 43:10; 44:6; 45:5–6, 21–22; 46:9; 1 Cor. 8:4, 6). That runs counter to the pluralistic religiosity of our world, which rejects the concept of any exclusive religious truth. We are taught by the spirit of our age that the gods of the Christians, Jews, Moslems, Buddhists, and Hindus are to be charitably considered equally valid. If that were true, there would be many ways of salvation, and hence no need for evangelism. But since there is only one true God, then He is the One in whom all must believe to be saved. There is no other name under heaven by which sinners may be saved (Acts 4:12). Evangelistic prayer recognizes that all must come to the one true God.

EVANGELISTIC PRAYER IS CONSISTENT WITH THE PERSON OF CHRIST

Not only is there only one God, but **one mediator also between God and men, the man Christ Jesus.** *Mesitēs* (**mediator**) refers to one who intervenes between two individuals to restore peace, or ratify a covenant. The concept of a mediator is seen in Job's lament, "There is no umpire between us, who may lay his hand upon us both" (Job 9:33). Because Christ is the only mediator, all must come to God through Him (Acts 4:12). There isn't an endless series of aeons, or subgods, as the Gnostics taught. We do not approach God through the intercession of angels, saints, or Mary. Only through **the man Christ Jesus** can men draw near to God. The absence of the article before *anthrōpos* (**man**) suggests the translation, "Christ Jesus, Himself man." As the perfect God-man, he brings God and man together. Hebrews 8:6 calls Him "the mediator of a better covenant," while Hebrews 9:15 and 12:24 describe Him as the mediator of the new covenant. All men who come to God must come through Him.

EVANGELISTIC PRAYER REFLECTS THE FULLNESS OF CHRIST'S ATONEMENT

Our Lord freely **gave** His life when He died for our sins. In John 10:17–18 He said,

> For this reason the Father loves Me, because I lay down My life that I may take it again. No one has taken it away from Me, but I lay it down on My own initiative. I have authority to lay it down, and I have authority to take it up again. This commandment I received from My Father.

He voluntarily went to the cross and **gave** all of **Himself,** not merely something He possessed.

Ransom is a rich theological term, describing Christ's substitutionary death for us. It is not the simple word for **ransom,** *lutron,* but *antilutron,* the added preposition intensifying the meaning. Christ did not merely pay a ransom to free us; He became the victim in our place. He died our death, and bore our sin. He **gave Himself.**

The phrase **gave Himself as a ransom for all** is a comment on the *sufficiency* of the atonement, not its *design.* To apply a well-known epigram, the ransom paid by Christ to God for the satisfaction of His justice is sufficient for all, but efficacious for the elect only. Christ's atonement is therefore unlimited as to its sufficiency, but limited as to its application.

Real benefits accrue **for all** because of Christ's all-sufficient atoning work. The gospel may be preached indiscriminately to all (Mark 16:15); the water of life and the offer of divine mercy are extended freely to all (Rev. 22:17); Christ is set forth as Savior for all to embrace (1 Tim. 4:10; 1 John 4:14). Moreover, in a temporal sense, the entire race was spared from immediate destruction and judgment when Adam sinned (a privilege not afforded to the angels who fell—Heb. 2:16), and individual sinners experience delay in God's judgment on their sins. Nineteenth-century theologian William G. T. Shedd wrote,

> The atonement is sufficient in value to expiate the sin of all men indiscriminately; and this fact should be stated because it is a fact. There are no claims of justice not yet satisfied; there is no sin of man for which an infinite atonement has not been provided. . . . Therefore the call to 'come' is universal." (*Dogmatic Theology* [reprint; Nashville: Thomas Nelson, 1980], 2:482)

That does not mean that all will be saved. Again, "many are called, but few are chosen" (Matt. 22:14). Christ's death was *sufficient* to cover the sins of all people, but it is applied to the elect alone. The price paid was infinite. If billions more had been added to the number of the elect, Christ would not have been required to suffer one more stroke of divine wrath to pay the price for their sin. On the other hand, "had there been but one sinner, Seth, elected of God, this whole divine sacrifice would have been needed to expiate His guilt" (R. L. Dabney, *The Five Points of Calvinism* [reprint; Harrisonburg, Va.: Sprinkle, 1992], 61).

So the infinite price our Savior paid was certainly sufficient for all. "Christ's expiation . . . is a divine act. It is indivisible, inexhaustible, sufficient in itself to cover the guilt of all the sins that will ever be committed on earth" (Dabney, 61). Therefore salvation can sincerely and legitimately be offered to all, though only the elect will respond. Shedd writes, "The extent to which a medicine is offered is not limited by the number of persons favorably disposed to buy it and use it. Its adaptation to disease is the sole consideration in selling it, and consequently it is offered to everybody" (*Dogmatic Theology,* 2:482).

It is crucial to understand that the atoning work of Christ fully accomplishes everything God declared He would accomplish in eternity past with regard to the salvation of sinners. God's sovereign purposes are not thwarted in any degree by the unbelief of those who spurn Christ. "I am God," He states, "and there is no other; I am God, and there is no one like Me, declaring the end from the beginning and from ancient times things which have not been done, saying, 'My purpose will be established, and I will accomplish all My good pleasure'" (Isa. 46:9–10). The atonement of Christ does not represent a failed attempt to save anyone who will not be saved. All those whom God purposed to save from eternity past will be saved (cf. John 17:12).

Yet it is worth reiterating once more that while God's saving *purpose* is limited to the elect, His *desire* for the salvation of sinners is as broad as the human race. He **desires all men to be saved and to come to the knowledge of the truth.** And so Christ **gave Himself as a ransom** sufficient **for all.** How graphically the atoning work of Christ reveals to us the heart of God for the salvation of sinners!

That is why Paul refers to the atonement as **the testimony borne** by Christ **at the proper time.** This thought precisely parallels Galatians 4:4–5, "But when the fulness of the time came, God sent forth His Son, born of a woman, born under the Law, in order that He might redeem those who were under the Law." Christ **gave Himself as a ransom** at exactly **the proper time** in God's redemptive plan. His redemptive work is the most eloquent **testimony** ever **borne** to God's saving desire for all sinners. Evangelistic prayer for all men therefore reflects the heart of God, and honors Christ's work on the cross.

EVANGELISTIC PRAYER IS IN ACCORD WITH PAUL'S DIVINE COMMISSION

And for this, Paul writes in verse 7, **I was appointed a preacher and an apostle. This** refers to the great truths that God is our Savior, Christ is our mediator, and Christ gave Himself as a ransom, as discussed in the preceding verses. Paul's divine commission was based on those truths. **Preacher** derives from the verb *kērussō,* which means to herald, proclaim, or speak publicly. The ancient world had no news media, so announcements were made in the city square. Paul was a public herald proclaiming the gospel of Jesus Christ. An apostle was a messenger, sent on behalf of Christ. If the gospel message was exclusive, that would undercut Paul's calling.

Paul reinforces the truthfulness of his calling **as a teacher of the Gentiles in faith and truth** with the parenthetical statement in verse 7. He affirms **I am telling the truth, I am not lying.** In case some doubted his teaching in this passage, he insists that he is speaking the truth.

We, too, are called to proclaim the gospel to the lost world. That call, like Paul's divine commission, is based on God's desire that all be saved. Evangelistic prayer acknowledges our responsibility.

THE ATTITUDE OF EVANGELISTIC PRAYER

Therefore I want the men in every place to pray, lifting up holy hands, without wrath and dissension. (2:8)

Therefore indicates that this verse goes with the preceding section, not with what follows. The change of subject comes in verse 9, as the word "likewise" shows (cf. 3:8, 11). Having stressed the importance of evangelistic prayer, Paul now tells us with what attitude we are to pray. **Want** is from *boulomai,* and could be translated "I command," or "I purpose." **Men** is from *anēr,* and means men as opposed to women. Men are the leaders when the church meets for corporate worship. When prayer is offered for the lost during those times, the men are to do it. In the synagogues, only men were permitted to pray, and that was carried over into the church. The phrase **in every place** appears four times in Paul's writings (cf. 1 Cor. 1:2; 2 Cor. 2:14; 1 Thess. 1:8). All four times it refers to the official assembly of the church.

Some might argue that this teaching contradicts 1 Corinthians 11:5, where Paul permits women to pray and proclaim the Word. That passage, however, must be interpreted in light of 1 Corinthians 14:34–35, which forbids women to speak in the assembly. Women *are* permitted to pray and proclaim the Word, but not "in church"—that is, when the church meets for its corporate worship services. That in no way marks women as spiritually inferior (cf. Gal. 3:28). Not even all *men* proclaim the Word in the assembly, only those so called and gifted. (For a further discussion of this issue, see my book *Different By Design* [Wheaton, Ill.: Victor, 1994].)

The Old Testament saints frequently prayed **lifting up** their **hands** (cf. 1 Kings 8:22; Neh. 8:6; Pss. 63:4; 134:2; 141:2; Isa. 1:15). But Paul's emphasis here is not on a particular posture for prayer. The **hands** symbolize the activities of life, thus **holy hands** represent a holy life. That is a prerequisite for effective prayer (cf. Ps. 66:18). **Holy** translates *hosios,* which means "unpolluted," or "unstained by evil." Those who pray for the lost must not be characterized by **wrath and dissension.** They must be holy in heart and deed.

The greatest example of evangelistic praying is our Lord Himself. Isaiah 53:12 tells us He "interceded for the transgressors." On the cross He prayed, "Father, forgive them; for they do not know what they are doing" (Luke 23:34). God answered those prayers with three thousand converts on the Day of Pentecost, and countless thousands more through the centuries.

Do we pray for the lost like that? Do we have the passion that inspired John Knox to cry out, "Give me Scotland or I die"? Is our attitude that of George Whitefield, who prayed, "O Lord, give me souls or take my soul"? Can we, like Henry Martyn, say, "I cannot endure existence if Jesus is to be so dishonored"?

God honors evangelistic prayer. Standing among those who killed Stephen was a young man named Saul of Tarsus. Could it be that the great apostle's salvation was in answer to Stephen's prayer, "Lord, do not hold this sin against them"? Evangelism begins with evangelistic prayer.

God's Plan for Women in the Church

7

Likewise, I want women to adorn themselves with proper clothing, modestly and discreetly, not with braided hair and gold or pearls or costly garments; but rather by means of good works, as befits women making a claim to godliness. Let a woman quietly receive instruction with entire submissiveness. But I do not allow a woman to teach or exercise authority over a man, but to remain quiet. For it was Adam who was first created, and then Eve. And it was not Adam who was deceived, but the woman being quite deceived, fell into transgression. But women shall be preserved through the bearing of children if they continue in faith and love and sanctity with self-restraint. (2:9–15)

The role of women in the church is a topic that is hotly debated today. Unfortunately, the debate has left the pages of Scripture to find its resolution. The traditional doctrines are being swept away by the flood tides of evangelical feminism. Churches, schools, and seminaries are rapidly abandoning truths they have held since their inceptions. Dozens of books are being written defending the new "truth" regarding the role of women. Ironically, some of the authors of those books formerly held to the traditional, biblical view. But under the pressure of feminism they have abandoned biblical accuracy in favor of the culture. The biblical passages on women's roles are being culturally reinterpreted, ignored because of the alleged anti-female bias of the biblical authors, or dismissed as the additions of later redactors.

The ultimate source of those attacks is the archenemy of God, Satan. His goal, as always, is to overthrow God's plan and corrupt His design. He is behind the effort to entice women away from their God-created roles in society, in the family, and in the church. Such a satanic enterprise is not new—in fact it was an issue in the church at Ephesus, because it was an issue in the Roman world of that time.

In a church plagued with false doctrine and false leaders, it is not surprising to find them struggling over gender roles. Some women were leading impure lives (cf. 5:6, 11–15; 2 Tim. 3:6), and their indecency carried over into the worship service. Under the pretense of gathering to worship God, women were flaunting themselves and becoming serious distractions from worship. Their actions revealed that the intent of their heart was evil. Since worship is central to the life of the church, it was high on Paul's list of issues for Timothy to confront.

Following his discussion of the role of the men when the church is called to evangelistic prayer (2:1–8), Paul turns to the subject of women in worship. He addresses their appearance, attitude, testimony, role, design, and contribution.

The Appearance of Women

Likewise, I want women to adorn themselves with proper clothing . . . not with braided hair and gold or pearls or costly garments; (2:9a, c)

Likewise refers to verse 8, and marks the transition to a new aspect within the same overall subject (cf. 3:8, 11). Having discussed the conduct of men in the gathering of the church, he now turns to that of women.

The verb in this sentence must be supplied from verse 8. As noted in the discussion of that verse, **want** is from *boulomai,* and could be translated "I command," or "I purpose." Paul is not expressing his opinion or giving advice. His words carry divine authority. Men are commanded to pray and **likewise** women are mandated to adorn themselves in a manner fitting worship of God.

Adorn is from *kosmeō,* from which the English word "cosmetic" derives. It means "to arrange," "to put in order," or "to make ready." A woman must arrange herself appropriately to join God's people as they worship. Part of that important preparation involves the outside, the wearing of **proper clothing. Proper** translates *kosmiō,* which, like *kosmeō,* derives from the noun *kosmos. Kosmos* is often translated "world," but it really means "order," or "system." It is the antonym of "chaos." *Katastolē* (**clothing**) encompasses not only the clothing itself, but also the look—the whole demeanor. Women are to come to the corporate worship ready to face the Lord. They must not come in slovenly disarray or personal display because of an unbecoming wardrobe or demeanor. There is a place for lovely clothes that reflect the humble grace of a woman, as evidenced in Proverbs 31:22, "Her clothing is fine linen and purple." Proper adornment on the outside reflects a properly adorned heart.

From the general principle in the first part of verse 9, Paul moves to specifics in the latter part of the verse. In so doing, he hints at some of the practices that were causing confusion in the assembly. He starts with commenting about **braided hair,** a term that can generally mean "hair styles." His point is not that women should be indifferent to their hair. That would contradict what he had just said about careful preparation to put oneself in order. Paul's intent is not to forbid certain kinds of hairdos, as if some reflected a more worshipful attitude than others. He is confronting any gaudy, ostentatious hairdo that would distract attention from the Lord and the purposes that are holy. Women in that culture often wove **gold, pearls,** or other jewelry through their hairdos to call attention to themselves and their wealth or beauty.

There is nothing wrong with owning jewelry. Solomon's bride in Song of Solomon wore gold and silver jewelry (Song 1:10–11; 4:9), as did Rebekah (Gen. 24:53). There is an appropriate time and place for that, as affirmed by the words of Isaiah 61:10: "I will rejoice greatly in the Lord, my soul will exult in my God; for He has clothed me with garments of salvation, He has wrapped me with a robe of righteousness, as a bridegroom decks himself with a garland, and as a bride adorns herself with her jewels." But jewelry was (and is) often used as a way of flaunting a woman's wealth or calling attention to herself in an unwholesome way. It is that preoccupation which Paul forbids in the place of worship.

When a woman dresses for the worship service to attract attention to herself, she has violated the purpose of worship (cf. 1 Peter 3:3–4). The fourth-century church father John Chrysostom wrote,

> And what then is modest apparel? Such as covers them completely and decently, and not with superfluous ornaments; for the one is decent and the other is not. What? Do you approach God to pray with broidered hair and ornaments of gold? Are you come to a ball? to a marriage-feast? to a carnival? There such costly things might have been seasonable: here not one of them is wanted. You are come to pray, to

> ask pardon for your sins, to plead for your offences, beseeching the Lord, and hoping to render him propitious to you. Away with such hypocrisy! (Cited in Alfred Plummer, "The Pastoral Epistles," in *The Expositor's Bible,* ed. W. Robertson Nicoll [New York: A. C. Armstrong & Son, 1903], 101)

Another way women in Paul's day flaunted their wealth and drew attention to themselves was by wearing **costly garments.** The expensive dresses worn by wealthy women could cost up to 7,000 denarii. Pliny the Elder, a first-century Roman historian, described a dress of Lollia Paulina, wife of the Emperor Caligula, which was worth several hundred thousand dollars by today's standards (*Natural History* 9.58). Dresses of the common women could cost as much as 500–800 denarii. To put that into perspective, the average daily wage of a common laborer was one denarius. Because of the extreme expense, most women probably owned only two or three nice dresses in their lives. For a wealthy woman to enter the worship service wearing an expensive dress would shift the focus of attention to her. It could also stir up envy on the part of the poorer women (or their husbands).

Such showy displays were criticized even by non-Christian writers. In his sixth satire, the first-century Roman poet Juvenal wrote,

> There is nothing that a woman will not permit herself to do, nothing that she deems shameful, and when she encircles her neck with green emeralds and fastens huge pearls to her elongated ears, so important is the business of beautification; so numerous are the tiers and stories piled one another on her head! In the meantime she pays no attention to her husband!

In his work *The Sacrifices of Cain and Abel,* the first-century Jewish philosopher Philo described a prostitute. He portrayed her as wearing many gold chains and bracelets, with her hair done up in elaborate and gaudy braids. Her eyes were marked with pencil lines, her eyebrows smothered in paint. She wore expensive clothes embroidered lavishly with flowers.

The wearing of expensive clothes and jewelry that drew attention away from the Lord was obviously inappropriate for women in the church. They were supposed to be demonstrating humble godliness, not appearing like prostitutes or showy pagan women. To come to church so attired was at best a distraction from honoring God, and at worst an attempt to seduce the men of the church.

How does a woman discern the sometimes fine line between proper dress and dressing to be the center of attention? The answer starts in the intent of the heart. A woman should examine her motives and goals for the way she dresses. Is her intent to show the grace and beauty of womanhood? Is it to show her love and devotion to her husband and his goodness to her? Is it to reveal a humble heart devoted to worshiping God? Or is it to call attention to herself, and flaunt her wealth and beauty? Or worse, to attempt to allure men sexually? A woman who focuses on worshiping God will consider carefully how she is dressed, because her heart will dictate her wardrobe and appearance.

The Attitude of Women

modestly and discreetly, (2:9a)

These two attitudes are to characterize a woman's approach to her appearance in worship. *Aidōs* (**modestly**) appears only here in the New Testament. It refers to modesty mixed with humility. At its core is the idea of shame (cf. the Authorized Version's translation "shamefacedness"). A godly woman would be ashamed and feel guilt if she distracted someone from worshiping God, or contributed to someone's lustful thought. A woman characterized by this attitude will dress so as not to be the source of any temptation. The word also has the connotation of rejecting anything dishonorable to God. Some would even suggest the meaning of the term as grief over a sense of sin. A godly woman hates sin so much that she would avoid anything that would engender sin in anyone. This is certainly consistent with the words of our Lord, who said,

> Whoever causes one of these little ones who believe in Me to stumble, it is better for him that a heavy millstone be hung around his neck, and that he be drowned in the depth of the sea. Woe to the world because of its stumbling blocks! For it is inevitable that stumbling blocks come; but woe to that man through whom the stumbling block comes! . . . See that you do not despise one of these little ones, for I say to you, that their angels in heaven continually behold the face of My Father who is in heaven. (Matt. 18:6–7, 10)

Better to be dead than lead another believer into sin!

The basic sense of *sōphrosunēs* (**discreetly**) is self-control, especially over sexual passions. It, too, is a rare word, appearing twice in this passage (cf. 2:15), and in Acts 26:25. The Greeks valued this virtue highly. Euripides called it "the fairest gift of the gods" (Marvin R. Vincent, *Word Studies in the New Testament* [Grand Rapids: Eerdmans,

1946], 4:224). Plato, in *The Republic,* called it one of the four cardinal virtues. Women are to exercise control so that neither their passions nor anyone else's are excited.

THE TESTIMONY OF WOMEN

but rather by means of good works, as befits women making a claim to godliness. (2:10)

Those women who profess godliness should support that testimony with their demeanor and appearance. Beyond those areas, they are to support it by being adorned **by means of good works.** *Agathōn* (**good**) refers to **works** that are genuinely good, not merely good in appearance. That **befits women making a claim to godliness. Making a claim** is from *epangellō,* which means "to make a public announcement." **Good works** must mark Christian women, who by virtue of their profession of love to Jesus Christ have publicly committed themselves to pursuing **godliness. Godliness** translates *theosebeia,* which refers to reverence to God. To affirm that you are a Christian is to claim to love, worship, honor, and fear the Lord. A woman cannot claim to fear God and yet disregard what His Word says about her behavior. She cannot contradict God's design for her in the church and yet claim to love Him.

THE ROLE OF WOMEN

Let a woman quietly receive instruction with entire submissiveness. But I do not allow a woman to teach or exercise authority over a man, but to remain quiet. (2:11–12)

Paul continues his discussion of women's duties by defining their role as learners rather than teachers during the public worship. While they are not to be the public teachers in that context, neither are they to be shut out of the learning process as was generally the case in ancient times. The verb in verse 11 is an imperative form of *manthanō* ("to learn," "to be informed"), from which the Greek word translated "disciple" or "learner" derives. When Paul says **let a woman . . . receive instruction,** he is not requesting, rather he commands that the women be taught. That Paul is here discussing the order of the church (cf. 3:15) shows the learning he speaks of was to take place in that context (cf. Acts 2:42). It should be noted that despite the claims of some to the contrary, teaching and worship are not mutually exclusive. Rather, knowledge of God and His Word helps stimulate worship. Worship is to be in spirit and in truth (cf. John 4:20–24).

It may seem obvious to us that women should be taught God's Word, since they are spiritually equal in Christ and the commands of the New Testament are to all (1 Peter 2:1–2). It was not at all obvious, however, to those who came from a Jewish background. First-century Judaism did not hold women in high esteem. While not barred from attending synagogue, neither were they encouraged to learn. In fact, most rabbis refused to teach women, and some likened it to throwing pearls to pigs.

Nor was the status of women in Greek society much better. William Barclay writes,

> The respectable Greek woman led a very confined life. She lived in her own quarters into which no one but her husband came. She did not even appear at meals. She never at any time appeared on the street alone; she never went to any public assembly. (*The Letters to Timothy, Titus, and Philemon* [Philadelphia: Westminster, 1975], 67)

The existence of such a mind-set at Ephesus may have contributed to the reaction of the women against such denigration. Unfortunately, some went too far, overreacting to their suppression by seeking a dominant position. Before Paul confronts that overreaction, however, he affirms their right to learn.

The prevalent Jewish tradition about women did not come from the Old Testament. The Old Testament affirmed that women have a spiritual status equal to that of men. The Mosaic law was given to all Israel, women as well as men (Deut. 1:1). Both were to teach it to their children (Deut. 6:4–7; Prov. 6:20). The protection of the law applied equally to women (cf. Ex. 21:28–32). Women had inheritance rights (Num. 36:1–12). Men and women alike participated in the Jewish religious feasts (cf. Ex. 12:3; Deut. 16:9–15). The single greatest spiritual vow, the Nazarite vow, was open to both men and women (Num. 6:2). Women were involved in spiritual service (Ex. 38:8; Neh. 7:67). Nor did God hesitate to deal directly with women (Gen. 3:13: 16:7–13; Judg. 13:3).

Spiritual equality between the sexes did not, however, do away with the difference in their roles. There were no queens in either Israel or Judah (Athaliah was a usurper). It is true that Deborah served as a judge (Judg. 4:4–5:31). Her case, however, was unique. Dr. Robert L. Saucy comments,

> There may be instances when the regular pattern of God's order may have to be set aside due to unusual circumstances. When, for exam-

> ple, the husband and father is absent, the woman of the house assumes the headship of the family. So it would appear, there may be unusual circumstances when male leadership is unavailable for one reason or another. At such times God may use women to accomplish his purposes even as he used Deborah. ("The Negative Case Against the Ordination of Women," in Kenneth S. Kantzer and Stanley N. Gundry, eds., *Perspectives on Evangelical Theology* [Grand Rapids: Baker, 1979], 285)

It is significant that Deborah declined to lead the military campaign against the Canaanites, deferring instead to a man, Barak. No women served as priests. None of the authors of the Old Testament were women. No woman had an on-going prophetic (speaking before people) ministry like that of Elijah, Elisha, or the other prophets. While Miriam (Ex. 15:20), Deborah (Judg. 4:4), Huldah (2 Kings 22:14), and Isaiah's wife (Isa. 8:3) are called prophetesses, none had a permanent calling to that office. Miriam, Deborah, and Huldah gave only one recorded prophecy, and Isaiah's wife none. She is called a prophetess because she gave birth to a child whose name had prophetic meaning. A fifth woman mentioned as a prophetess, Noadiah, was a false prophetess (Neh. 6:14). While God spoke through women on a few limited occasions, no woman had an on-going role of preaching and teaching.

The New Testament, like the Old, teaches the spiritual equality and differing roles of the sexes. Galatians 3:28 teaches the absolute spiritual equality of men and women in Christ. While many use that verse to justify women assuming leadership roles in the church, the context shows that Paul is speaking of salvation (cf. Gal. 3:22, 24, 26, 27). Again Saucy writes,

> The interpretive question [in Gal. 3:28] is: What is the distinction between male and female which is overcome in Christ? To phrase it another way in light of the apostle's statement "for you are all one in Christ Jesus," what is the "oneness" which male and female share in Christ? We would like to suggest . . . that the answers to these questions do not concern the functional order between man and woman at all. Rather the issue, as in the other two pairs mentioned [Jews and Greeks, slaves and freemen], concerns spiritual status before God. . . . To impart the issue of the functional orders of human society into this passage is to impute a meaning not justified by a valid contextual exegesis. There is therefore no more basis for abolishing the order between man and woman in the church from Galatians 3:28 than for abolishing an order between believing parents and children or believing citizens and rulers. For they are all one in Christ in or out of the organization of the church. (Saucy, 281–82)

That interpretation is further strengthened by the use of the general terms "male" and "female." In every Pauline passage dealing with functional roles, the terms "man" and "woman," or "husband" and "wife" appear. "Why, if the apostle is speaking of the functional relationship in Galatians 3:28, does he not use the language which he uses in every other passage? Why does he not say, 'there is neither man nor woman' in Christ rather than 'male' and 'female'?" (Saucy, 283). Oneness in Christ did not obliterate the distinctions between Jews and Gentiles. Nor did it remove the functional differences between slaves and masters (cf. 1 Cor. 7:20–24). Why, then, should we assume it did so between men and women?

In no way does the New Testament treat women as spiritual inferiors. The first person Jesus revealed His messiahship to was a woman (John 4:25–26). Jesus healed women (Mark 5:25–34; Luke 13:11–13). In contrast to the prevailing practice of the rabbis, He taught women (Luke 10:38–42). Women ministered to Jesus and the disciples (Luke 8:2–3). Following His resurrection, Jesus appeared first to a woman (Mark 16:9; John 20:11–18). Women and men were involved in the prayer services of the early church (Acts 1:13–14). Peter reminds men that women are to be "[granted] honor as fellow [heirs] of the grace of life" (1 Peter 3:7). The fruit of the Spirit (Gal. 5:21–22) are for both men and women. In short, all the promises, commands, and blessings of the New Testament apply equally to women and men.

As in the Old Testament, spiritual equality does not preclude differing roles. There are no women pastor-teachers, evangelists, or elders in the New Testament. None of the authors of the New Testament were women. The New Testament nowhere records a sermon or teaching of a woman. While the daughters of Philip are said to have prophesied (Acts 21:9), neither the occasion nor the message is defined. There is no reason to assume they had an on-going preaching ministry, or that they taught during the public worship. They, like Mary the mother of Jesus (Luke 1:46ff.), or Anna (Luke 2:36–39), delivered some message of truth elsewhere. As noted in chapter 6 of this volume, a comparison of 1 Corinthians 11:5 and 14:34 indicates women are permitted to pray and speak the Word, but Paul here makes clear that such allowance is not in the assembly of the church.

When the church gathers, however, women are to listen to the men who teach **quietly . . . with entire submissiveness.** *Hēsuchia* appears at the beginning of verse 11 (**quietly**), and the end of verse 12 (**quiet**), thus bracketing Paul's teaching on the role of women with the principle of silence. **Submissiveness** translates *hupotagē*, which means "to line up under." **With entire** emphasizes the complete subjection called for. In the context of the worship, then, women are to be silent and content in the role of the learner.

Some have tried to evade the plain meaning of the text by arguing that *hēsuchia* means a meek and quiet spirit. Women, they contend, can preach or teach as long as they do it with the proper attitude. Some go to the opposite extreme and use this text as a prohibition against any talking during church by women. Neither of those revisionist interpretations is valid, however. The context makes the meaning unmistakable to the honest reader.

In verse 12, Paul actually interprets the meaning of verse 11. He defines exactly what he means by women staying quiet in the worship: **But I do not** (as the apostle of Jesus Christ, who speaks through me) **allow a woman to teach or exercise authority over a man.** Women are to keep quiet in the sense of not teaching. They are to demonstrate subjection by not usurping the authority of the elder or preacher. That is true not because women are in any sense inferior to men, but because God's law commands it (1 Cor. 14:34), in line with His design for the weaker vessels. Those who insist that subordination and equality are mutually exclusive would do well to consider Christ's relationship to the Father. While on earth, Jesus assumed a subordinate role, yet He was in no way inferior. First Corinthians 11:3 states, "But I want you to understand that Christ is the head of every man, and the man is the head of a woman, and God is the head of Christ."

Epitrepō (**allow**) is always used in the New Testament to speak of permitting someone to do what they desire to do. Paul's choice of words may imply that some women in Ephesus desired to be the public preachers, and thus have authority over the congregation—as in today's church. Paul, however, speaking as the official apostle of Jesus Christ, does not **allow** that. The role of the elder as evangelist or pastor-teacher is only for men.

The present infinitive *didaskein* (**to teach**) would best be translated "to be a teacher." The noted Greek grammarians H. E. Dana and Julius R. Mantey wrote the following on the distinction between the aorist infinitive and the present infinitive:

> It is well to notice particularly the difference between the aorist and present infinitive. The aorist infinitive denotes that which is eventual or particular, while the present infinitive indicates a condition or process. Thus *pisteusai* [aorist] is to exercise faith on a given occasion, while *pisteuein* [present] is to be a believer. (*A Manual Grammar of the Greek New Testament* [Toronto: MacMillian, 1957], 199)

By using the present infinitive instead of the aorist, Paul does not forbid women to teach under appropriate conditions and circumstances, but to fill the office and role of the pastor or teacher in the life of the church.

Paul also adds the prohibition that forbids women to **exercise authority over a man.** *Authentein* (**exercise authority over**), another present infinitive, appears only here in the New Testament. Some have attempted to evade the force of Paul's prohibition by arbitrarily supposing that *authentein* should properly be translated "abusive authority." Women, according to that view, can exercise authority over men so long as it is not abusive authority. A study of the extrabiblical uses of *authentein,* however, makes clear that the word means simply authority. It carries no negative connotation, such as abusive or domineering authority. Paul, then, in an unqualified directive, forbids women from exercising any type of authority over men in the church. It is the "elders [clearly men, since 1 Tim. 3:2 states they must be 'the husband of one wife'] who rule" (1 Tim. 5:17).

That does not entirely rule out women teaching. Priscilla and Aquila both instructed Apollos (Acts 18:26), but in private and not in the worship of the church. And women can and must teach other women (cf. Titus 2:3–4). Nor does it mean women cannot pray, merely that they are not to lead the prayers during the public worship of the church. It does not mean that women do not have spiritual gifts in the area of public speaking and leadership. The issue is where they exercise those gifts.

Some question whether women can fill leadership roles on the mission field in the absence of men. It is significant that Paul, who wrote this passage, was himself the greatest missionary the world has ever seen. Yet he made no exceptions for the mission field. God does not violate His principles for the sake of expediency.

Through the years there have been a number of good examples of how to cope with a shortage of men on the mission field. I know missionary women personally who found themselves in a situation where no men were present and they alone were biblically trained to handle the Word. Rather than violate the Scripture, they would prepare the message or lesson and teach it to a native man, who would be the preacher when the church gathered.

Women must stop believing the devil's lie that the only role of significance is that of leadership. People usually desire places of prominence not to humbly serve others, but to boost their own egos and gain power and control. Leaders, however, bear a heavy burden and responsibility, and the subordinate role often is one of greater peace and happiness. Subordination is not punishment, but privilege.

The Design of Women

For it was Adam who was first created, and then Eve. And it was

not Adam who was deceived, but the woman being quite deceived, fell into transgression. (2:13–14)

A popular view today is that woman's subordinate role is a corruption of God's perfect design that was the result of the Fall. Since the effects of the curse are intended to be reversed in Christ, it is argued, differing male and female roles should be abolished. Paul, however, establishes woman's subordinate role not in the Fall, but in the divine order of original creation. **For it was Adam who was first created,** he writes, **and then Eve.** God made woman after man to be his suitable helper (Gen. 2:18). The priority of man's role is obvious.

Nor was Paul's teaching prompted by some cultural situation at Ephesus and hence not applicable today, as some argue. He not only appeals here to the creation account in Genesis 2, but also taught this same truth to the Corinthians (1 Cor. 11:8–9).

Paul does not derive women's role from the Fall, but he uses that event as further corroboration of God's intention. He points out that **it was not Adam who was deceived, but the woman being quite deceived, fell into transgression.** Genesis 3:1–7 chronicles the tragic account of what happened when Eve usurped the headship role:

> Now the serpent was more crafty than any beast of the field which the Lord God had made. And he said to the woman, "Indeed, has God said, 'You shall not eat from any tree of the garden'?" And the woman said to the serpent, "From the fruit of the trees of the garden we may eat; but from the fruit of the tree which is in the middle of the garden, God has said, 'You shall not eat from it or touch it, lest you die.'" And the serpent said to the woman, "You surely shall not die! For God knows that in the day you eat from it your eyes will be opened, and you will be like God, knowing good and evil." When the woman saw that the tree was good for food, and that it was a delight to the eyes, and that the tree was desirable to make one wise, she took from its fruit and ate; and she gave also to her husband with her, and he ate. Then the eyes of both of them were opened, and they knew that they were naked; and they sewed fig leaves together and made themselves loin coverings.

The whole human race thus fell into depravity and judgment. Eve was not suited by nature to assume the position of ultimate responsibility. When she stepped out from under the protection and leadership of Adam, she was highly vulnerable and fell. And, of course, when Adam violated his leadership role and followed Eve (though **it was not** he **who was deceived**), the perversion of God's order was complete. The Fall resulted, then, not simply from disobedience to God's command, but from violating God's appointed roles for the sexes. That is not to say that Adam was less culpable than Eve, or that she was more defective. Although he was not deceived by Satan, as was Eve, Adam still chose to disobey God. As the head of their relationship, he bore ultimate responsibility. That is why the New Testament relates the Fall to Adam's sin, not Eve's (Rom. 5:12–21; 1 Cor. 15:21–22). Headship by the man, then, was part of God's design from the beginning, and he bears the responsibility for its success or failure. The tragic experience of the garden encounter with the serpent confirmed the wisdom of that design.

THE CONTRIBUTION OF WOMEN

But women shall be preserved through the bearing of children if they continue in faith and love and sanctity with self-restraint. (2:15)

Preserved is from *sōzō*, the common New Testament word for salvation. The word can also mean "to rescue," "to preserve safe and unharmed," "to heal," "to set free," or "to deliver from." It appears a number of times in the New Testament without reference to spiritual salvation (cf. Matt. 8:25; 9:21–22; 10:22; 24:22; 27:40, 42, 49; 2 Tim. 4:18). Paul obviously does not intend to teach that women are eternally saved from the wages of sin **through the bearing of children.** That would contradict the New Testament's teaching that salvation is by grace through faith alone (cf. Rom. 3:19–20). The future tense and the use of the plural pronoun **they** indicate that he was not even referring to Eve. The plural and the absence of any connection to the context show Paul was not referring to Mary, the mother of Jesus, as some suggest.

Paul teaches here that although a woman precipitated the Fall and women bear that responsibility, yet they may be **preserved** from that stigma through childbearing. The rescue, the delivery, the freeing of women from the stigma of having led the race into sin happens when they bring up a righteous seed. What a perfect counter! Women are far from being second-class citizens because they have the primary responsibility for rearing godly children. Mothers spend far more time with their children than do their fathers, and thus have the greater influence. Fathers cannot know the intimate relationship with their children that their mother establishes from pregnancy, birth, infancy, and early childhood. Paul's point is that while a woman may have led the race into sin, women have the privilege of leading the race out of sin to godliness. That does not mean that God wants all women to bear children; some He doesn't even want married (1 Cor. 7:25–40). Paul speaks in general terms. The pain associated with childbirth was the punishment for the woman's sin (Gen. 3:16), but the joy and privilege of child rearing delivers women from the stigma of that sin.

For women to reverse the blight that has befallen them in the Fall and fulfill their calling they need to raise a godly seed. To do that, they must **continue in faith and love,** where their salvation really rests. And they must continue in **sanctity** (holiness) **with self-restraint** (the same word translated "discreetly" in verse 9). It is the very appearance, demeanor, and behavior demanded of believing women in the church that becomes their deliverance from any inferior status, as they live godly and raise godly children.

In this passage we see how God has perfectly balanced the roles of the sexes. (For a complete discussion of the design of God for men and women in the church, see my book *Different by Design* [Wheaton, Ill.: Victor, 1994].) Men are to be the leaders in the church and the family. Women are kept from any accusation of inferiority through the godly influence they have in the lives of their precious children. For the church to depart from this divine order is to perpetuate the disaster of the Fall.

Called to Lead the Church

8

It is a trustworthy statement: if any man aspires to the office of overseer, it is a fine work he desires to do. (3:1)

Paul moves from discussing the congregation (2:1–15) to dealing with the pastors. The ministry, effectiveness, and testimony of any church is largely a reflection of its leaders. The principle of Hosea 4:9, "And it will be, like people, like priest" is still true. People do not normally rise above the level of their leaders. So important is it that those who lead the church be highly qualified spiritually that the detailed list of their specific qualifications is given twice in Paul's letters, here and in Titus 1. Church leadership is at the core of New Testament teaching, since the Lord came into this world to build the church (Matt. 16:18).

There is an inseparable link between the character of a church and the quality of its leadership. Leaders must set a godly example for the church to follow. Our Lord said in Luke 6:40, "Everyone, after he has been fully trained, will be like his teacher." Paul urged the Corinthians to "be imitators of me" (1 Cor. 4:16; cf. 1 Cor. 11:1). To the Philippians he wrote, "The things you have learned and received and heard and seen in me, practice these things" (Phil. 4:9).

The church at Ephesus had been blessed with leadership of the highest caliber. It was founded by Paul, who ministered there for three years (Acts 20:31). During that time he trained a core of godly leaders (Acts 20:17ff.) to lead the church after he left. As he foresaw, however, false leaders arose after his departure from Ephesus (Acts 20:29–30). After his release from his first Roman imprisonment, Paul returned to Ephesus and dealt with two prominent ones (1:20). Leaving Timothy to deal with the rest and the other issues in the church, he set out for Macedonia (1:3). Not long afterward, he wrote this letter to Timothy, directing him with a strategy to correct and build up the Ephesian church. At the heart of that task was the crucial need to reestablish a godly leadership. Choosing the right elders was to be done by measuring men against a divinely inspired checklist of qualifications.

The qualifications Paul gives in 3:2–7 are set against the backdrop of the unqualified leaders in Ephesus. He places God's standards against what the Ephesians had allowed the leadership to degenerate into. Some of the leaders were teaching false doctrine (1:3; 4:1–3, 7; 6:3–5), turning aside to "fruitless discussion" (1:6). They misused the law and misunderstood the gospel (1:7–11). Some were women (2:12), though that was forbidden by God's Word. Others were guilty of sin, and needed public rebuke (5:20).

All the qualifications he lists are spiritual virtues, character traits that mark godly teachers and leaders. He says nothing about the duties of the leaders, but is concerned only with their spirituality, morality, and virtue as the necessary foundation to duty. The duties were clear, the qualifications needed to be clarified. All who serve as overseers or elders in the church must measure up to these standards, or face public discipline (5:20–24).

Before discussing the individual qualifications against which all pastors are to be measured, however, Paul gives some helpful insight into the call to spiritual leadership. This opening verse suggests six facets related to the call to ministry: It is an important calling, a limited calling, a compelling calling, a responsible calling, a worthy calling, and a demanding calling.

An Important Calling

It is a trustworthy statement: (3:1a)

As noted in chapter 3 of this volume, the phrase **a trustworthy statement** is unique to the Pastoral Epistles, appearing five times (cf. 1:15; 4:9; 2 Tim. 2:11; Titus 3:8). Each time, it introduces a basic truth of great importance and familiarity among believers. **A trustworthy state-**

ment is an obvious, self-evident truth that doesn't need proof. Because the phrase appears only late in Paul's ministry, it probably indicates axioms that had become creeds. While the **trustworthy statement** in this passage is about the issue of the call to the ministry, the others refer to doctrinal matters. Including this truth with those essential elements of Christian dogma shows the importance placed on the role of leadership by the early church. It was and is a serious and sacred trust.

In Paul's day the pastorate was not entered into lightly. Today people enter the ministry for a variety of reasons, not all of them commendable. Some are in it for the money, others for job security, prestige and respect, the privilege of working with Christians, or other unacceptable motivations. In the early church, however, conditions were very different. There was little money to be made, since the churches were poor and few Christians were rich. The ministry was not a position of prestige in society, since Christians, and especially preachers, were despised outcasts (cf. 1 Cor. 1:26). And since the church was a frequent target of persecution, those in leadership roles risked their lives.

The record of the developing church constantly affirms the importance of spiritual leadership. On their first missionary journey, Paul and Barnabas "appointed elders for them in every church" (Acts 14:23). Elders, along with the apostles, presided at the Jerusalem Council (Acts 15:2, 4, 6, 22, 23). As already noted, Paul had appointed elders at Ephesus (Acts 20:17, 28). Paul addressed the book of Philippians to "to all the saints in Christ Jesus who are in Philippi, including the overseers and deacons" (Phil. 1:1). He wrote to the Thessalonians, "We request of you, brethren, that you appreciate those who diligently labor among you, and have charge over you in the Lord and give you instruction, and that you esteem them very highly in love because of their work" (1 Thess. 5:12–13). In a similar vein the writer of Hebrews exhorted his readers to "obey your leaders, and submit to them; for they keep watch over your souls, as those who will give an account. Let them do this with joy and not with grief, for this would be unprofitable for you" (Heb. 13:17). Peter wrote

> Therefore, I exhort the elders among you, as your fellow elder and witness of the sufferings of Christ, and a partaker also of the glory that is to be revealed, shepherd the flock of God among you, exercising oversight not under compulsion, but voluntarily, according to the will of God; and not for sordid gain, but with eagerness; nor yet as lording it over those allotted to your charge, but proving to be examples to the flock. (1 Peter 5:1–3)

Since godly leaders have always been the backbone of the church, it is essential that they be qualified. In an unsuccessful church, the issue is all too often not poor programs or uncommitted people, but substandard leadership. Godly leaders are not produced by Bible colleges or seminaries; they merely give them the tools with which to work. Nor do pulpit committees or ordination councils make men fit for the ministry; they merely have the responsibility to recognize those who already are. Only the Holy Spirit can produce a true spiritual leader.

When Saul failed to be a godly king over Israel God sought out David, "a man after His own heart" (1 Sam. 13:14). In Ezekiel 22:30 God cries out, "I searched for a man among them who should build up the wall and stand in the gap before Me for the land, that I should not destroy it; but I found no one." George Liddell wrote,

> Give me a man of God—one man,
> Whose faith is master of his mind,
> And I will right all wrongs
> And bless the name of all mankind.
>
> Give me a man of God—one man,
> Whose tongue is touched with heaven's fire,
> And I will flame the darkest hearts
> With high resolve and clean desire.
>
> Give me a man of God—one man,
> One mighty prophet of the Lord,
> And I will give you peace on earth,
> Bought with a prayer and not a sword.
>
> Give me a man of God—one man,
> True to the vision that he sees,
> And I will build your broken shrines,
> And bring the nations to their knees.
>
> (Cited in J. Oswald Sanders,
> *Spiritual Leadership*, rev. ed.
> [Chicago: Moody, 1980], 17–18)

That is the kind of man God seeks to lead His redeemed people. Such men are "those who are willing to suffer for the sake of objectives great enough to demand their wholehearted obedience" (Sanders, *Spiritual Leadership*, 20).

Such a man was Samuel Logan Brengle, one of the early leaders of the Salvation Army. He wrote,

> [Spiritual leadership] is not won by promotion, but by many prayers and tears. It is attained by confessions of sin, and much heartsearching and humbling before God; by self-surrender, a courageous sacrifice of

> every idol, a bold, deathless, uncompromising and uncomplaining embracing of the cross, and by an eternal, unfaltering looking unto Jesus crucified. It is not gained by seeking great things for ourselves, but rather, like Paul, by counting those things that are gain to us as loss for Christ. That is a great price, but it must be unflinchingly paid by him who would be not merely a nominal but a real spiritual leader of men, a leader whose power is recognized and felt in heaven, on earth and in hell. (*The Soul-Winner's Secret* [London: The Salvation Army, 1918], 22)

The call to lead the church is so important that only the noblest need apply.

A Limited Calling

if any man (3:1b)

Church leadership is not for everyone. An essential requirement for a church leader is that he be a **man.** The indefinite pronoun *tis* (**any**) should be taken here as masculine, in agreement with the masculine form of the adjectives in verses 2–6. Also, a woman could hardly be a "one-woman man" (v. 2), nor did women in that day head households (vv. 5–6). Paul here applies the truth he taught in 2:11–15: women are not to be the leaders in the church. As already noted in chapter 7 of this volume, they have a vitally important role in the church, the home, and in society. That role, however, does not include leadership over God's people.

A Compelling Calling

aspires . . . desires (3:1c, g)

Those who seek the office of overseer must have a Spirit-given, compelling desire for it. **Aspires** is from *oregō,* a rare word, appearing only here, 1 Timothy 6:10, and Hebrews 11:16 in the New Testament. It means "to reach out after," or "to stretch out oneself to grasp something." The term does not speak of internal motives, but only describes the external act. Here it describes someone who is taking steps to become an overseer.

Desires is from *epithumeō,* which means "a passionate compulsion," in this context for good rather than for evil. In contrast to *oregō,* this verb refers to the inward feeling of desire. Taken together, the two terms describe the man who outwardly pursues the ministry because of a driving compulsion on the inside.

Some men seek spiritual oversight in the church because people they respect have encouraged them to do so. Others pursue it because they have decided the ministry is their best option. They love the Lord and His church, so they attend Bible college or seminary to prepare for service. Because they are not driven by an internal passion for the ministry, however, it can become a mere academic exercise for them.

On the other hand, some have a great passion for the ministry, but lack self-control and devotion to priorities for preparation. They can't seem to get their lives disciplined enough to get on track to achieve their desire.

The man truly called to the ministry is marked by both an inward consuming passion and a disciplined outward pursuit. For him the ministry is not the best option, it is the only option. There is nothing else he could do with his life that would fulfill him. Accordingly, he works diligently to prepare himself to be qualified for service. While some may be called later in life, from that point on nothing else will do.

As already noted, some seek the office of overseer for wrong motives, such as money, power, or prestige. The true motive for seeking the ministry was described by Patrick Fairbairn: "The seeking here intended . . . must be of the proper kind, not the prompting of a carnal ambition, but the aspiration of a heart which has itself experienced the grace of God, and which longs to see others coming to participate in the heavenly gift" (*Pastoral Epistles* [Minneapolis: James & Klock, 1976], 136). It is not the office the truly called seek, but the work itself. Samuel Brengle wrote that "the final estimate of men shows that history cares not for the rank or title a man has borne, or the office he has held, but only the quality of his deeds and the character of his mind and heart" (C. W. Hall, *Samuel Logan Brengle* [New York: The Salvation Army, 1933], 274).

Simply put, ambition for office corrupts, desire for service purifies. Our Lord described the true character of spiritual service in Mark 10:42–44:

> And calling [the disciples] to Himself, Jesus said to them, "You know that those who are recognized as rulers of the Gentiles lord it over them; and their great men exercise authority over them. But it is not so among you, but whoever wishes to become great among you shall be your servant; and whoever wishes to be first among you shall be slave of all."

In a striking sermon known as "The Sermon of the Plow," the noted English Reformer Hugh Latimer blasted the passionless, self-promoting clergy of his day:

> And now I would ask you a strange question; who is the most diligent bishop and prelate in all England; that passes all the rest in doing his office? I can tell, for I know who it is; I know him well. But now I think I see you listening and hearkening that I should name him. There is one that passes all the other [sic], and is the most diligent prelate and preacher in all England. And will ye know who it is? I will tell you—it is the Devil. He is the most diligent preacher of all others; he is never out of his diocese; he is never away from his cure; you shall never find him unoccupied; he is ever in his parish; he keeps residence at all times; you shall never find him out of the way; call for him when you will, he is ever at home. He is the most diligent preacher in all the realm; he is ever at his plough; nor lording or loitering can hinder him; he is ever applying his business; you shall never find him idle, I warrant you. . . . Where the devil is resident, and has his plough going, there away with books and up with candles; away with bibles and up with beads; away with the light of the gospel and up with the light of candles, yea at noonday; . . . up with man's traditions and his laws, down with God's traditions and his most holy word. . . . Oh that our prelates would be as diligent to sow the corn of good doctrine as Satan is to sow cockle and darnel! . . . There never was such a preacher in England as he is.
>
> The prelates are lords . . . and no labourers; but the devil is diligent at his plough. He is no unpreaching prelate; he is no lordly loiterer from his cure; but a busy ploughman. . . . Therefore, ye unpreaching prelates, learn of the devil: to be diligent in doing of your office. . . . If you will not learn of God, nor good men, to be diligent in your office, learn of the devil. (Cited in John R. W. Stott, *Between Two Worlds* [Grand Rapids: Eerdmans, 1982], 27–28)

The church must be led by men of passion who are compelled to the ministry.

A Responsible Calling

the office of overseer (3:1d)

Having oversight of the church is no small task, but rather a sobering responsibility. Hebrews 13:17 warns that leaders must give an account to God for how faithfully they have led, while James adds that because they teach they face a stricter judgment (James 3:1). Overseer translates *episkopos,* the term rendered bishop by the Authorized Version. In our day "bishop" has been encumbered with much ecclesiastical trapping. In the New Testament, however, the terms "bishop" (or overseer) referred to the same role as pastor and elder (cf. Acts 20:28; Titus 1:5–9; 1 Peter 5:1–2).

Some have suggested that *episkopos* derives its sense from the city administrator, inspector, or financial manager of Greek culture. Its New Testament usage, however, more closely parallels that of the Essene Jews of the Qumran community. The overseers among the Essenes preached, taught, presided, exercised care and authority, and enforced discipline. Those functions more closely mirror that of the New Testament overseer than the more narrow use of the term in Greek culture.

What are the responsibilities of the overseer? They are to rule (1 Tim. 5:17), to preach and teach (1 Tim. 5:17), to pray for the sick (James 5:14), to care for the church (1 Peter 5:1–2), to be examples for others to follow (1 Peter 5:1–2), to set church policy (Acts 15:22ff.), and to ordain other leaders (1 Tim. 4:14).

A Worthy Calling

it is a fine work (3:1e)

The ministry is a **fine** (*kalos*), noble, honorable, excellent, high-quality **work.** It is a most worthy and glorious calling, as godly men have always recognized. The fourteenth-century English reformer John Wycliffe wrote,

> The highest service that men may attain to on earth is to preach the Word of God. This service falls peculiarly to priests, and therefore God more straightly demands it of them. . . . And for this cause, Jesus Christ left other works and occupied himself mostly in preaching, and thus did his apostles, and for this, God loved them. . . .
>
> The church, however, is honoured most by the preaching of God's Word, and hence this is the best service that priests may render unto God. . . . And thus, if our bishops preach not in their own persons, and hinder true priests from preaching, they are in the sins of the bishops who killed the Lord Jesus Christ. (Cited in Clyde E. Fant, Jr., and William M. Pinson, Jr., eds., *20 Centuries of Great Preaching* [Waco, Tex.: Word, 1971], 1:234)

The seventeenth-century American Puritan Cotton Mather agreed:

> The office of the Christian ministry, rightly understood, is the most honourable, and important, that any man in the whole world can ever sustain; and it will be one of the wonders and employments of eternity to consider the reasons why the wisdom and goodness of God assigned this office to imperfect and guilty man! . . . The great design and intention of the office of a Christian preacher are to restore the throne and dominion of God in the souls of men; to display in the most lively colours, and proclaim in the clearest language, the wonderful perfections, offices and grace of the Son of God; and to attract the souls of men into a state of everlasting friendship with him. . . . It is a work which an angel might wish for, as an honour to his character; yea, an office which every angel in heaven might covet to be employed in for a thousand years to come. It is such an honourable, important and useful office, that if a man be put into it by God, and made faithful and successful through life, he may look down with disdain upon a crown, and shed a tear of pity on the brightest monarch on earth. (Cited in Stott, *Between Two Worlds,* 31)

The twentieth-century English preacher Will Sangster wrote of the ministry:

> Called to preach! . . . Commissioned of God to teach the Word! A herald of the great King! A witness of the eternal gospel! Could any work be more high and holy? To this supreme task God sent His only begotten Son. In all the frustration and confusion of the times, is it possible to imagine a work comparable in importance with that of proclaiming the will of God to wayward men? . . .
>
> Not by accident, nor yet by the thrustful egotism of men, was the pulpit given the central place in the Reformed Churches. It is there of design and devotion. It is there by the logic of things. It is there as "*the throne of the Word of God.*" (W. E. Sangster, *The Craft of the Sermon* [Philadelphia: Westminster, 1951], 24, 17; italics in original)

The work of preaching and leading the church, which our Lord purchased with His blood, is the highest and the greatest and the most glorious calling to which anyone can ever be called.

A Demanding Calling

work (3:1f)

Those looking for an easy time will not find it in the ministry. The ministry is **work,** a demanding, lifelong task. Paul commanded Timothy to "do the *work* of an evangelist" (2 Tim. 4:5). He reminded the

Thessalonians to "appreciate those who diligently *labor* [from *kopiaō*—"to work to the point of exhaustion"] among you, and have charge over you in the Lord" (1 Thess. 5:12). Paul told the Colossians, "We proclaim Him, admonishing every man and teaching every man with all wisdom, that we may present every man complete in Christ. And for this purpose also I labor, striving according to His power, which mightily works within me" (Col. 1:28–29). The ministry is no nine-to-five occupation that one can walk away from and forget each evening. Its work is neverending and dependent on maximum effort and the power of Christ at work in the man.

The work of the ministry is such a serious undertaking that no man may enter it based solely on his own desire. Anyone who would lead the church must be set apart to that responsibility by the church when it clearly recognizes his giftedness, virtue, and service, by the standards given in verses 2–7. The sign that this recognition had occurred and a man had been set apart for the ministry in the early church was the laying on of hands (cf. 1 Tim. 4:14). The symbolism comes from the Old Testament, where the one offering a sacrifice identified with it by laying his hands on it. By laying hands on a candidate for the ministry, church leaders showed their unity and solidarity with him. They also gave him their commendation, support, and affirmation.

Paul strongly cautioned Timothy not to "lay hands upon anyone too hastily and thus share responsibility for the sins of others" (1 Tim. 5:22). Those who ordain an unworthy man to the ministry share the responsibility for his sin. The early church took ordination very seriously. In Acts 13:2 and 14:23 we read that prayer and fasting accompanied the setting apart of men for the ministry. It was done in the early years by the apostles (Acts 14:23) and later by the elders of each congregation.

So spiritual oversight begins with a divine calling. Men, driven by an inner passion, actively seek to serve the church. The congregation either affirms or rejects that calling based on how the man's life measures up to the standards the Holy Spirit has delineated in 3:2–7.

Qualities of a Godly Leader—part 1 Moral Qualities

9

An overseer, then, must be above reproach, the husband of one wife, temperate, prudent, respectable, hospitable, able to teach, not addicted to wine or pugnacious, but gentle, uncontentious, free from the love of money. (3:2–3)

Field Marshal Sir Bernard Law Montgomery was perhaps Britain's greatest military leader during World War II. He was thus eminently qualified to list the qualities necessary to a leader in war. According to Montgomery, such a leader should see the big picture and not become bogged down in details. He must not be petty. He must choose men well. He should trust those under him and let them get on with their jobs without interference. He must have the power of clear decision. He should inspire confidence. Finally, he must have a proper sense of religious truth and acknowledge it to his troops (Bernard L. Montgomery, *Memoirs of Field-Marshal Montgomery* [Cleveland: World, 1958], 74–83).

From a different perspective John R. Mott, a world leader in student circles in the early part of this century, gave the following list: Does he do little things well? Has he learned the meaning of priorities? How does he use his leisure? Has he intensity? Has he learned to take advantage of momentum? Has he the power of growth? What is his attitude toward discouragements? How does he face impossible situations? What are his weakest points? (Basil Matthews, *John R. Mott: World Citizen* [New York: Harper & Brothers, 1934], 332–98).

The Overarching Requirement of a Godly Leader

An overseer, then, must be above reproach, (3:2a)

Those lists, and many others like them, contain qualities every church overseer should possess. But pastoring God's people demands far more because the issue is not just leadership, but moral and spiritual example. Summing up that realm of requirement, Paul demands that **an overseer** in the church of Jesus Christ **must be above reproach.** The Greek particle *de* (**must**) emphasizes that this is an absolute necessity. A life without blame is the overarching requirement for leadership in the church.

Few have stated that truth as eloquently as the godly Richard Baxter, a pastor in the Puritan movement of seventeenth-century England:

> Take heed to yourselves, lest your example contradict your doctrine, and lest you lay such stumbling-blocks before the blind, as may be the occasion of their ruin; lest you unsay with your lives, what you say with your tongues; and be the greatest hinderers of the success of your own labours. . . . One proud, surly, lordly word, one needless contention, one covetous action, may cut the throat of many a sermon, and blast the fruit of all that you have been doing.
>
> Take heed to yourselves, lest you live in those sins which you preach against in others, and lest you be guilty of that which daily you condemn. Will you make it your work to magnify God, and, when you have done, dishonour him as much as others? Will you proclaim Christ's governing power, and yet contemn it, and rebel yourselves? Will you preach his laws, and wilfully break them? If sin be evil, why do you live in it? if it be not, why do you dissuade men from it? If it be dangerous, how dare you venture on it? if it be not, why do you tell men so? If God's threatenings be true, why do you not fear them? if they be false, why do you needlessly trouble men with them, and put them into such frights without a cause? Do you 'know the judgment of God, that they who commit such things are worthy of death;' and yet will you do them? 'Thou that teachest another, teachest thou not thyself? Thou that sayest a man should not commit adultery,' or be drunk, or covetous, art thou such thyself? 'Thou that makest thy boast of the law, through breaking the law dishonourest thou God?' What! shall the same tongue speak evil that speakest against evil? Shall those lips censure, and

> slander, and backbite your neighbour, that cry down these and the like things in others? Take heed to yourselves, lest you cry down sin, and yet do not overcome it; lest, while you seek to bring it down in others, you bow to it, and become its slaves yourselves: 'For of whom a man is overcome, of the same is he brought into bondage.' 'To whom ye yield yourselves servants to obey, his servants ye are to whom ye obey, whether of sin unto death, or of obedience unto righteousness.' O brethren! it is easier to chide at sin, than to overcome it. (*The Reformed Pastor* [Edinburgh: Banner of Truth, 1979], 63, 67–68)

Anepilēmptos (**above reproach**) means "not able to be held." The man who is above reproach cannot be arrested and held as if he were a criminal; there is nothing for which to accuse him. In Titus 1:6, the same idea of being above reproach is conveyed, but a different term (*anengklētos*—"unreprovable") is used. The present participle *einai* (**be**) indicates he is in a present state of being above reproach. Obviously, it does not mean he has not committed sins in his life. What it does mean is that his life has not been marred by some obvious sinful defect in character which would preclude him setting the highest standard for godly conduct. He must be a model for the congregation to follow (cf. Phil. 3:17; 2 Thess. 3:9; Heb. 13:7; 1 Peter 5:3). He also must not give the enemies of the church reason to attack its reputation.

Pastors must take great care to remain above reproach for several reasons. First, they are the special targets of Satan, and he will assault them with more severe temptation than others. Those on the front lines of the spiritual battle will bear the brunt of satanic opposition.

Second, their fall has a greater potential for harm. Satan knows that when a shepherd falls, the effect on the sheep is devastating.

Third, leaders' greater knowledge of the truth, and accountability to live it, brings greater chastening when they sin.

Fourth, elders' sins are more hypocritical than others' because they preach against the very sins they commit.

Leaders need an abundance of God's grace and power because of their greater responsibility and visibility.

To protect themselves leaders must spend in-depth time in the study of God's Word. They must be "constantly nourished on the words of the faith [Scripture] and of the sound doctrine" (1 Tim. 4:6). The psalmist wrote, "Thy word I have treasured in my heart, that I may not sin against Thee" (Ps. 119:11). A leader must continuously expose his life to the light of the Word of God. He must also be a man of prayer, and be accountable to others in spiritual fellowship.

The church is called to be committed to maintaining leadership that is godly. The church is responsible to measure men by the standard of **above reproach.** The all too common practice today is to forgive a leader who sins and immediately restore him to his ministry. The church, like God, must not hesitate to forgive those who truly repent. To immediately restore them to the ministry, however, lowers the standard that God expects leaders to follow. And since leaders serve as the pattern of holiness and virtue for the congregation, the standard for the entire church is lowered.

In 3:2–7, Paul lists four areas in which a man aspiring to church leadership may be evaluated as to whether he is **above reproach.** These have to do with his moral character, home life, spiritual maturity, and public reputation.

THE MORAL CHARACTER OF A GODLY LEADER

the husband of one wife, temperate, prudent, respectable, hospitable, able to teach, not addicted to wine or pugnacious, but gentle, uncontentious, free from the love of money. (3:2b–3)

In spelling out specifically what it means to be above reproach, Paul lists qualities of the overseer's character.

The overseer or elder must first be above reproach in relation to women. He must be **the husband of one wife.** The Greek text literally reads "a one-woman man." Paul is not referring to a leader's marital status, as the absence of the definite article in the original indicates. Rather, the issue is his moral, sexual behavior. Many men married only once are not one-woman men. Many with one wife are unfaithful to that wife. While remaining married to one woman is commendable, it is no indication or guarantee of moral purity.

Some may wonder why Paul begins his list with this quality. He does so because it is in this area, above all others, where leaders seem most prone to fall. The failure to be a one-woman man has put more men out of the ministry than any other sin. It is thus a matter of grave concern.

Various interpretations have been offered that evade the meaning of this standard. Some have argued that its intent is to forbid polygamy. A man could not, however, even be a member of the church if he was a polygamist, let alone a leader. If that were all Paul meant, it would be an unnecessary prohibition. Further, polygamy was not an issue in Ephesus. It was uncommon in Roman society, in part because sexual encounters outside of marriage as well as divorces were easily obtainable. Nor was polygamy a feature of first-century Jewish society.

Others maintain that Paul here forbids remarriage after the death of a spouse. As already noted, however, this standard, like all the rest, refers to moral character, not marital status. Further, the Scriptures permit and honor second marriages under the proper circumstances. Paul expected younger widows to remarry and raise a family (1 Tim. 5:14), and widows could be described as one-man women (5:9). In 1 Corinthians 7:39 he wrote, "A wife is bound as long as her husband lives; but if her husband is dead, she is free to be married to whom she wishes, only in the Lord."

Still others hold that this qualification excludes divorced men from spiritual leadership. That again ignores the fact that Paul is not here referring to marital status. Nor does the Bible forbid all remarriage after a divorce. In Matthew 5:31–32 and 19:9, our Lord permitted remarriage when a divorce was caused by adultery. Paul gave a second occasion when remarriage is permitted, when the unbelieving spouse initiates the divorce (1 Cor. 7:15). While God hates all divorce (Mal. 2:16), He is gracious to the innocent party in those two situations. (For a complete exposition of the relevant passages on divorce, see *Matthew 1–7*, MacArthur New Testament Commentary [Chicago: Moody, 1985], and *1 Corinthians*, MacArthur New Testament Commentary [Chicago: Moody, 1984.) Since remarriage in and of itself is not a sin, it is not necessarily a blight on a man's character. If divorce resulted from a man's inability to lead his family (v. 5), however, then it is a disqualification.

Nor does Paul intend to exclude single men from the ministry. If that was his point here, he would have disqualified himself, since he was single (1 Cor. 7:8).

A one-woman man is a man devoted in his heart and mind to the woman who is his wife. He loves, desires, and thinks only of her. He maintains sexual purity in both his thought life and his conduct. That qualification was especially important in Ephesus, where sexual evil was rampant. Many, if not most, of the congregation had at one time or another fallen prey to sexual evil. If that was before a man came to Christ, it wasn't a problem (cf. 2 Cor. 5:17). If it happened after his conversion, even before he assumed a leadership role, it was a problem. If it happened after he assumed a leadership role, it was a definite disqualification. Those same standards apply to men in positions of spiritual leadership today. Scripture makes clear that sexual sin is a reproach that never goes away. Proverbs 6:32–33 says of the adulterer, "The one who commits adultery with a woman is lacking sense; he who would destroy himself does it. Wounds and disgrace he will find, and his reproach will not be blotted out." Paul also indicates that failure to keep the body pure and controlled results in being disqualified for preaching (1 Cor. 9:27).

A leader in God's church must also be **temperate.** *Nēphalios* (**temperate**) literally means "wineless," or "unmixed with wine." While it is true that wine "makes man's heart glad" (Ps. 104:15), it also has the potential for great harm. That is why it was commonly diluted with water in biblical times. Even so, it retained its potential for harm to those who drank it unmixed or to excess. Proverbs 20:1 warns, "Wine is a mocker, strong drink a brawler, and whoever is intoxicated by it is not wise." Proverbs 23:29–35 graphically describes one snared by wine:

> Who has woe? Who has sorrow? Who has contentions? Who has complaining? Who has wounds without cause? Who has redness of eyes? Those who linger long over wine, those who go to taste mixed wine. Do not look on the wine when it is red, when it sparkles in the cup, when it goes down smoothly; at the last it bites like a serpent, and stings like a viper. Your eyes will see strange things, and your mind will utter perverse things. And you will be like one who lies down in the middle of the sea, or like one who lies down on the top of a mast. "They struck me, but I did not become ill; they beat me, but I did not know it. When shall I awake? I will seek another drink."

Noah (Gen. 9:20–27) and Amnon (2 Sam. 13:28–29) are examples of those affected by wine.

Leviticus 10:9 forbids priests from drinking wine when performing their priestly duties. Those taking a Nazirite vow also could not drink wine (Num. 6:3). Kings and other rulers were to abstain from drinking (Prov. 31:4), because it could dull their senses and affect their judgment.

In a metaphorical sense, *nēphalios* means "alert," "watchful," "vigilant," or "clear-headed." That may be its primary sense in this passage. A leader must be one who thinks clearly. He must possess the inner strength to refrain from any excess that would dull his alertness. William Hendriksen writes, "His pleasures are not primarily those of the senses . . . but those of the soul" (*New Testament Commentary: The Pastoral Epistles* [Grand Rapids: Baker, 1981], 122). **Temperate** men are desperately needed in today's church. They will be to her what the sons of Issachar in 1 Chronicles 12:32 were to Israel, "men who understood the times, with knowledge of what Israel should do."

Third, a leader in the church must be **prudent.** This quality is the result of being temperate. The **prudent** man is well-disciplined, and knows how to correctly order his priorities. He is a person who is serious about spiritual things. That does not mean he is cold and humorless, but that he views the world through God's eyes. The realities that the world is lost, disobedient to God, and bound for hell leave little room for frivolity in his ministry. Such a man has a sure and steady mind. He is not rash in judgment, but thoughtful, earnest, and cautious. He follows Paul's counsel in Philippians 4:8: "Whatever is true, whatever is honorable, whatever is right, whatever is pure, whatever is lovely, whatever is of good repute, if there is any excellence and if anything worthy of praise, let your mind dwell on these things." His mind will be controlled by God's truth, not the whims of the flesh. Jesus Christ will reign supreme over every area of his life.

Fourth, an overseer must be **respectable.** *Kosmios* (**respectable**) carries the idea of "orderly." A man **prudent** in mind will have a **respectable,** or orderly life. His well-disciplined mind leads to a well-disciplined life. "The ministry is no place for the man whose life is a continual confusion of unaccomplished plans and unorganized activities" (Homer A. Kent, Jr., *The Pastoral Epistles* [Winona Lake, Ind.: BMH Books, 1982], 127). As noted in chapter 7 of this volume, the word *kosmos,* from which *kosmios* derives, is the opposite of "chaos." A spiritual leader must not have a chaotic, but an orderly lifestyle. If he cannot order his own life, how can he bring order to the church (v. 5)?

Fifth, church leaders must be **hospitable.** That word translates *philoxenos,* a compound word from the Greek words for "to love," and "strangers." The word thus literally means "to love strangers." It is a frequently commanded Christian virtue (cf. Rom. 12:13; Heb. 13:2; 1 Peter 4:9). It does not refer to entertaining friends, but showing hospitality to strangers. Our Lord said in Luke 14:12,

> When you give a luncheon or a dinner, do not invite your friends or your brothers or your relatives or rich neighbors, lest they also invite you in return, and repayment come to you. But when you give a reception, invite the poor, the crippled, the lame, the blind, and you will be blessed, since they do not have the means to repay you; for you will be repaid at the resurrection of the righteous.

Persecution, poverty, orphans, widows, and traveling Christians made hospitality essential in New Testament times. They had no hotels or motels, and the inns were notoriously evil. Often they were brothels, or places where travelers were robbed or beaten. William Barclay wrote of them,

> In the ancient world, inns were notoriously bad. In one of Aristophane's plays Heracles asks his companion where they will lodge for the night; and the answer is: "Where the fleas are fewest." Plato speaks of the inn-keeper being like a pirate who holds his guests to ransom. Inns tended to be dirty and expensive and, above all, immoral. The ancient world had a system of what were called *Guest Friendships.* Over generations families had arrangements to give each other accommodations and hospitality. Often the members of the families came in the end to be unknown to each other by sight and identified themselves by

> means of what were called *tallies.* The stranger seeking accommodation would produce one half of some object; the host would possess the other half of the tally; and when the two halves fitted each other the host knew that he had found his guest, and the guest knew that the host was indeed the ancestral friend of his household.
>
> In the Christian church there were wandering teachers and preachers who needed hospitality. There were also many slaves with no homes of their own to whom it was a great privilege to have the right of entry to a Christian home. It was of the greatest blessing that Christians should have Christian homes ever open to them in which they could meet people like-minded to themselves. (*The Letters to Timothy, Titus, and Philemon* [Philadelphia: Westminster, 1975], 82; italics in original)

The door of the Christian home, as well as the heart of the Christian family, ought to be open to all who come in need. That is especially true of the overseer. Elders are not elevated to a place where they are unapproachable. They are to be available. A pastor's life and home are to be open so that his true character is manifest to all who come there, friend or stranger.

The overseer in the church must be **able to teach.** Here is the only qualification that relates specifically to his giftedness and function. *Didaktikos* (**able to teach**) appears only here and in 2 Timothy 2:24 in the New Testament. An elder must be a highly skilled teacher, who works hard in his studies and proclamation (cf. 5:17). That is the one qualification that sets him apart from the deacons. Since, as noted below, the primary duty of the overseer is to preach and teach the Word of God, being gifted for that is crucial.

Some may wonder why Paul includes this qualification in the midst of a list of moral qualities. He does so because effective teaching is woven into the moral character of the teacher. What a man is cannot be divorced from what he says. "He that means as he speaks," writes Richard Baxter, "will surely do as he speaks" (*The Reformed Pastor,* 63).

To preach and teach God's Word is the primary task of elders (1 Tim. 4:6, 11, 13, 16; 5:17; 2 Tim. 2:15, 24; Titus 2:1). It was for that purpose that they were given to the church (Eph. 4:11–14). While all believers are responsible to pass on the truths they have learned in God's Word, not all have gifts for preaching and teaching (1 Cor. 12:29). Those who aspire to pastoral duty, however, must be so gifted.

What criteria identify a man as a skilled teacher?

First, as noted above, a skilled teacher must have the gift of teaching. It is not that natural ability that makes one a good teacher; the gift of teaching is the Spirit-given enablement to teach effectively the truths of God's Word. Timothy had the gift of teaching (1 Tim. 4:14; 2 Tim. 1:6).

Second, a skilled teacher must have a deep understanding of doctrine. "A good servant of Christ Jesus," Paul wrote to Timothy in 1 Timothy 4:6, "[is] constantly nourished on the words of the faith and of . . . sound doctrine." Richard Baxter writes,

> He must not be himself a babe in knowledge, that will teach men all those mysterious things which must be known in order to salvation. O what qualifications are necessary for a man who hath such a charge upon him as we have! How many difficulties in divinity to be solved! and these, too, about the fundamental principles of religion! How many obscure texts of Scripture to be expounded! How many duties to be performed, wherein ourselves and others may miscarry, if in the matter, and manner, and end, we be not well informed! How many sins to be avoided, which, without understanding and foresight, cannot be done! What a number of sly and subtle temptations must we open to our people's eyes, that they may escape them! How many weighty and yet intricate cases of conscience have we almost daily to resolve! And can so much work, and such work as this, be done by raw, unqualified men? (*The Reformed Pastor*, 68–69)

The deeper the reservoir of doctrinal knowledge a man has, the more skilled and applicable will be his teaching.

Third, a skilled teacher must have an attitude of humility. To teach the truth with an arrogant attitude would only serve to undermine the very truths being taught. Paul reminded Timothy that "the Lord's bond-servant must not be quarrelsome, but be kind to all, able to teach, patient when wronged, with gentleness correcting those who are in opposition, if perhaps God may grant them repentance leading to the knowledge of the truth" (2 Tim. 2:24–25).

Fourth, a skilled teacher is marked by a life of holiness. Paul exhorted Timothy to "discipline yourself for the purpose of godliness" (1 Tim. 4:7), and to "pursue righteousness, godliness, faith, love, perseverance and gentleness" (1 Tim. 6:11). He must be credible and live what he teaches. Paul exhorted Timothy to "in speech, conduct, love, faith and purity, show yourself an example of those who believe" (1 Tim. 4:12). The teacher must be the prototype of what he asks his people to be.

Fifth, a skilled teacher must be a diligent student of Scripture. In the familiar passage in 2 Timothy 2:15, Paul writes, "Be diligent to present yourself approved to God as a workman who does not need to be ashamed, handling accurately the word of truth."

Sixth, a skilled teacher must avoid error. This criterion is closely related to numbers three and five listed above. It is tragic when men, seeking preparation for the ministry, attend a school that doesn't honor God's Word. While they may survive with the basics of their faith intact, they will almost invariably lose their convictions. Paul repeatedly warned Timothy to avoid false doctrine (1 Tim. 4:7; 6:20; 2 Tim. 2:16), wise counsel for us as well.

Finally, a skilled teacher must have strong courage and consistent convictions. He must not abandon the truth and shipwreck his faith (cf. 1 Tim. 1:18–19; 4:11, 13). At the close of his ministry, he should be able to say with Paul, "I have fought the good fight, I have finished the course, I have kept the faith" (2 Tim. 4:7).

Another requirement for one who desires to be an elder is that he **not** be **addicted to wine.** This quality is not concerned with whether or not he gets drunk. Obviously, someone given to drunkenness would in no way be qualified for the ministry. An elder who is **not addicted to wine** is a man who does not have a reputation as a drinker. He doesn't frequent bars or involve himself in the scenes associated with drinking.

The Bible points out the tragic consequences when leaders are drinkers. Isaiah blasted the spiritual leaders of Israel for this very sin: "And these also reel with wine and stagger from strong drink: The priest and the prophet reel with strong drink, they are confused by wine, they stagger from strong drink; they reel while having visions, they totter when rendering judgment" (Isa. 28:7). Isaiah 56:9–12 adds,

> All you beasts of the field, all you beasts in the forest, come to eat. His watchmen are blind, all of them know nothing. All of them are dumb dogs unable to bark, dreamers lying down, who love to slumber; and the dogs are greedy, they are not satisfied. And they are shepherds who have no understanding; they have all turned to their own way, each one to his unjust gain, to the last one. "Come," they say, "let us get wine, and let us drink heavily of strong drink; and tomorrow will be like today, only more so."

A man who is a drinker has no place in the ministry. He is a poor example, and will surely be the cause of serious sin and disaster in the lives of others who follow his example as drinkers, justifying their indulgence because of their leader. A leader must be a man whose associations are radically different from those of the world, and whose example leads others to righteous conduct, not sin.

In ancient times most people consumed wine, since it was the staple liquid to drink. The water was impure, and mixing the wine with water not only significantly diluted the alcohol content, but purified the water. A mixture of eight parts water to one part wine was common, so as to avoid any dissipating effect. Timothy was even reluctant to take the mixed wine, so as not to set an example that could cause someone to stumble. Thus, he was committed to abstinence, and Paul had to tell him, "no longer drink water exclusively, but use a little wine for the sake of your stomach and your frequent ailments" (5:23). Drinking only water was contributing to his poor health.

Nor may an elder be **pugnacious.** *Mē plēktēs* (**pugnacious**) literally means "not a giver of blows," or "not a striker." A leader in the church must not be one who reacts to difficulty with physical violence. He must not settle disputes with blows. He must react to situations calmly, coolly, and gently (cf. 2 Tim. 2:24–25).

Instead of being **pugnacious,** a leader must be **gentle.** *Epieikēs* (**gentle**) describes the person who is considerate, genial, forbearing, and gracious, who easily pardons human failure. Such a person remembers good, not evil. He does not keep a list of all the wrongs done to him, or hold a grudge. Many men leave the ministry because they can't accept criticism. A leader, when wronged, must have no thought of retaliation.

Uncontentious translates *amachos,* which means "peaceful," or "reluctant to fight." It refers not so much to physical violence as to a quarrelsome person. To have a contentious person in leadership will result in disunity and disharmony, seriously hindering the effectiveness of that leadership team.

Finally, a leader must be **free from the love of money.** It is a perverse corruption of the ministry to be in it for money. Love of money is what is at the heart of all motivation for false teachers (cf. 1 Thess. 2:5; 1 Peter 5:2; 2 Peter 2:1–3, 14; Jude 16, etc.). Paul reminded Timothy that

> godliness actually is a means of great gain, when accompanied by contentment. For we have brought nothing into the world, so we cannot take anything out of it either. And if we have food and covering, with these we shall be content. But those who want to get rich fall into temptation and a snare and many foolish and harmful desires which plunge men into ruin and destruction. For the love of money is a root of all sorts of evil, and some by longing for it have wandered away from the faith, and pierced themselves with many a pang. (1 Tim. 6:6–10)

Paul was **free from the love of money.** He assured the Ephesian elders that, during his three years of ministry in their city, he had "coveted no one's silver or gold or clothes" (Acts 20:33; cf. 1 Cor.

9:1–16; 2 Cor. 11:9; 12:15–16; 1 Thess. 2:5). A leader must not be greedy, stingy, or financially ambitious. "The earth-bound desires of a covetous spirit always clip the wings of faith and love" (Geoffery B. Wilson, *The Pastoral Epistles* [Edinburgh: Banner of Truth, 1982], 50).

Those aspiring to an overseer's role in the church must be measured against these moral qualities before they are ordained to serve. May God give us morally qualified men to lead the church through these dark times.

10 Qualities of a Godly Leader—part 2 Home Life, Spiritual Maturity, Public Reputation

He must be one who manages his own household well, keeping his children under control with all dignity (but if a man does not know how to manage his own household, how will he take care of the church of God?); and not a new convert, lest he become conceited and fall into the condemnation incurred by the devil. And he must have a good reputation with those outside the church, so that he may not fall into reproach and the snare of the devil. (3:4–7)

The most important qualities leaders can demonstrate are not intelligence, a forceful personality, glibness, diligence, vision, administrative skills, decisiveness, courage, humor, tact, or any other similar natural attribute. Those all play a part, but the most desirable quality for any leader is integrity.

While integrity is most desirable in secular leadership, its absence is fatal to spiritual leadership. Underlining this, John Stott writes,

> Communication is by symbol as well as speech. For "a man cannot only preach, he must also live. And the life that he lives, with all its lit-

> tle peculiarities, is one of two things: either it emasculates his preaching or it gives it flesh and blood" [J. H. Bavinck, *An Introduction to the Science of Missions* (Phillipsburg, N.J.: Presb. & Ref., 1960), 93]. We cannot hide what we are. Indeed, what we are speaks as plainly as what we say. When these two voices blend, the impact of the message is doubled. But when they contradict each other, even the positive witness of the one is negatived by the other. This was the case with the man Spurgeon describes as a good preacher but a bad Christian: he "preached so well and lived so badly, that when he was in the pulpit everybody said he ought never to come out again, and when he was out of it they all declared he never ought to enter it again." [*Lectures to My Students* (Grand Rapids: Zondervan, 1980), 1:12–13]. It is at this point that a practical problem presents itself to us. Pastors are told to be models of Christian maturity. (*Between Two Worlds* [Grand Rapids: Eerdmans, 1982], 264)

All leadership seeks to accomplish one goal: influence. Leaders seek to influence people to achieve their objectives. Influence is a direct result of teaching and example. What a man is will influence his followers to be fully committed to what he says. Teaching sets the nails into the mind, but example is the hammer that drives them in deep. Not surprisingly, the Scripture has much to say about the power of example to influence behavior, both for good and for evil. In Leviticus 18:3 God warned Israel not to follow the example of their pagan neighbors: "You shall not do what is done in the land of Egypt where you lived, nor are you to do what is done in the land of Canaan where I am bringing you; you shall not walk in their statutes." Deuteronomy 18:9 repeats that warning: "When you enter the land which the Lord your God gives you, you shall not learn to imitate the detestable things of those nations." Proverbs 22:24–25 warns, "Do not associate with a man given to anger; or go with a hot-tempered man, lest you learn his ways, and find a snare for yourself." The power of an evil ruler to influence his subordinates is seen in Proverbs 29:12: "If a ruler pays attention to falsehood, all his ministers become wicked." Hosea echoed that warning: "And it will be, like people, like priest; so I will punish them for their ways, and repay them for their deeds" (Hos. 4:9). Our Lord gave this indictment of the Scribes and Pharisees in Matthew 23:1–3:

> Then Jesus spoke to the multitudes and to His disciples, saying, "The scribes and the Pharisees have seated themselves in the chair of Moses; therefore all that they tell you, do and observe, but do not do according to their deeds; for they say things, and do not do them."

The Bible also encourages us to follow godly examples. Paul commended the Thessalonians for becoming "imitators of us and of the Lord" (1 Thess. 1:6). To the Philippians he wrote, "The things you have learned and received and heard and seen in me, practice these things" (Phil. 4:9). He encouraged both Timothy (1 Tim. 4:12) and Titus (Titus 2:7) to be good examples for their people to follow. Hebrews 13:7 exhorts us to follow the example of godly leaders, while James 5:10 points us to the example of the prophets. Peter admonishes elders to be examples to their flocks (1 Peter 5:3).

The power of example can be seen in the influence of two of Israel's kings. Repeatedly, godly kings of the southern kingdom are said to have followed the example of David (cf. 1 Kings 3:3; 15:11; 2 Kings 18:1–3; 22:1–2; 2 Chron. 29:1–2; 34:1–2), while wicked kings of the northern kingdom are said to walk in the sins of Jeroboam (cf. 1 Kings 16:1–2, 18–19, 25–26, 30–31; 2 Kings 3:1–3; 10:29, 31; 13:1–2, 6, 10–11; 14:23–24; 15:8–9, 17–18, 23–24, 27–28; 17:22).

It is not enough for a leader in the church to teach the truth, he must also model it. Richard Baxter writes,

> It is not likely that the people will much regard the doctrine of such men, when they see that they do not live as they preach. They will think that he doth not mean as he speaks, if he do not live as he speaks. They will hardly believe a man that seemeth not to believe himself. (*The Reformed Pastor* [Edinburgh: Banner of Truth, 1979], 84)

Integrity is living what you teach and preach. That is why all the qualifications for leaders given in this passage describe their moral character. It is not the typical list a corporate analyst might come up with, because the issue is not leadership skills, but spiritual example. One who would lead people to Christlikeness must be a pattern of godly behavior for his people to follow. He must be above reproach in his moral life (see chapter 9 of this volume), home life, spiritual maturity, and public reputation.

The Home Life of a Godly Leader

He must be one who manages his own household well, keeping his children under control with all dignity (but if a man does not know how to manage his own household, how will he take care of the church of God?); (3:4–5)

It is not enough for the overseer to have an exemplary personal life, he must also have an exemplary home life. He must not be, like Talkative in Pilgrim's Progress, "a saint abroad, and a devil at home" (John Bunyan, *Pilgrim's Progress* [reprint; Grand Rapids: Zondervan, 1976], 76). The family is the proving ground for leadership skills.

Throughout history, there have been those who advocated celibacy for spiritual leaders. Such a faction existed in Ephesus (cf. 4:3). In contrast, however, the Word of God assumes that a leader will be married and have a family. Although that does not eliminate single men, it is nevertheless the norm. Spiritual leaders are to be successful leaders in the family.

Manages means "presides," or "has authority over." The same word is translated "rule" in 5:17, showing the link between leading the home and leading the church. In the home, as in the church, it is God's plan for men to assume the leadership role (cf. 2:9–15).

Well is from *kalos,* a rich word that could also be translated "excellently." Its meaning can be better understood by comparing it to *agathos. Agathos* means "inherently," "morally," or "practically good." *Kalos* takes that a step further and adds the idea of aesthetically good, beautiful, and appealing to the eye. An elder must be one whose leadership in the home is not only intrinsically good, but also visibly good.

It is possible for a man to meet the moral qualifications for a pastor, yet be disqualified because of his evident lack of leadership in the home. A man who came to Christ later in life, after his wife and children had established patterns of behavior, and had a home in chaos, could serve the Lord, but not as an elder or a deacon (3:12).

Household includes an elder's family and more, because it reaches to everything connected with the home. He must be a good steward of his house and his finances—all the people and resources over which he has responsibility. Someone, for example, who managed his family well, but mismanaged his money and possessions, would be disqualified. The man who serves as a pastor must demonstrate that he can lead people to salvation and sanctification because he has done that in his own home—which is a model, a pattern for all homes to follow.

Further, a leader in the church must keep **his children under control with all dignity.** That qualification is not meant to exclude men without children, but merely assumes they will be present. *Hupotagē* (**under control**) is a military term. It speaks of lining up in rank under one in authority. An elder's children are to be respectful, well-disciplined, and believers (Titus 1:6). **Dignity** includes courtesy, humility, and competence. It could be translated "respect," or "stateliness." An elder's children must bring honor to their parents. The obvious implication is that his family is ordered, disciplined, not rebellious, as Paul adds in Titus 1:6, "not accused of dissipation or rebellion." He also demands in that same verse that the elder have "children who believe." The point is that one given the task of leading men and women to justification, sanctification, and service in the church must have shown in the home that he is capable of such leadership.

There are four keys to producing children who bring honor to their parents. First, a father must exercise the authority that makes it advisable for his children to obey. Disobedience must be met with immediate negative consequences. Proverbs 13:24 says, "He who spares his rod hates his son, but he who loves him disciplines him diligently" (cf. Prov. 22:15; 23:13–14; 29:15).

Second, a father must have enough wisdom to make it natural and reasonable for his children to obey. Authority must not be arbitrary, but tempered with reasonableness. Children may not challenge their father's authority, yet should understand why they are expected to behave in a certain way.

Third, a father must show a love that makes it delightful to obey. Children should be motivated to obey because they do not want their intimate love relationship with him to be hindered.

Fourth, a father must be able to convince his children of the urgency, priority, and privileges of salvation and obedience to the Word of God.

The reason a church leader must have a well-managed home is obvious: **If a man does not know how to manage his own household, how will he take care of the church of God?** The phrase **church of God** should be taken as a reference to a local assembly (cf. 1 Cor. 1:2; 2 Cor. 1:1). **Take care of** is from *epimelomai,* a broad term that is used in our Lord's parable of the good Samaritan (Luke 10:34–35). An elder is responsible for leading people to God, to holiness, to obedience, and to witness—crucial matters that must be tested in his own home. Resolving conflict, building unity, maintaining love, and serving each other are essentials to church life that are challenges also in the home. If he succeeds in his family, he is likely to succeed in God's family. If not, he is disqualified.

The Spiritual Maturity of a Godly Leader

and not a new convert, lest he become conceited and fall into the condemnation incurred by the devil. (3:6)

Since one of the great dangers facing the overseer is pride, humility is an essential qualification. *Neophutos* (**new convert**) appears only here in the New Testament. It is used in extrabiblical Greek to refer to a newly planted tree, hence its metaphorical use here. An elder must not be newly baptized as a Christian, **lest he become conceited.** Placing him in a leadership role would expose him to the temptation of pride. That would be especially true if he were elevated in a respected, established church like Ephesus. That this qualification is absent from the list in Titus 1 may reflect the fact that the churches on Crete were relatively new, made up of new believers. In that case, placing younger converts in leadership would not so readily lead to pride, since their fellow elders would be relatively new. An elder, then, is to be drawn from the most spiritually mature in the congregation, but that maturity must be viewed in relationship to each individual congregation. The relative measure of spiritual maturity in an established church in the United States varies from that in a first-generation church in a third-world nation.

Conceited is from *tuphoō,* which derives from a root word meaning "smoke." The verb means "to puff up like a cloud of smoke." Putting a new convert into a position of spiritual leadership is apt to puff him up, to put his head in the clouds. That would place him in grave danger of falling **into the condemnation incurred by the devil.** That does not mean an individual is condemned by Satan, since the Bible never portrays him as a judge. It is best taken as an objective genitive; he falls into the same kind of judgment pronounced by God on Satan. The context, which deals with the danger of pride, also lends support to that interpretation. The judgment or condemnation of the devil was a demotion from a high position due to his sinful pride. That is the danger awaiting the man placed in a position of spiritual leadership before he is ready. As Proverbs 16:18 warns, "Pride goes before destruction, and a haughty spirit before stumbling."

It was pride that brought Satan down. Not content with being the highest ranking angel, he sought to exalt himself above God (cf. Ezek. 28:11–19; Isa. 14:12–14). The five "I wills" of Isaiah 14:12–14 clearly show his pride. As a result, Satan, who had "the seal of perfection" and was "full of wisdom and perfect in beauty" (Ezek. 28:12), who had been on the "holy mountain of God" and served as "the anointed cherub who covers" (Ezek. 28:14), was "cast . . . as profane from the mountain of God" (Ezek. 28:16; cf. Rev. 12:9).

What happened to Satan could easily happen to an immature Christian elevated to eldership. It is that danger which Paul warns Timothy against. The antidote to pride is humility, which is the mark of a spiritually mature leader (Matt. 23:11–12). The church must not lift up those whom the Lord will later have to cut down.

THE PUBLIC REPUTATION OF A GODLY LEADER

And he must have a good reputation with those outside the church, so that he may not fall into reproach and the snare of the devil. (3:7)

The godly character of an elder must not be manifested only in his personal life, the church, and his home. He must also **have a good reputation with those outside the church. Reputation** translates *marturia,* from which our English word "martyr" derives. The word speaks of a certifying testimony. An elder's character is to be certified by the testimony of those outside the church. A man chosen to lead the church must maintain a reputation in the community for righteousness, moral character, love, kindness, generosity, and goodness. All will certainly not agree with his theology, and he will no doubt face antagonism when he takes a stand for God's truth. Nevertheless, those outside the church must recognize him as a man of impeccable reputation. How can a man have a spiritual impact on his community if that community does not respect him? Such an individual can do nothing but bring **reproach** or disgrace on the cause of Christ.

In Romans 2:23–24, Paul delivered a scathing indictment of Israel: "You who boast in the Law, through your breaking the Law, do you dishonor God? For 'the name of God is blasphemed among the Gentiles because of you,' just as it is written." Israel, meant to be a light to the nations, instead caused them to blaspheme.

The Bible expects every believer's life to be a positive testimony to the watching world, and that is especially true of those in pastoral positions. Paul exhorted the Philippians to "prove yourselves to be blameless and innocent, children of God above reproach in the midst of a crooked and perverse generation, among whom you appear as lights in the world" (Phil. 2:15). Colossians 4:5 urges believers to "conduct yourselves with wisdom toward outsiders." Peter wrote, "Keep your behavior excellent among the Gentiles, so that in the thing in which they slander you as evildoers, they may on account of your good deeds, as they observe them, glorify God in the day of visitation" (1 Peter 2:12).

By having a good reputation in the community, an elder will avoid **the snare of the devil.** The genitive here is subjective, and refers to the snare set by Satan. God does not set traps for his people (cf. James 1:13), but Satan would like nothing better than to set a trap to discredit a leader in the church. D. Edmond Hiebert writes,

> For one who has an unsavory reputation in the community, to be placed by the church into a prominent place of authority would be to

> draw upon himself and the church the reproach of the world. The suspicion and censure thus arrayed against him and the church might easily weaken and discourage the elder. Thus weakened and disheartened he might readily fall an easy prey into some skillfully laid snare of the Devil, who is here vividly pictured as a hunter of souls. Such a fall would cause great harm to his own soul and bring terrible damage to the church. The enemy's aim has always been to destroy the leaders of the church. Hence great care must be exercised in the selection of its leaders. (*First Timothy* [Chicago: Moody, 1957], 68)

Leaders face many temptations from the very nature of their position, without unnecessarily adding others. First, they face the temptation to discouragement. Failing to live up to the high standards they set for themselves can bring discouragement. People who fail to grow or respond, who fall away, or fail to live up to the leader's expectations can also be a source of discouragement.

Second, leaders are tempted to indifference. That temptation is an outgrowth of the first one. Some leaders respond to discouragement by distancing themselves from people who could wound them with disappointments.

Third, leaders face the temptation of what might be termed "busy laziness." They take the path of least resistance and do what they want to do, not what they need to do. Though they appear to be busy, they are in reality lazy, since they do not discipline themselves to do what needs to be done.

Fourth, leaders are tempted to compromise. They avoid saying what ought to be said for the sake of pleasing men.

Finally, leaders face all the temptations common to other Christians. They, more than anyone, need to keep the armor of God on at all times (cf. Eph. 6:11).

To elevate someone prematurely to a leadership role is to expose him to temptation over and above that normally faced by leaders. A man in such a position is all too likely to fall into Satan's snare.

Ephesus needed to choose carefully its leaders, and so do we. We need to pray that God will raise up the men of His choosing. The future of the church depends on it.

An anonymous poet captured the process God uses to build His leaders in the following words:

> When God wants to drill a man
> And thrill a man
> And skill a man,

When God wants to mold a man
To play the noblest part;
When He yearns with all His heart
To create so great and bold a man
That all the world shall be amazed,
Watch His methods, watch His ways!
How He ruthlessly perfects
Whom He royally elects!
How He hammers him and hurts him,
And with mighty blows converts him
Into trial shapes of clay which
Only God understands;
While his tortured heart is crying
And he lifts beseeching hands!
How He bends but never breaks
When his good He undertakes;
How He uses whom He chooses
And with every purpose fuses him;
By every act induces him
To try His splendour out—
God knows what He's about!

Called to Serve the Church

11

Deacons likewise must be men of dignity, not double-tongued, or addicted to much wine or fond of sordid gain, but holding to the mystery of the faith with a clear conscience. And let these also first be tested; then let them serve as deacons if they are beyond reproach. Women must likewise be dignified, not malicious gossips, but temperate, faithful in all things. Let deacons be husbands of only one wife, and good managers of their children and their own households. For those who have served well as deacons obtain for themselves a high standing and great confidence in the faith that is in Christ Jesus. (3:8–13)

When God raises up people to serve His church, He looks for those whose hearts are right with him. His concern is not about talents or abilities, but spiritual virtue.

The men God has chosen to serve His people have always had hearts devoted to Him. Nehemiah 9:8 says of Abraham, "Thou didst find his heart faithful before Thee." When Samuel searched for a successor to Saul, the Lord reminded him that "the Lord looks at the heart" (1 Sam. 16:7). Saul, chosen largely because he was "a choice and handsome man, and there was not a more handsome person than he among the sons of Israel" (1 Sam. 9:2), had turned out to be a disaster. To replace him, God "raised up David to be their king, concerning whom He also testified and said, 'I have found David the son of Jesse, a man after My heart, who will do all My will'" (Acts 13:22; cf. 1 Sam. 13:14). When he turned over the kingdom to his son Solomon, David advised him to "know the God of your father, and serve Him with a whole heart and a willing mind" (1 Chron. 28:9). Godly King Jehoshaphat of Judah was blessed by God because he "set [his] heart to seek God" (2 Chron. 19:3). God used King Josiah to lead a spiritual revival because his heart was tender and he humbled himself before the Lord (2 Kings 22:19). Ezra was used by God because he "set his heart to study the law of the Lord, and to practice it, and to teach His statutes and ordinances in Israel" (Ezra 7:10). The apostle Paul described his conduct among the Thessalonians as devout, upright, and blameless (1 Thess. 2:10). It is such men, men of integrity, purity, and virtue, that God chooses to lead His people.

Having discussed such spiritual qualifications for elders in 3:1–7, Paul now turns to those of deacons in 3:8–13. The standard for deacons is in no way inferior to that required of elders. Elders who lead and deacons who serve perform different functions, but the spiritual qualifications required for both are essentially identical. There is no drop-off in spiritual quality or maturity from overseers to deacons. The only difference is that overseers are "able to teach" (3:2).

Diakonos (**deacon**) and the related terms *diakoneō* ("to serve"), and *diakonia* ("service") appear approximately 100 times in the New Testament. Only here and in Philippians 1:1 are they transliterated "deacon" or "deacons." The rest of the time they are translated by various English words. Only in those two passages is the deacon elevated to official status. The rest of the time the terms are used in a general, nonspecific sense.

The original meaning of this word group had to do with performing menial tasks such as waiting on tables. That definition gradually broadened until it came to include any kind of service in the church. The word group's versatility can be seen in its divergent usage in the New Testament. *Diakonos, diakoneō,* and *diakonia* are variously translated "administration," "cared for," "minister," "servant," "serve," "service," "preparations," "relief," "support," and "deacon," among others. The root idea of serving food comes across in John 2:5, where *diakonos* is used of the waiters at a wedding. *Diakoneō* is used in the same sense in Luke 4:39, where Peter's mother-in-law served a meal. Luke 10:40; 17:8; and John 12:2 also use this word group to refer to serving food.

Diakonos is used to refer to soldiers and policemen who enforce justice (Rom. 13:4). In John 12:26, Jesus equated following Him with serving Him. Anything done in obedience to Him is spiritual service. In the general sense of the term, all Christians are deacons, for all are to be actively serving Christ and His church.

That is Paul's point in 1 Corinthians 12:5, where he writes that "there are varieties of ministries" (*diakoniōn*). Every Christian is to be involved in some form of spiritual service. Leaders, through both teaching and modeling, are to equip believers to perform that service (Eph. 4:12).

But *diakonos, diakonia,* and *diakoneō* are also used in a second, more specific sense. The list of spiritual gifts in Romans 12:6–8 includes a gift for service. Those with that gift are specially equipped for service, though they may not hold the office of deacon. Stephanas and his family were so gifted. Paul wrote of them, "they have devoted themselves for ministry (*diakonia*) to the saints" (1 Cor. 16:15).

The third use of this word group refers to the officially recognized responsibility of deacons. Everyone is a deacon in the general sense, some are specially gifted by the Holy Spirit for service, but still others hold the office of deacon. They model spiritual service for everyone else. They work alongside the elders, implementing their preaching, teaching, and oversight in the practical life of the church.

The only discussion of the office of deacon is in 1 Timothy 3:8–13, though there is a possible reference to it in Philippians 1:1. Some hold that Paul was officially identified as a deacon. While Paul was a servant in the general sense of the word, he held the office of apostle (Rom. 11:13; cf. 2 Cor. 10–12). Others have argued, based on 1 Timothy 4:6, that Timothy was a deacon. In 2 Timothy 4:5, however, Paul seems to identify Timothy as an evangelist. Others have proposed Tychicus (cf. Eph. 6:21), but Paul's use of *diakonos* (Eph. 3:7) and *diakonia* (Eph. 4:12) in a general, nonrestrictive sense makes doubtful the use of *diakonos* in Ephesians 6:21 as a strict reference to the office. There is likewise no reason to assume that the use of *diakonos* in reference to Epaphras (Col. 1:7) is limited to the specific office.

Many hold that the seven men chosen to oversee the distribution of food in Acts 6 were the first official deacons. The text, however, nowhere calls them deacons. In fact, the only use of *diakonia* in Acts 6 is in reference to the apostles (v. 4), and to the serving of food (v. 1). That again emphasizes its general usage. Nor are any of the seven ever called deacons elsewhere in Scripture. The book of Acts nowhere uses the term *diakonos* (**deacon**), which seems strange if an order of deacons was initiated in Acts 6. Elders are mentioned several times in Acts (cf. 11:30; 14:23; 15:2, 4, 6, 22–23; 16:4; 20:17), making the omission of any reference to deacons even more significant. All seven men were apparently Hellenistic Jews, since all have Greek names. It is unlikely that an order of deacons at the Jerusalem church would not include any Palestinian Jews. Finally, they were in many respects more like elders than deacons. Stephen and Philip, the only two mentioned elsewhere in Acts, were evangelists (cf. Acts 6:8; 8:5ff.; 21:8). These seven men were chosen for a specific task. They did not hold the office of deacon, though their function of serving certainly foreshadowed that of the later deacons.

Paul wrote 1 Timothy some thirty years after the birth of the church on the day of Pentecost. The church had grown and developed to the point that there was a need for official deacons. They would function as models of spiritual virtue and service. To ensure that those given that responsibility were worthy, Paul lists several qualifications they must be measured by. As with elders, those qualifications relate to their spiritual character, not their function. In fact, no specifics are given in Scripture as to the duties of deacons. They were to carry out whatever tasks were assigned to them by the elders or needed by the congregation. In 3:8–13, Paul lists those qualifications for both male deacons and female deacons (deaconesses). He then closes by mentioning the reward for those who serve faithfully.

Qualifications for Deacons

Deacons likewise must be men of dignity, not double-tongued, or addicted to much wine or fond of sordid gain, but holding to the mystery of the faith with a clear conscience. And let these also first be tested; then let them serve as deacons if they are beyond reproach. . . . Let deacons be husbands of only one wife, and good managers of their children and their own households. (3:8–10, 12)

Likewise is a key transition word that serves to introduce a new category within the overall topic of church leaders. Having discussed elders in 3:1–7, Paul now gives five areas in which a deacon must be qualified.

PERSONAL CHARACTER

Deacons likewise must be men of dignity, not double-tongued, or addicted to much wine or fond of sordid gain, (3:8)

Men of dignity translates *semnos,* which could also be translated "serious," or "stately." Semnos contains the idea of being serious in mind as well as in character. It comes from a root word (*sebomai*) that means "to venerate," or "to worship." Those characterized by it have a majestic quality of character that makes people stand in awe of them. A synonym of *semnos, hieroprepēs,* "expresses that which beseems a sacred person, thing, or act" (Richard C. Trench, *Synonyms of the New Testament* [Grand Rapids: Eerdmans, 1983], 348). A deacon must not be a silly, flippant person, one who makes light of serious matters. Although not a cold, joyless person, a deacon understands the seriousness of life.

After that positive trait come three negative ones. A deacon must **not** be **double-tongued.** *Dilogos* (**double-tongued**) appears only here in the New Testament. Some think it refers to a gossip, a person who has, so to speak, not one but two tongues going. It seems best, however, to interpret it as a prohibition against saying one thing to one person and another thing to someone else. A deacon's speech must not be hypocritical, but be characterized by integrity, consistency, and honesty. A man who tells different stories to different people will quickly lose their confidence, and manifest a duplicitous and manipulative motive.

A second prohibition forbids deacons from being **addicted to much wine.** *Prosechō* (**addicted to**) means "to turn one's mind to," or "to occupy oneself with," hence the NASB translation **addicted to.** The present active participle indicates this is to be the deacon's habitual practice. He is not to be preoccupied with drink, nor to allow it to influence his life. Some may wonder why the Lord did not call for total abstinence. As Homer Kent points out, however,

> It is extremely difficult for the twentieth-century American to understand and appreciate the society of Paul's day. The fact that deacons were not told to become total abstainers, but rather to be temperate, does not mean that Christians today can use liquor in moderate amounts. The wine employed for the common beverage was very largely water. The social stigma and the tremendous social evils that accompany drinking today did not attach themselves to the use of wine as the common beverage in the homes of Paul's day. Nevertheless, as the church grew and the Christian consciousness and conscience developed, the dangers of drinking came to be more clearly seen. The principle laid down elsewhere by Paul that Christians should not do anything to cause a brother to stumble came to be applied to the use of wine. Raymond states it this way:
>
> > If an individual by drinking wine either causes others to err through his example or abets a social evil which causes others to succumb to its temptations, then in the interests of Christian love he ought to forego the temporary pleasures of drinking in the interests of heavenly treasures. (Irwin Woodworth Raymond, *The Teaching of the Early Church on the Use of Wine and Strong Drink* [New York: Columbia Univ., 1927], 88)

> Certainly in present-day America, the use of wine by a Christian would abet a recognized social evil, and would set a most dangerous example for the young and the weak. To us, Paul would undoubtedly say, "No wine at all." (Homer A. Kent, Jr., *The Pastoral Epistles* [Winona Lake, Ind.: BMH Books, 1982], 133)

A deacon must also not be **fond of sordid gain.** He must not use his office as a means to make money. That was an important quality in the early church, since deacons would routinely handle money as part of their official duties. They would distribute money to widows, orphans, and others in need. The temptation would always be there to steal from those funds, as did Judas (John 12:4–6). It was essential, then, that deacons be free from any love of money that could compromise their honesty.

SPIRITUAL LIFE

but holding to the mystery of the faith with a clear conscience. (3:9)

Paul uses the word **mystery** frequently in his writings. It refers to revealed truth previously hidden, but now manifested (cf. Rom. 16:25; 1 Cor. 15:51; Eph. 3:3–6; 6:19; Col. 1:26). **The mystery of the faith** is the New Testament revelation. Such truth was not revealed in the Old Testament. It encompasses the mystery of the Incarnation of Christ (1 Tim. 3:16), of the indwelling of Christ in believers (Col. 1:26–27), of the unity of Jews and Gentiles in Christ (Eph. 1:9; 3:4–6), of the saving gospel (Col. 4:3), of lawlessness (2 Thess. 2:7), and of the rapture of the church (1 Cor. 15:51–52).

The faith is the content of New Testament revealed truth. A deacon must hold to it **with a clear conscience,** that is, a conscience that does not accuse him. It is not enough merely to believe the truth (cf. James 2:19), deacons must also live it. And the stronger the theological and biblical knowledge and obedience, the stronger the affirmation of conscience. Every deacon (and every Christian) should strive to be able to say with Paul, "For our proud confidence is this, the testimony of our conscience, that in holiness and godly sincerity, not in fleshly wisdom but in the grace of God, we have conducted ourselves in the world, and especially toward you" (2 Cor. 1:12).

The conscience is a human faculty given by God to every person, which is designed to warn each person when they have violated moral law (cf. Rom. 2:14–15). It either accuses or excuses. It either produces guilt, shame, fear, remorse, and despair over sin, or assurance, peace, and joy due to righteousness. The deacon who has a clear conscience is enjoying the latter three.

CHRISTIAN SERVICE

And let these also first be tested; then let them serve as deacons (3:10a)

Dokimazō (**let [them] be tested**) means "to approve after testing." The present tense of the verb indicates an ongoing test, not a one-time test, or probationary period. Deacons are to be continually tested before they officially **serve as deacons.** The test in view here is the general assessment of a believer's service by the church. Once they become officially recognized as deacons, this evaluation goes on. **Also** refers to the discussion of elders in 3:1–7. They, too, are to be continually evaluated by the church.

MORAL PURITY

if they are beyond reproach. Let deacons be husbands of only one wife, (3:10b, 12a)

Deacons, no less than elders, must be **beyond reproach.** *Anegklētos* (**beyond reproach**) means "not arraigned" (as in a court), or "unblamable." They differ in function from elders in that elders are the primary teachers of the church, while deacons help in applying their teaching. Nevertheless, the spiritual requirements for both are the same. Deacons must not have any blot on their lives, nothing for which they could be accused, arraigned, and disqualified.

Paul reiterates another key element from the qualifications given for elders. Deacons, too, must **be husbands of only one wife.** The Greek text literally reads "one-woman men" (cf. 3:2). They must not be unfaithful to their wives either in their actual conduct with other women, or in their minds. As with elders, the issue is moral character, not marital status. They are models of sexual purity.

HOME LIFE

and good managers of their children and their own households. (3:12b)

Deacons, like elders, must prove their spiritual character in the home. They are to be **good managers** not only **of their children,** but also of their money, possessions, and everything associated with **their own households.** As with elders' children, the children of deacons must be believers.

QUALIFICATIONS FOR DEACONESSES

Women must likewise be dignified, not malicious gossips, but temperate, faithful in all things. (3:11)

Whether the **women** in view here are deacons' wives or a separate order of female deacons has been much disputed. The following points show that women in general, not necessarily deacons' wives are in view here. First, the use of **likewise** (cf. 1 Tim. 2:9; 3:8; Titus 2:3, 6) argues strongly for seeing a third and distinct group here in addition to elders and deacons. Second, there is no possessive pronoun or definite article connecting these **women** with deacons. Third, Paul gave no qualifications for elders' wives. Why would he do so for deacons' wives? Fourth, Paul did not use the word "deaconesses" because there was no such word in the Greek language; the masculine form of *diakonos* was used of both men and women (cf. Rom. 16:1). A different term, *diakonissa,* was used for "deaconess" in postbiblical Greek (Marvin R. Vincent, *Word Studies in the New Testament* [Grand Rapids: Eerdmans, 1946], 3:176). Using the term **women** was the only way Paul could distinguish them from the male deacons. Finally, their qualifications parallel those of the male deacons.

Women who serve the church must first be **dignified.** Paul uses the same word here that he used in verse 8 to describe male deacons. Female deacons, like their male counterparts, must lead serious lives. People should hold them in awe because of their spiritual devotion. They are **not** to be **malicious gossips.** *Diabolos* (**malicious gossips**) means "slanderer." It is often used to describe Satan, and is translated "devil" (cf. Matt. 4:1). Deaconesses must control their tongues. Like elders (v. 2) and male deacons (v. 8), the women are to be **temperate.** They are not to be drinkers, but sober in judgment. Finally, they must be **faithful in all things.** They must be absolutely trustworthy. That qualification may include the idea of not being "fond of sordid gain" (cf. v. 8). Like male deacons, females would have occasion to handle money while performing their duties. Women who were not **faithful** in every dimension of responsibility could not be trusted with this privileged service.

The Rewards of Faithful Service

For those who have served well as deacons obtain for themselves a high standing and great confidence in the faith that is in Christ Jesus. (3:13)

Two rewards await those men and women **who have served well as deacons.** First, they **obtain for themselves a high standing.** *Bathmos* (**standing**) literally refers to an elevated stand. Here it is used metaphorically to speak of those who are a step above everyone else. In our vernacular, we might say they are put on a pedestal. That is not sinful pride, because deacons do not seek it, yet are worthy of it. Those who serve in humility will be exalted by God (James 4:10; 1 Peter 5:6), and by the church (1 Thess. 5:12–13). Faithful deacons will be respected and honored by those they serve. It is only by commanding such respect that deacons can be examples, since respected people are the ones emulated.

Second, they will gain **great confidence in the faith that is in Christ Jesus.** *Parrēsia* (**great confidence**) is often used of boldness of speech (cf. Acts 4:13). **The faith that is in Christ Jesus** refers to the sphere of Christian truth, the family of believers. Successful service breeds confidence and assurance among the people served. Those who serve God well and see His power and grace operative in their lives will be emboldened for even greater service.

Conduct in the Church

12

I am writing these things to you, hoping to come to you before long; but in case I am delayed, I write so that you may know how one ought to conduct himself in the household of God, which is the church of the living God, the pillar and support of the truth. And by common confession great is the mystery of godliness:

> **He who was revealed in the flesh,**
> **Was vindicated in the Spirit,**
> **Beheld by angels,**
> **Proclaimed among the nations,**
> **Believed on in the world,**
> **Taken up in glory.** (3:14–16)

Vince Lombardi, the Hall of Fame coach of the Green Bay Packers football team, was notorious for his emphasis on fundamentals. His teams won championships because they could block, tackle, and execute better than anyone else. It is said that once, frustrated by his team's poor performance, he held up a football and said, "Gentlemen, this is a football!"

Like Coach Lombardi, the apostle Paul knew well the importance of going back to the fundamentals. He penned this letter to Timothy because the church at Ephesus was starting to drift away from the basic truths of the Christian faith. Like the Ephesians, we need regularly to be reminded of the foundational truths of our faith. The church today sponsors a bewildering variety of highly specialized ministries, everything from race track evangelism to bowling leagues for blind bowlers. People can get lost in the superficial. Further, the Bible contains such an inexhaustible treasure of knowledge that some seem to become lost in its depths. It is all too easy for churches and believers to get so involved with peripheral matters or theological minutiae that they lose sight of the primary matters. Paul writes this passage as a reminder that the church must give its attention to the essential truths.

These verses also mark a turning point in 1 Timothy. They come at the end of the first three chapters, which contain positive instruction, and before the last three chapters, which contain negative warnings. Verse 15 gives the heart of the church's mission, verse 16 the heart of its message. Before taking us to those crucial realities, however, Paul gives some background information in verses 14 and 15.

The Theme of 1 Timothy

I am writing these things to you, hoping to come to you before long; but in case I am delayed, I write so that you may know how one ought to conduct himself (3:15a)

When Paul says **I am writing** and **I write** he is introducing the purpose of the epistle, the general reason for his concern. He is writing to instruct about how believers are to behave in the church. The antecedent of **these things** has been variously interpreted. Some suggest the material in chapter 3 about church leaders. Others would include Paul's remarks about men and women in chapter 2, or his teaching about false doctrine in chapter 1. But since nothing in the context places limits on the phrase, and because it seems clear that he is stating his theme in a very general way, it is best to interpret it as broadly as possible, to include the entire epistle. Conduct in the church is the theme.

The comparative adverb *tachion* (**before long**) could be better translated "more quickly," or "sooner." Paul would then be saying he was **hoping to come to** Timothy more quickly than he had first thought or planned. The last half of verse 14 could, however, be interpreted as a concessive clause. In that case, Paul was saying, "I am writing these things, although I hoped to come to you sooner." The third class conditional clause **but in case I am delayed** lends support to that latter interpretation. Since it now appeared Paul would be unable to come as soon as he had originally wished, and maybe not at all, he wrote this letter to strengthen Timothy in leading the church. Whether Paul ever returned to Ephesus is not known. In his epistle to Titus, probably written about the same time as 1 Timothy, he expressed his intent to spend the winter at Nicapolis. Nicapolis was west of Macedonia, Ephesus east.

You is singular, indicating that this passage, like 1:18–20, is a personal word to Timothy. He must **know** if he is to teach the church. **Know** is from *oida,* a word used to describe "the possession of knowledge or skill necessary to accomplish a desired goal" (Fritz Rienecker and Cleon L. Rodgers, Jr., *A Linguistic Key to the Greek New Testament* [Grand Rapids: Zondervan, 1982], 624). It is not mere intellectual knowledge Paul has in mind, but the practical knowledge of **how one ought to conduct himself.** Paul here broadens his instruction to include not only Timothy, but also everyone else. The present infinitive form of *anastrephō* (**to conduct himself**) speaks of a consistent pattern of life. Behaving in the church as God desires certainly calls for understanding several essential realities.

The Master of the Church

in the household of God, which is the church of the living God, (3:15b)

It is basic to understand that the church belongs to God. In no sense is it a human institution. It is God's church, His family.

Although *oikos* (**household**) could be translated "house," and refer to a building, the NASB rendering **household** is preferable. *Oikos* is so used in 3:4, 5, 12; 2 Timothy 1:16; and Titus 1:11. Paul's metaphor here is not that of a building, but of a family. Believers are members of God's household, and the responsibility to conduct themselves accordingly is heaven's mandate to them. In Ephesians 2:19, Paul emphasizes the same truth: "So then you are no longer strangers and aliens, but you are fellow citizens with the saints, and are of God's household." The idea of the church as the household of God also appears in Galatians 6:10; Hebrews 3:6; and 1 Peter 4:17.

Paul further defines the assembly of believers as **the church of the living God,** or "the living God's church." The absence of the definite article with **church** stresses its character. The church by its very nature belongs to the living God. In fact, Paul told the Ephesian elders at the gathering at Miletus that the church of God was truly His because He had "purchased [it] with His own blood" (Acts 20:28). In his letter to Ephesus, he had called the church "God's own possession, to the praise of His glory" (Eph. 1:14; cf. Titus 2:14; 1 Peter 2:9; Rev. 5:9). The identification of the Creator as **the living God** has a rich Old Testament heritage. Joshua told the Israelites, "By this you shall know that the living God is among you, and that He will assuredly dispossess from before you the Canaanite, the Hittite, the Hivite, the Perizzite, the Girgashite, the Amorite, and the Jebusite" (Josh. 3:10). David was incensed that Goliath should "taunt the armies of the living God" (1 Sam. 17:26). The psalmist wrote, "My soul thirsts for God, for the living God; when shall I come and appear before God?" (Ps. 42:2), and, "My soul longed and even yearned for the courts of the Lord; my heart and my flesh sing for joy to the living God" (Ps. 84:2). Jeremiah wrote, "The Lord is the true God; He is the living God and the everlasting King" (Jer. 10:10). The description of the Ephesian assembly as the living God's church was especially apropos. It was the island of light in a dark sea of pagan worship. Crucial to behaving properly is the knowledge that the assembly of saints is the living God's church in the world of dead idols, and that it is mandated and empowered for a divine mission and a divine message.

The Mission of the Church

the pillar and support of the truth. (3:15c)

The imagery of these terms for the church would not have been lost on the Ephesians. The impressive temple of the goddess Diana (Artemis), one of the seven wonders of the ancient world, was located in the city. William Barclay gives the following description of it: "One of its features was its pillars. It contained one hundred and twenty-seven pillars, every one of them the gift of a king. All were made of marble, and some were studded with jewels and overlaid with gold" (*The Letters to Timothy, Titus, and Philemon* [Philadelphia: Westminster, 1975], 89). Each **pillar** acted as a tribute to the king who donated it. The honorary significance of the pillars, however, was secondary to their function of holding up the immense structure of the roof.

Hedraiōma (**support**) appears only here in the New Testament and refers to the foundation on which a structure rests. Thus in Paul's metaphor the church is the foundation and pillar that holds up the truth. As the foundation and pillars of the Temple of Diana were a testimony to the error of pagan false religion, so the church is to be a testimony to God's truth. That is its mission in the world—its reason for existing here. For failing to do that, Israel has been temporarily set aside.

The truth is the divine revelation, including the truth of the gospel, the content of the Christian faith. It is the solemn responsibility of every church to solidly, immovably, unshakably uphold the truth of God's Word. The church does not invent the truth, and alters it only at the cost of judgment. It is to support and safeguard it. It is the sacred, saving treasure given to sinners for their forgiveness, and to believers for their sanctification and edification, that they might live for the glory of God. The church has the stewardship of Scripture, the duty to guard it as the most precious possession on earth. Churches that tamper with, misrepresent, depreciate, relegate to secondary place, or abandon biblical truth destroy their only reason for existing and experience impotence and judgment.

Although it is the collective responsibility of the gathered believers to support the Word, that cannot occur unless each individual believer is committed to that duty. How do believers uphold the truth? First, by believing it. Paul gave testimony to Felix saying, "I do serve the God of our fathers, believing everything that is in accordance with the Law, and that is written in the Prophets" (Acts 24:14). His belief in God's Word extended to the New Covenant revelation, as Paul made clear when he spoke to the Corinthians: "We also believe, therefore also we speak" (2 Cor. 4:13). The many exhortations to hear the word also refer to hearing with faith. Jesus said in Matthew 13:9, "He who has ears, let him hear" (cf. Rev. 2:7, 11, 17, 29; 3:6, 13, 22). Christians cannot uphold the Word if they do not hear it and believe.

Second, by memorizing it. The psalmist wrote, "Thy word I have treasured in my heart, that I may not sin against Thee" (Ps. 119:11). It is not enough to hear the Word, it must be hidden away in the memory. Only then can believers "always [be] ready to make a defense to everyone who asks [them] to give an account for the hope that is in [them]" (1 Peter 3:15).

Third, by meditating on it. Joshua 1:8 says, "This book of the law shall not depart from your mouth, but you shall meditate on it day and night, so that you may be careful to do according to all that is written in it; for then you will make your way prosperous, and then you will have success." In addition to hearing and memorizing the Word, believers must meditate on it.

Fourth, by studying it. In his second letter to Timothy, Paul urged him to "be diligent to present yourself approved to God as a workman who does not need to be ashamed, handling accurately the word of truth" (2 Tim. 2:15).

Fifth, by obeying it. Jesus said in Luke 11:28, "Blessed are those who hear the word of God, and observe it." It does little good to hear the Word, memorize it, meditate on it, and study it if we do not obey it.

Sixth, by defending it. Paul told the Philippians that he was "appointed for the defense of the gospel" (Phil. 1:16). The truth will always be attacked, and the church must be ready to defend it.

Seventh, by living it. Paul reminded Titus that believers are to "adorn the doctrine of God our Savior in every respect" (Titus 2:10).

Having a mind controlled by the Word of God produces godly behavior (Col. 3:16ff.).

Finally, by proclaiming it. In obedience to our Lord's command, believers are to "go therefore and make disciples of all the nations, baptizing them in the name of the Father and the Son and the Holy Spirit, teaching them to observe all that I commanded you; and lo, I am with you always, even to the end of the age" (Matt. 28:19–20).

The supreme mission of the church is to uphold the precious legacy of God's Word. What a privilege to support the truth given us by our Savior (cf. John 17:14).

The Message of the Church

And by common confession great is the mystery of godliness:

> **He who was revealed in the flesh,**
> **Was vindicated in the Spirit,**
> **Beheld by angels,**
> **Proclaimed among the nations,**
> **Believed on in the world,**
> **Taken up in glory.** (3:16)

The Word of God is a vast, inexhaustible storehouse of spiritual truth. Out of all that truth, what is most essential for the church to uphold and proclaim? Paul gives the answer in verse 16: The message of Jesus Christ. That is the core of what we teach and preach. In Luke 24:46–47, Jesus said to the disciples, "Thus it is written, that the Christ should suffer and rise again from the dead the third day; and that repentance for forgiveness of sins should be proclaimed in His name to all the nations, beginning from Jerusalem." That became the theme of apostolic preaching. In Acts 10:37–43 Peter said,

> You yourselves know the thing which took place throughout all Judea, starting from Galilee, after the baptism which John proclaimed. You know of Jesus of Nazareth, how God anointed Him with the Holy Spirit and with power, and how He went about doing good, and healing all who were oppressed by the devil; for God was with Him. And we are witnesses of all the things He did both in the land of the Jews and in Jerusalem. And they also put Him to death by hanging Him on a cross. God raised Him up on the third day, and granted that He should become visible, not to all the people, but to witnesses who were chosen beforehand by God, that is, to us, who ate and drank with Him after He arose from the dead. And He ordered us to preach to the people, and solemnly to testify that this is the One who has been appointed by God

as Judge of the living and the dead. Of Him all the prophets bear witness that through His name everyone who believes in Him receives forgiveness of sins.

Paul, too, made Jesus Christ the central theme in his preaching. To the Corinthians he wrote, "we preach Christ crucified" (1 Cor. 1:23), and, "For I determined to know nothing among you except Jesus Christ, and Him crucified" (1 Cor. 2:2). In his second epistle to them he added, "For the Son of God, Christ Jesus, who was preached among you by us—by me and Silvanus and Timothy—was not yes and no, but is yes in Him" (2 Cor. 1:19), and "We do not preach ourselves but Christ Jesus as Lord, and ourselves as your bond-servants for Jesus' sake" (2 Cor. 4:5). In Galatians 6:14 he said, "May it never be that I should boast, except in the cross of our Lord Jesus Christ, through which the world has been crucified to me, and I to the world." Even when Christ was preached from wrong motives, he rejoiced (Phil. 1:18).

Because Paul emphasizes the person and work of Christ in 1 Timothy (cf. 1:1; 2:5–6; 6:15–16), that truth may well have been under attack in Ephesus. In this magnificent six-line hymn, Paul rehearses in familiar terms the central truths about Jesus Christ.

Common confession comes from *homologeō,* which means "to say the same thing." This is a truth upon which everyone agrees; it is the unanimous conviction of all believers that **great is the mystery of godliness.** That phrase may be a parallel to the common confession of the pagan worshipers in Ephesus, "Great is Artemis [Diana] of the Ephesians!" (Acts 19:28).

As already noted, a **mystery** was a hidden, sacred truth that is revealed in the New Testament. The **mystery of godliness** parallels the "mystery of the faith" (v. 9). It refers to the great truth of salvation and righteousness through Christ, which produces **godliness** (*eusebeia*) in those who believe. It is also possible to understand **the mystery of godliness** as a reference to Jesus, who was the very revelation of true and perfect "godlikeness," since He was God. **Godliness,** then, first refers to the incarnation and secondly to those who are saved and become the godly in Christ.

As already noted, the lines that follow are undoubtedly from an early church hymn. That is evident from its uniformity (the six verbs are all third person singular aorists), rhythm, and parallelism. The first parallel is between the flesh and the Spirit, the second between angels and nations (men), and the third between the world and glory, or earth and heaven.

The Authorized Version opens the hymn with "God." The earliest and best manuscripts, however, read *hos* (**He who**), not *theos*

("God"). (For a discussion of the textual issue see Bruce M. Metzger, *A Textual Commentary on the Greek New Testament* [New York: United Bible Societies, 1975], 641.) Although no antecedent for *hos* is given, the hymn can only be describing Jesus Christ, who is the purest **mystery of godliness**—the hidden God revealed perfectly. This marvelous hymn gives us six truths about our Lord.

First, Jesus Christ was **revealed in the flesh.** God became man in the person of Jesus of Nazareth. *Phaneroō* (**revealed**) does not mean "to bring into existence," or "to create," but "to make visible." It thus affirms Christ's preexistence (cf. John 8:58; 17:5). At the Incarnation, Jesus "although He existed in the form of God . . . emptied Himself, taking the form of a bond-servant, and [was] made in the likeness of men" (Phil. 2:6–7). Our Lord Jesus Christ made the invisible God visible to human eyes (cf. 1:17; 6:16; John 14:9; Col. 1:15; Heb. 1:3).

Flesh does not refer here to sinful, fallen human nature, as it does in Romans 7. Rather it refers merely to humanness (cf. John 1:14; Rom. 1:3; Gal. 4:4). Jesus was "made in the likeness of men . . . and . . . found in appearance as a man" (Phil. 2:7–8). "Since then the children share in flesh and blood, He Himself likewise also partook of the same" (Heb. 2:14), and therefore "is not ashamed to call them brethren" (Heb. 2:11). That does not mean He was sinful, but that He was fully human. "We do not have a high priest who cannot sympathize with our weaknesses, but One who has been tempted in all things as we are, yet without sin" (Heb. 4:15).

It is at precisely this point that the cults and false religions of the world deceive. Satan invariably attacks the Person of Christ, denying that He is the living, eternal God in human flesh.

Second, Jesus Christ **was vindicated in the Spirit.** *Dikaioō* (**vindicated**) means "to justify," or "to declare righteous." Though the translators decided to capitalize **Spirit,** making it refer to the third member of the Trinity, it could also refer to Jesus. That would mean that Jesus Christ was **vindicated**—declared to be righteous—with respect to His spiritual nature. This reality is why the Father said, "This is My beloved Son, in whom I am well-pleased" (Matt. 3:17). First John 2:1 calls Him "Jesus Christ the righteous." He was "tempted in all things as we are, yet without sin" (Heb. 4:15). Hebrews 5:9 relates that "having been made perfect, He became to all those who obey Him the source of eternal salvation," while Hebrews 7:26 describes Him as "holy, innocent, undefiled, separated from sinners and exalted above the heavens."

Jesus Christ was a sinless sacrifice on our behalf: "He made Him who knew no sin to be sin on our behalf, that we might become the righteousness of God in Him" (2 Cor. 5:21). "How much more will the blood of Christ, who through the eternal Spirit offered Himself without blemish to God, cleanse your conscience from dead works to serve the living God" (Heb. 9:14)? "For you have been called for this purpose, since Christ also suffered for you, leaving you an example for you to follow in His steps, who committed no sin, nor was any deceit found in His mouth" (1 Peter 2:21–22).

Our Lord was the God-Man. In His human nature, He was fully man, in His divine nature, He was fully God.

It is also possible that the translation of **Spirit** in the upper case is correct and is referring to Christ's vindication by the Holy Spirit. In Romans 1:4 Paul tells us that Jesus Christ "was declared the Son of God with power by the resurrection from the dead, according to the spirit of holiness." His resurrection by the Spirit proved His sinlessness. If He had any sin of His own, He would have stayed dead as the penalty for that sin. The affirmation of His perfect righteousness came when the Holy Spirit raised Him from the dead.

It may well be that Paul here encompasses both realities. Jesus Christ was **vindicated** both by His sinless life of obedience to God which declared His righteousness, and by the testimony of the Holy Spirit, who affirmed His righteousness again by raising Him from the dead.

Third, Jesus Christ was **beheld by angels.** *Horaō* (**beheld**) means "to see," "to visit," "to observe," or "to be attendant to." Throughout our Lord's earthly ministry, the **angels** observed Him, and attended to Him. They were there at His birth, announcing it to Joseph and the shepherds. They ministered to Him at His temptation, and strengthened Him in Gethsamane. At His death and resurrection, which is the focal point of this passage, **angels** observed Him. The fallen angels saw Him. First Peter 3:18–20 describes that event:

> For Christ also died for sins once for all, the just for the unjust, in order that He might bring us to God, having been put to death in the flesh, but made alive in the spirit; in which also He went and made proclamation to the spirits now in prison, who once were disobedient, when the patience of God kept waiting in the days of Noah.

After His death on the cross, our Lord visited the place where certain demons are kept imprisoned, and proclaimed His triumph over them (cf. Col. 2:15).

The holy angels also were involved. An angel rolled away the stone at the door of His tomb (Matt. 28:2). Angels appeared to the women, affirming that Jesus had risen (Luke 24:4–7). Finally, two angels attended Christ's ascension (Acts 1:10–11). Angels were involved in our Lord's earthly life from beginning to end. That, too, signified divine approval of the incarnate Messiah.

Fourth, Jesus Christ was **proclaimed among the nations.** Before His ascension, He commanded the disciples to "go therefore and make disciples of all the nations, baptizing them in the name of the Father and the Son and the Holy Spirit, teaching them to observe all that I commanded you; and lo, I am with you always, even to the end of the age" (Matt. 28:19–20). In Acts 1:8 He told them, "you shall be My witnesses both in Jerusalem, and in all Judea and Samaria, and even to the remotest part of the earth." There was to be no nation left without the gospel message. Jesus Christ is the Savior of the whole world (cf. John 3:16; 4:42; 2 Cor. 5:19–20; 1 John 2:2; 4:14).

Fifth, Jesus Christ was **believed on in the world.** The plan of God was fulfilled as the apostles' proclamation resulted in saving faith in many lives. At the first public preaching of the gospel after Christ's resurrection, 3,000 people were saved (Acts 2:41). In the days that followed, thousands more **believed on** Him. The gospel was preached throughout Judea, then to the Samaritans, to an Ethiopian eunuch, to Cornelius the Gentile, and ultimately across the Gentile world by Paul and his associates.

Finally, Jesus Christ was **taken up in glory.** Acts 1:9–10 describes the event:

> After He had said these things, He was lifted up while they were looking on, and a cloud received Him out of their sight. And as they were gazing intently into the sky while He was departing, behold, two men in white clothing stood beside them; and they also said, "Men of Galilee, why do you stand looking into the sky? This Jesus, who has been taken up from you into heaven, will come in just the same way as you have watched Him go into heaven."

"When He had made purification of sins," Hebrews 1:3 says, "He sat down at the right hand of the Majesty on high." To the Philippians Paul wrote,

> Being found in appearance as a man, He humbled Himself by becoming obedient to the point of death, even death on a cross. Therefore also God highly exalted Him, and bestowed on Him the name which is above every name, that at the name of Jesus every knee should bow, of those who are in heaven, and on earth, and under the earth, and that every tongue should confess that Jesus Christ is Lord, to the glory of God the Father (Phil. 2:8–11).

Jesus' ascension showed that the Father was pleased with Him and accepted His work.

In six short stanzas, this hymn summarizes the gospel. God became man, died for our sins, triumphed over death, was honored by angels and feared by demons, and ascended into heaven. This message was preached all over the world and many believed and were saved. That is the heart of the message it is our mission to proclaim to the world.

There once was an old church in England. A sign on the front of the building read "We preach Christ crucified." After a time, ivy grew up and obscured the last word. The motto now read, "We preach Christ." The ivy grew some more, and the motto read, "We preach." Finally, ivy covered the entire sign, and the church died. Such is the fate of any church that fails to carry out its mission in the world.

Falling Away from the Faith

13

But the Spirit explicitly says that in later times some will fall away from the faith, paying attention to deceitful spirits and doctrines of demons, by means of the hypocrisy of liars seared in their own conscience as with a branding iron, men who forbid marriage and advocate abstaining from foods, which God has created to be gratefully shared in by those who believe and know the truth. For everything created by God is good, and nothing is to be rejected, if it is received with gratitude; for it is sanctified by means of the word of God and prayer. (4:1–5)

Since creation, the earth has been the battleground between God and Satan. God calls mankind to respond to His Word, and Satan tries to lure them to follow lies. Some claim satanic perversions to be the truth from God. Sadly, even some who profess to follow God's truth turn away from it.

Such deviations from the true faith are nothing new. Among the many examples of apostasy in the Old Testament was King Amaziah of Judah. Second Chronicles 25:2 says of him, "he did right in the sight of the Lord, yet not with a whole heart." His religion was mere external behavior; in his heart he did not know God. Soon he was lured away into idolatry. Second Chronicles 25:14 tells the tragic story: "Now it came about after Amaziah came from slaughtering the Edomites that he brought the gods of the sons of Seir, set them up as his gods, bowed down before them, and burned incense to them." At the close of his life, his epitaph read, "Amaziah turned away from following the Lord" (2 Chron. 25:27).

The New Testament also has its share of apostates, men like Judas Iscariot (John 6:70–71) and Demas (2 Tim. 4:10). The church at Ephesus had seen Hymenaeus and Alexander depart from the faith (1:18–20). Church history from New Testament times until our own day is replete with examples of apostates. They have turned aside to follow **deceitful spirits and doctrines of demons.** It is fallen angels, those demonic beings, who energize all false religion. Like their evil master, Satan, their deception is effective because they disguise themselves as angels of light (2 Cor. 11:14).

When men worship idols, they are in reality worshiping the demons behind those idols. Leviticus 17:7 says, "They shall no longer sacrifice their sacrifices to the goat demons with which they play the harlot." Deuteronomy 32:17 laments that Israel "sacrificed to demons who were not God," while Psalm 106:36–37 shows the depravity of such worship. Israel "served their idols, which became a snare to them. They even sacrificed their sons and their daughters to the demons." "The things which the Gentiles sacrifice," Paul wrote to the Corinthians, "they sacrifice to demons" (1 Cor. 10:20).

The presence of apostate false teachers at Ephesus is indicated from 1:3–7, 18–20. In chapters 2 and 3, Paul dealt with some of the ramifications of their false teaching and corruption of the church. He countered their deceptions with the divine design for men and women in the church, and the spiritual qualifications for true church leaders. Chapter 3 closed with a creedal statement affirming what apostates most directly deny and what is the central truth of the Christian faith: the Person and work of Jesus Christ. In chapter 4, Paul returns to his discussion of the false teachers themselves. The battle lines are thus sharply drawn. While not always popular in our day of toleration and "love," there is a biblical mandate to deal directly and firmly with false teaching. Any tolerance of error regarding God's revelation is a direct form of dishonor to Him. "For Thou hast magnified Thy word according to all Thy name" (Ps. 138:2). Professing believers who would not speak a blasphemous or degrading word against God Himself out of reverence for His name will nevertheless readily misrepresent and pervert His Word, which is to be equally exalted.

THE CERTAINTY OF APOSTASY

some will fall away from the faith, (4:1c)

The key to unlock this passage is the phrase in verse 1, **some will fall away from the faith.** There will be those, like Judas, Demas, and the false disciples of John 6:66, and those often warned in Hebrews, who abandon the faith. **Fall away** is from *aphistēmi,* which means "to depart from," or "to remove oneself from the position originally occupied to another place." It is a stronger term than either the word translated "straying" in 1:6, or the one translated "suffered shipwreck" in 1:19, and refers to a purposeful, deliberate departure from a former position. This term can refer to a simple geographical leaving (cf. Luke 2:37; 4:13; Acts 5:37; 12:10). But in the spiritual sense, it refers to those who come very close to the truth that saves, only to leave. Jesus used this verb when He described some who hear the gospel as being like seed falling on soil that has rockbed below the surface: "Those on the rocky soil are those who, when they hear, receive the word with joy; and these have no firm root; they believe for a while, and in time of temptation fall away (*aphistemi*)" (Luke 8:13). Here it is used to describe apostasy, to identify the tragic reality that some will act like Judas and turn their face from eternal joy to choose hell.

An apostate is not someone struggling to believe, but one who willfully abandons the biblical faith he had once professed. As already noted, **the faith** refers to the content of divine revelation that constitutes what Christians believe (cf. Jude 3). This phrase, then, describes an apostate, a rejector of Christ from within the ranks of the church.

In this passage, Paul gives us six features of apostasy: its predictability, its chronology, its supernatural source, its human purveyors, its content, and its error.

THE PREDICTABILITY OF APOSTASY

But the Spirit explicitly says (4:1a)

Whereas apostasy should sadden and outrage believers, it should neither shock nor surprise them, because **the Spirit explicitly says** that it will occur. This prediction is part of His ongoing revelation in Scripture on the subject of apostasy. In the Old Testament, He warned of the consequences of apostasy (Deut. 28:15:ff.; Ezek. 20:38), and gave numerous examples of apostates (Ex. 32; 1 Sam. 15:11; Neh. 9:26; Ps. 78). The New Testament also warns of apostasy, particularly at the time of the end just before the Lord's return. Our Lord warned of false christs who would deceive many (Matt. 24:4–12). Paul wrote to the Thessalonians about the wholesale departure from the faith that will take place during the future time of tribulation (2 Thess. 2:3–12). Peter and Jude warned of mockers, who, in the end time would depart from the faith (2 Peter 3:3; Jude 18). The apostle John cautioned that "it is the last hour; and just as you heard that antichrist is coming, even now many antichrists have arisen; from this we know that it is the last hour" (1 John 2:18; cf. 4:1–6). But apostasy, though escalated in the end time, is not limited to that era. The writer of Hebrews exhorted his readers, "Take care, brethren, lest there should be in any one of you an evil, unbelieving heart, in falling away from the living God" (Heb. 3:12; cf. 5:11–6:8; 10:26–31).

Paul knew that Ephesus would not be spared efforts to deceive people into abandoning the truth. In his farewell address to the Ephesian elders in Acts 20:29–30 he said, "I know that after my departure savage wolves will come in among you, not sparing the flock; and from among your own selves men will arise, speaking perverse things, to draw away the disciples after them."

As the revelation from the Spirit in Scripture shows, apostasy is predictable, and inevitable. There will always be those who make a temporary response to the gospel, but have no genuine faith in God. We should not be surprised when they leave, and should remember the words of John, "They went out from us, but they were not really of us; for if they had been of us, they would have remained with us; but they went out, in order that it might be shown that they all are not of us" (1 John 2:19).

The Chronology of Apostasy

that in later times (4:1b)

Paul defines the time frame in which apostasy will take place as the **later times.** The **later times** include, but are not limited to, the eschatological future. The first coming of Christ ushered in the **later** or last **times,** which was the Messianic era. First John 2:18 supports this fact when it says simply, "Children, it is the last hour." First Peter 1:20 states that Christ "has appeared in these last times for the sake of you." The writer of Hebrews informs us that God "in these last days has spoken to us in His Son" (Heb. 1:2), and "now once at the consummation of the ages [Christ] has been manifested to put away sin by the sacrifice of Himself" (Heb. 9:26). From the first coming of our Lord to His return, through all this age of the church, apostasy will occur and escalate toward the end when "most people's love will grow cold" (Matt. 24:12).

THE SOURCE OF APOSTASY

paying attention to deceitful spirits and doctrines of demons (4:1d)

As already noted, apostasy is generated by demonic beings. Ephesians 6:12 says that the battle for the truth and the kingdom of heaven is a struggle "not against flesh and blood, but against the rulers, against the powers, against the world forces of this darkness, against the spiritual forces of wickedness in the heavenly places." **Paying attention to** is from *prosechō.* The verb expresses more than merely listening to something. It means "to assent to," "to devote oneself to," or "cling to something." The present tense of the participle shows that apostates continually cling to demonic teaching. They understand the facts of the gospel intellectually, and outwardly identify with the Christian faith. Since their hearts are not right with God and they do not have the Spirit to teach and protect them (cf. Jude 19), however, they are lured away by *deceitful spirits. Planos* (**deceitful**) comes from the root word from which our English word "planet" derives. It carries the idea of wandering, and thus came to mean "seducing," or "deceiving." Demons are called **deceitful** because they cause men to wander from the orbit of the truth. The Holy Spirit leads people into saving truth (cf. John 16:13), while these unholy spirits lead them into damning error.

Apostates are not actually the victims of sophisticated university professors, false religious leaders, or wickedly clever writers or speakers. They are the victims of demonic spirits, purveying lies from the depths of hell through such humans. False teaching is thus something far more than a human aberration, it is nothing less than the **doctrines of demons.** The subjective genitive indicates this is not teaching about demons, but teaching done by them. Satan and his agents have concocted all manner of lying theologies to confuse and deceive. To sit under false teaching that contradicts the truth of Scripture is to be taught by demons, and to put one's mind and soul in jeopardy. It is no wonder, then, that the Bible cautions against exposing oneself to false doctrine.

In his second epistle, the apostle John wrote,

> Many deceivers have gone out into the world, those who do not acknowledge Jesus Christ as coming in the flesh. This is the deceiver and the antichrist. Watch yourselves, that you might not lose what we have accomplished, but that you may receive a full reward. Anyone who goes too far and does not abide in the teaching of Christ, does not have God; the one who abides in the teaching, he has both the Father and the Son. If anyone comes to you and does not bring this teaching, do

> not receive him into your house, and do not give him a greeting; for the one who gives him a greeting participates in his evil deeds. (vv. 7–11)

We are to rescue those under the influence of false teaching like we would snatch a stick out of the fire, being careful not to get burned ourselves (Jude 23).

Deuteronomy 13:12–18 gives us a very straightforward warning about apostasy:

> If you hear in one of your cities, which the Lord your God is giving you to live in, anyone saying that some worthless men have gone out from among you and have seduced the inhabitants of their city, saying, "Let us go and serve other gods" (whom you have not known), then you shall investigate and search out and inquire thoroughly. And if it is true and the matter established that this abomination has been done among you, you shall surely strike the inhabitants of that city with the edge of the sword, utterly destroying it and all that is in it and its cattle with the edge of the sword. Then you shall gather all its booty into the middle of its open square and burn the city and all its booty with fire as a whole burnt offering to the Lord your God; and it shall be a ruin forever. It shall never be rebuilt. And nothing from that which is put under the ban shall cling to your hand, in order that the Lord may turn from His burning anger and show mercy to you, and have compassion on you and make you increase, just as He has sworn to your fathers, if you will listen to the voice of the Lord your God, keeping all His commandments which I am commanding you today, and doing what is right in the sight of the Lord your God.

That sobering warning shows how seriously God wants us to view apostasy. It was to be cut out of the nation of Israel like cancer from a human body.

The history of demonic seduction dates back to Satan's successful tempting of Eve in the Garden of Eden. Throughout human history, culminating in the terrible influence of demons in the Tribulation (Rev. 9:2–11; 13:14; 16:14; 18:2, 23; 19:20; 20:2, 3, 8, 10), **deceitful spirits** will ply **doctrines of demons.** Through God's mercy, however, true believers will not succumb (Ps. 44:18; Heb. 6:9; 10:39; Jude 24–25).

The Purveyors of Apostasy

by means of the hypocrisy of liars seared in their own conscience as with a branding iron (4:2)

Demonic false teaching is purveyed through human agents. While the source is supernatural, the agents are natural. The phrase **the hypocrisy of liars** translates two nouns in the Greek text and could be rendered "hypocritical or deceitful lie-speakers." To purvey their hellish teachings, demons use human deceivers who speak their lies. They may be religious leaders, and appear outwardly good and devout. They may teach in an ostensibly Christian college or seminary. They may pastor a church, or write theological books or commentaries. Though they wear the mask of religion (even Christianity) and wear a mask of piety, they do not serve God, but Satan. They blaspheme God. Sitting under such teachers has no redeeming value, and it results in being exposed to spiritual gangrene (2 Tim. 2:17–18).

The false teachers are able to go about their devilish business without restraint because they are **seared in their own conscience as with a branding iron.** Some argue that Paul's metaphor here is that of a slave branded with his owner's mark. The false teachers, according to that view, carried Satan's brand in their consciences. It seems better, however, to understand this as a reference to the burning or numbing of their consciences. *Kautēriazō* (**seared**) was used by the Greek medical writer Hippocrates to speak of cauterization. The false teachers can carry out their hypocrisy because their consciences have been destroyed. **Conscience** is the faculty that affirms or condemns an action (cf. Rom. 2:14–15). It is the sensitivity to right and wrong that controls behavior. Paul looked to his conscience as the divinely given witness to the condition of his soul (cf. Acts 23:1; 24:16; Rom. 9:1; 2 Cor. 1:12; 2 Tim. 1:3). The apostle has already stated that false teachers reject "a good conscience" (1:19), which is the very goal Paul pursued (1:5). The false teachers' consciences have been so ignored and misinformed that they have become like scar tissue burned senseless, which cease to function. With scarred consciences, they feel no guilt or remorse as they purvey their false doctrines.

The Content of Apostasy

men who forbid marriage and advocate abstaining from foods, (4:3a)

Anything contrary to Scripture can be the entry point of demonic teaching. We might have expected the apostle to follow his severe comments about demon doctrine with examples like denying the Trinity or the deity of the Savior, or rejecting salvation by grace. But Satan is so subtle and seeks to gain a foothold on territory more easily yielded. Paul gives a sample of what was being taught at Ephesus. The deceivers there were focusing on two seemingly minor teachings: that spirituality demanded avoiding **marriage** and **abstaining from foods.** As is typical of satanic deception, both of those teachings contain an element of truth. There is nothing wrong with singleness, and such a state may aid spiritual service. First Corinthians 7:25–35 honors those designed by God to be single. Nor is fasting wrong; it is an important accompaniment to prayer (cf. Matt. 6:16–17; 9:14–15). The deception comes in seeing those as essential elements of salvation. The devising of human means of salvation is a hallmark of all false religion.

The teaching that self-denial on the physical level was essential for true spirituality characterized the Essenes. They were a Jewish sect that appeared in Palestine as early as the second century B.C. They formed the Qumran community, near the Dead Sea, where the Dead Sea Scrolls were found. They practiced asceticism, denying marriage and enforcing special dietary regulations. It is possible their influence was being felt in Ephesus.

Another possible influence was the philosophic dualism that characterized much contemporary Greek philosophy. That view held that matter was evil, and spirit good. Marriage and food, being aspects of the evil material world, were to be shunned. Such teaching may have influenced the Ephesians, as it did the Corinthians (cf. 1 Cor. 7:1–7, 28–38; 15:12). In the second century, this false teaching developed into the dangerous heresy known as Gnosticism. Gnostics boasted of a secret, hidden knowledge. They believed they were the initiated ones, who had transcended the mundane and touched the reality of God. They rejected the body as part of the evil, physical world. Gnosticism was to pose a serious threat to the orthodox faith for several centuries.

The emphasis on externalism that marked the Ephesian apostates is typical of all satanic false religion. From the animism of primitive tribes to the sophistication of major world religions, men rely on good works, outward ritual, and self denial. William Barclay comments,

> This was an ever-recurring heresy in the Church; in every generation men arose who tried to be stricter than God. When the *Apostolic Canons* came to be written, it was necessary to set it down in black and white: "If any overseer, priest or deacon, or anyone on the priestly list, abstains from marriage and flesh and wine, not on the ground of asceticism (that is, for the sake of discipline), but through abhorrence of them as evil in themselves, forgetting that all things are very good, and that God made man male and female, but blaspheming and slandering the workmanship of God, either let him amend, or be deposed and cast out of the Church. Likewise a layman also" (*Apostolic Canons* 51). Irenaeus, writing towards the end of the second century, tells how certain followers of Saturninus "declare that marriage and generation are

> from Satan. Many likewise abstain from animal food, and draw away multitudes by a feigned temperance of this kind (Irenaeus, *Against Heresies,* 1, 24, 2). This kind of thing came to a head in the monks and hermits of the fourth century. They went away and lived in the Egyptian desert, entirely cut off from men. They spent their lives mortifying the flesh. One never ate cooked food and was famous for his "fleshlessness." Another stood all night by a jutting crag so that it was impossible for him to sleep. Another was famous because he allowed his body to become so dirty and neglected that vermin dropped from him as he walked. Another deliberately ate salt in midsummer and then abstained from drinking water. "A clean body," they said, "necessarily means an unclean soul." (*The Letters to Timothy, Titus, and Philemon* [Philadelphia: Westminster, 1975], 93–94)

Such teaching is both false and dangerous. Paul rejects it in Colossians 2:16–23:

> Therefore let no one act as your judge in regard to food or drink or in respect to a festival or a new moon or a Sabbath day—things which are a mere shadow of what is to come; but the substance belongs to Christ. Let no one keep defrauding you of your prize by delighting in self-abasement and the worship of the angels, taking his stand on visions he has seen, inflated without cause by his fleshly mind, and not holding fast to the head, from whom the entire body, being supplied and held together by the joints and ligaments, grows with a growth which is from God. If you have died with Christ to the elementary principles of the world, why, as if you were living in the world, do you submit yourself to decrees, such as, "Do not handle, do not taste, do not touch!" (which all refer to things destined to perish with the using)—in accordance with the commandments and teachings of men? These are matters which have, to be sure, the appearance of wisdom in self-made religion and self-abasement and severe treatment of the body, but are of no value against fleshly indulgence.

Believers are complete in Christ and do not need to practice physical self-denial to gain salvation from sin and righteousness before God.

The Error of Apostasy

which God has created to be gratefully shared in by those who believe and know the truth. For everything created by God is good, and nothing is to be rejected, if it is received with gratitude; for it is sanctified by means of the word of God and prayer. (4:3b–5)

The fundamental error of such apostate teaching is that it rejects divine revelation. *All* false teaching is a denial of God's Word. All through the Pastoral Epistles, Paul confronts false teachers for their treatment of Holy Scripture (cf. 1 Tim. 1:3–11; 6:3–5, 20–21; 2 Tim. 2:14–18; 23–26; 3:13–17; 4:1–4; Titus 1:9–16; 3:9–11). Contrary to the false teaching plaguing Ephesus, God created both marriage and food and pronounced them good (cf. Gen. 1:28–31; 2:18–24; 9:3). God created marriage and food to be **gratefully shared in by those who believe and know the truth.** How then can it be right to deny them to men? God made marriage and food for the same reason He made everything else—to give man joy and to bring Himself glory (cf. 1 Cor. 10:31). Unbelievers, while they enjoy marriage ("the grace of life"—1 Peter 3:7) and food, do not fulfill that ultimate intention and praise God for them. So in the truest sense, God made marriage and food for **those who believe and know the truth,** because they are the ones who will glorify Him for such gracious goodness. How foolish to abstain from his kindness and thus deny God the right to be glorified for their enjoyment!

The Ephesian deceivers refused to recognize that **everything created by God is good.** They flatly denied the goodness of God's creation, which would have led them to understand that **nothing is to be rejected, if it is received with gratitude.** Paul once again emphasizes that God's purpose in giving good things to men is so that, in their enjoyment of those gifts, they would praise Him. By gratefully receiving God's gracious gifts, believers fulfill that noble intention for which those things were created. The doxology of Romans 11:36 sums up this perspective: "For from Him and through Him and to Him are all things. To Him be the glory forever. Amen."

At the close of creation week, God pronounced everything He had created "good" (Gen. 1:31). Those good things from God that believers gratefully receive are **sanctified by means of the word of God and prayer.** To be **sanctified** is to be set apart for holy use. The **means** by which that is accomplished are **the word of God and prayer. Prayer** obviously refers to the thanksgiving that expresses gratitude. **The word** seems to refer to the very word in Genesis 1:31, that everything God made was good. There is a double sanctifying, or setting apart from all that is sinful. But it is also possible that Paul has in mind more than Genesis 1:31, namely, the New Testament gospel.

In the Pastoral Epistles, the **word of God** refers to the message of salvation (cf. 2 Tim. 2:9; Titus 2:5). Through that message, believers have come to know the truth in Christ. Part of that truth is that Christ has abolished the dietary laws. According to Mark 7:19, our Lord "declared all foods clean" (cf. Acts 10:9–15; Rom. 14:1–12; Col. 2:16–17). The dietary regulations were temporary, intended to teach Israel the importance of discernment and to isolate the nation from the pagan societies around them. To reimpose them now would be to manufacture a works righteousness system that denies the work of Christ and dishonors God. If believers understand that the gospel has abolished the dietary laws, and in **prayer** offer God thanks, they can receive all His good gifts, and He will be glorified.

Mandatory celibacy and abstinence from foods in general or particular is the teaching of demons. It denies the goodness of God's creation, and robs Him of the glory and praise He is due for that goodness. It also is a denial of God's truth, as revealed in His Word. Mere externalism neither pleases God nor promotes genuine spirituality.

Apostasy is an ever-present danger to the church. Believers can avoid the false teaching that feeds it only by giving heed to God's Word. They would do well to pay attention to the warning issued by the writer of Hebrews: "Do not be carried away by varied and strange teachings; for it is good for the heart to be strengthened by grace, not by foods, through which those who were thus occupied were not benefitted" (Heb. 13:9).

Qualities of an Excellent Minister —part 1

14

In pointing out these things to the brethren, you will be a good servant of Christ Jesus, constantly nourished on the words of the faith and of the sound doctrine which you have been following. But have nothing to do with worldly fables fit only for old women. On the other hand, discipline yourself for the purpose of godliness; for bodily discipline is only of little profit, but godliness is profitable for all things, since it holds promise for the present life and also for the life to come. It is a trustworthy statement deserving full acceptance. For it is for this we labor and strive, because we have fixed our hope on the living God, who is the Savior of all men, especially of believers. Prescribe and teach these things. (4:6–11)

Pastors are often evaluated on the basis of the wrong criteria. Their effectiveness is frequently gauged by the size of their church, their building program, their popularity, their educational background, the number of books they have written, or their radio or TV exposure.

While such things may have some significance, none of them are biblically valid criteria for assessing a man of God. The Puritan genius John Owen wrote, "A minister may fill his pews, his communion roll, the mouths of the public, but what that minister is on his knees in secret before God Almighty, that he is and no more" (cited in I. D. E. Thomas, *A Puritan Golden Treasury* [Edinburgh: Banner of Truth, 1977], 192). The true criteria by which a man of God must be evaluated are found in the New Testament. In 4:6–16, Paul summarizes them. They form the standard by which every ministry is to be measured.

An Excellent Minister Is, Above All, a Servant

you will be a good servant of Christ Jesus, (4:6b)

It is helpful to use as an anchor for the passage the phrase in verse 6, **you will be a good servant of Christ Jesus.** That phrase holds the rest of the teaching in 4:6–16, as well as being one of the underlying themes of the entire epistle. *Kalos* (**good**) could also be translated "noble," "admirable," or "excellent." It is used in 3:1 to describe the ministry, and here to identify the man in that ministry. It takes a noble man to do the noble work. *Diakonos* (**servant**) is not here used in the technical sense of the office of deacon, but in its more general usage (cf. 1 Cor. 4:1–2; 2 Cor. 3:6; 6:4) of anyone who serves in any ministry on Christ's behalf.

Diakonos may be contrasted with another word frequently used to describe those who serve Christ, *doulos*. The latter word, often translated "slave," has the idea of submission and subjection. *Diakonos* has the idea of "serviceability," or "usefulness." Those who serve Christ are called to excellence in their usefulness to His cause.

Having discussed the inevitability of false teachers in 4:1–5, Paul now instructs Timothy in how to be, and to evaluate those suited to be, an effective minister of the Lord in the face of demonic opposition. In so doing, Paul focuses mostly on the positive traits that should characterize an excellent ministry. The way to defeat false doctrine is not only by denouncing and refuting it, but also by positively teaching and living the truth. The primary focus of the ministry is to be positive, to build up the people of God, because sanctification is more than avoiding error, it is being built up with truth.

So Paul calls Timothy to be an excellent servant of Jesus Christ, and to set a standard of virtue in faith, devotion, and conduct that others can follow. By so doing, people will be delivered from heresy and will be focused on the positive truth that makes them spiritually strong. In 4:6–16, Paul directs Timothy to consider his responsibilities by exhibiting eleven qualities that are to characterize the ministry of an excellent servant of Jesus Christ.

An Excellent Minister Warns His People of Error

In pointing out these things to the brethren, (4:6a)

While the ministry is not to be dominated by a negative attitude, that does not mean there is no place for warning. It is an essential element of the ministry. *Hupotithēmi* (**pointing out**) is a mild verb, meaning "to remind," or "to suggest." It could literally be translated, "to lay before." The verb does not have the idea of commanding people or forcing obedience. Rather, it refers to gentle, humble persuasion. The present tense of the participle indicates Timothy was to be continually warning his people.

That was a recurring theme in Paul's ministry. In Acts 20:29–32, he warned the Ephesian elders:

> I know that after my departure savage wolves will come in among you, not sparing the flock; and from among your own selves men will arise, speaking perverse things, to draw away the disciples after them. Therefore be on the alert, remembering that night and day for a period of three years I did not cease to admonish each one with tears. And now I commend you to God and to the word of His grace, which is able to build you up and to give you the inheritance among all those who are sanctified (cf. Rom. 15:15; 1 Cor. 4:14; Col. 1:28; 2:8).

Paul warned them of the errors that were to come. He did not, however, give an exhaustive exposition of those errors. Instead, he focused on the positive aspect of building up their faith through God's Word. Having that strong foundation, they would be able to handle any kind of error when it came.

These things are those Paul warned of in 4:1–5. Timothy is to warn of the danger of all features of unbiblical, demonic doctrine purveyed by false teachers. The people he is to warn are **the brethren,** God's people. Believers are not to be "children, tossed here and there by waves, and carried about by every wind of doctrine, by the trickery of men, by craftiness in deceitful scheming" (Eph. 4:14). He is to remind them that the way to deal with satanic false teaching is to be strong in the Word (1 John 2:14).

The failure to think biblically and theologically has cost the church dearly. It has allowed the infiltration of all sorts of error. That, in turn, has led to the church's becoming confused and weak. Convictionless preaching, consisting of watered down teaching, platitudes, and weak theology has replaced doctrinally strong expositional preaching. The resulting legacy has been one of charismatic confusion, psychological encroachment, mysticism, even psychic and occult influence. Much of that chaos can be attributed directly to the failure of pastors to think critically and preach with conviction. So many pastors have failed to draw the line clearly between truth and error and build their people up in the rich and sound doctrine of God's Word. Such weak preachers are often said to compensate by having what some call a "pastor's heart." A pastor's heart, however, is not measured by how good a man is at petting sheep, but by how well he protects them from wolves and feeds them so they grow to be mature and strong.

God holds those in positions of spiritual leadership accountable to warn their people. Ezekiel 3:17–21 relates God's warning to Ezekiel:

> Son of man, I have appointed you a watchman to the house of Israel; whenever you hear a word from My mouth, warn them from Me. When I say to the wicked, "You shall surely die"; and you do not warn him or speak out to warn the wicked from his wicked way that he may live, that wicked man shall die in his iniquity, but his blood I will require at your hand. Yet if you have warned the wicked, and he does not turn from his wickedness or from his wicked way, he shall die in his iniquity; but you have delivered yourself. Again, when a righteous man turns away from his righteousness and commits iniquity, and I place an obstacle before him, he shall die; since you have not warned him, he shall die in his sin, and his righteous deeds which he has done shall not be remembered; but his blood I will require at your hand. However, if you have warned the righteous man that the righteous should not sin, and he does not sin, he shall surely live because he took warning; and you have delivered yourself.

In 2 Timothy 4:1–5, Paul gave the following exhortation to Timothy:

> I solemnly charge you in the presence of God and of Christ Jesus, who is to judge the living and the dead, and by His appearing and His kingdom: preach the word; be ready in season and out of season; reprove, rebuke, exhort, with great patience and instruction. For the time will come when they will not endure sound doctrine; but wanting to have their ears tickled, they will accumulate for themselves teachers in accordance to their own desires; and will turn away their ears from the truth, and will turn aside to myths. But you, be sober in all things, endure hardship, do the work of an evangelist, fulfill your ministry.

A man of God must develop and preach strong convictions. He must continually warn his people of error as the need arises. He is the protector of his flock.

An Excellent Minister Is an Expert Student of Scripture

constantly nourished on the words of the faith and of the sound doctrine which you have been following. (4:6c)

This quality is basic to excellence in ministry, but is sadly lacking in the church today. Much contemporary preaching is weak and produces weak churches because it reflects a lack of biblical knowledge, and a minimal commitment to the study of Scripture. For many pastors, study is an unwelcome intrusion into their schedule. It interrupts the routine of administrative tasks and meetings with which they occupy themselves. They study only enough to make a sermon, not to feed their own hearts and think deeply and carefully on divine truth. The result is impotent sermons that fall on hard hearts and have little impact.

That has not always been the case, however. Throughout church history, most of the greatest theologians have been pastors. For example, in addition to their work of reforming the church, the Reformers had regular pastoral responsibilities. The leaders of the seventeenth-century English Puritan movement, men like John Owen, Richard Baxter, Thomas Goodwin, and Thomas Brooks, were pastors. As pastors, they were above all students of Scripture, not merely communicators, administrators, or counselors. Their understanding and interpretation of Scripture was marked by precision. They labored hard at teaching and preaching (cf. 5:17).

William Tyndale, the sixteenth-century English reformer and Bible translator, was an example of a man with a burning desire to study and understand God's Word. In prison shortly before he was martyred, he wrote a letter to the governor-in-chief asking for

> a warmer cap, a candle, a piece of cloth to patch my leggings. . . . But above all, I beseech and entreat your clemency to be urgent with the Procureur that he may kindly permit me to have my Hebrew Bible, Hebrew Grammar and Hebrew Dictionary, that I may spend time with that in study. (Cited in J. Oswald Sanders, *Spiritual Leadership*, rev. ed. [Chicago: Moody, 1980], 148)

It is to that expert study of Scripture that Paul called Timothy. The translation **constantly nourished** reflects the present tense of the participle. The continual experience of being **nourished** on the truths of God's word is essential. An excellent minister must read the Word, study it, meditate on it, and master its contents. Only then can he be "approved to God as a workman who does not need to be ashamed, handling accurately the word of truth" (2 Tim. 2:15).

The phrase **the words of the faith** reflects the body of Christian truth contained in Scripture. If the Word is "inspired by God and profitable for teaching, for reproof, for correction, for training in righteousness; that the man of God may be adequate, equipped for every good work" (2 Tim. 3:16–17), a minister must know it. No premium can be placed on biblical ignorance. The issue is not how good a communicator a man is, or how well he knows the culture and the contemporary issues, or even how well he knows the particular vicissitudes of his flock. The issue is how well he knows the Word of God, since God's revelation perfectly assesses all issues in every time and every life and addresses them with the divine will. It is through knowledge of the Word that the pastor fulfills his calling to lead his people through spiritual growth to Christlikeness (cf. 1 Peter 2:2).

Sound doctrine is that teaching which is firmly rooted in and yielded from the proper interpretation of Scripture, not human systems of theological or philosophical speculations. Exegetical theology must be the foundation of biblical and systematic theology. An excellent minister must be knowledgeable of biblical truth, both its depth and breadth.

Paul is quick to add that he knew it was that **sound doctrine** that Timothy had **been following.** The sincere faith of Timothy's grandmother, Lois, and mother, Eunice, had been passed on to him, causing Paul to write, "from childhood you have known the sacred writings which are able to give you the wisdom that leads to salvation through faith which is in Christ Jesus" (2 Tim. 3:15). Timothy had also been taught **sound doctrine** from Paul (cf. 2 Tim. 1:13; 2:1–2). Paul exhorted him to continue to follow the truths of God's Word he had been following all his life. Such an exhortation is needed because any man of God can be tempted to lose his heart for the Word and the work. This is implied in Paul's very personal concern for Timothy's loyalty in 6:20 and in his second letter to him (cf. 2 Tim. 1:6–8, 13, 14; 2:15–23; 3:16–4:4).

An excellent minister must be an excellent student of Scripture. He cannot give out what he does not take in.

An Excellent Minister Avoids the Influence of Unholy Teaching

But have nothing to do with worldly fables fit only for old women. (4:7a)

The flip side of being strong in the Word is avoiding false teaching. An excellent minister who is committed to the study of Scripture is correspondingly uninterested in and unwilling to have his strength dissipated by ungodly teaching. *Paraiteomai* (**have nothing to do with**) is a strong word, meaning "reject," or "put away" (cf. 2 Tim. 2:23; Titus

3:10). **Worldly** translates *bebēlos,* a word that describes what is radically separate from what is holy. It could be translated "unhallowed," and refers to anything that contradicts the Word of God. **Fables** translates *muthos,* from which our English word "myth" derives. Such **fables** are the opposite of biblical truth (cf. 2 Tim. 4:4). Paul sarcastically describes them as **fit only for old women.** Women were not usually allowed the educational opportunity men had, so this phrase comes from such a situation. That epithet was commonly used in philosophical circles as a term of disdain for a viewpoint lacking credibility and thus appealing only to uneducated, unsophisticated, and perhaps senile matrons. No intelligent man would hear it at all. The Ephesians would have understood Paul's use of the phrase.

The mind is a precious thing, and God expects those in leadership to have a pure mind, one saturated with His Word. There is no place for foolish, silly myths that are in reality the doctrines of demons. The excellent minister maintains his conviction and his clarity of mind by exposing himself to the Word of God (cf. Phil. 4:8; 2 Tim. 2:16), not to demonic lies that assault the Bible. Under the guise of advanced theological education and academic erudition, many a man's love of the truth has been destroyed, and a once clear mind has been hopelessly muddled.

An Excellent Minister Disciplines Himself for Godliness

On the other hand, discipline yourself for the purpose of godliness; for bodily discipline is only of little profit, but godliness is profitable for all things, since it holds promise for the present life and also for the life to come. It is a trustworthy statement deserving full acceptance. (4:7b–9)

There is no effective spiritual ministry apart from personal godliness, since ministry is the overflow of a godly life. J. Oswald Sanders wrote, "Spiritual ends can be achieved only by spiritual men who employ spiritual methods" (*Spiritual Leadership,* 40).

Spurgeon described in the following words the minister who, lacking godliness in his own life, would seek to lead others to it:

> A graceless pastor is a blind man elected to a professorship of optics, philosophising upon light and vision, discoursing upon and distinguishing to others the nice shades and delicate blendings of the prismatic colours, while he himself is absolutely in the dark! He is a dumb man elevated to the chair of music; a deaf man fluent upon symphonies and harmonies! He is a mole professing to educate eagles; a limpet

elected to preside over angels. (*Lectures to My Students,* first series [reprint; Grand Rapids: Baker, 1980], 4)

Discipline is from *gumnazō,* from which our English words "gymnasium" and "gymnastics" derive. It means "to train," or "to exercise." The word speaks of the rigorous, strenuous, self-sacrificing training an athlete undergoes.

Every Greek city had its gymnasium, and Ephesus was no exception. Youths customarily spent much of their time from ages sixteen to eighteen in physical training. That was vital, since life in those days involved much physical activity. There was a great emphasis on physical training and the glory of winning athletic events.

By using *gumnazō,* Paul plays off that cultural phenomenon and applies it to the spiritual realm. As Greek culture emphasized dedicated training of the body, Paul urged Timothy to **discipline** himself **for the purpose of godliness.** The present tense of the verb indicates that was to be Timothy's constant pursuit. Timothy was to train his inner man for **godliness.**

Eusebeia (**godliness**) expresses the reality of reverence, piety, and true spiritual virtue. It was a word much used by the philosophers of Paul's day. The Platonists defined it as "right conduct in regard to the gods." The Stoic definition was "knowledge of how God should be worshipped." Lucian said it described one who was "a lover of the gods," while Xenophon said it characterized someone who was "wise concerning the gods" (cf. Richard C. Trench, *Synonyms of the New Testament* [Grand Rapids: Eerdmans, 1976], 172–73). Thus even to the pagans *eusebeia* meant a concern for deity and a reverence for things holy.

That concept carried over into the Christian faith. **Godliness** is a right attitude and response toward the true Creator God; a preoccupation from the heart with holy and sacred realities. It is respect for what is due to God, and is thus the highest of all virtues. In 1 Timothy 6:3 it is said to be at the heart of truth. Second Peter 1:3 says that it comes from Christ, while 1 Timothy 6:11 balances that by teaching that believers must pursue it. According to Acts 3:12 it brings power, while 2 Timothy 3:12 indicates it brings trouble. First Timothy 6:5–6 says that it brings eternal (though not necessarily temporal) blessings. **Godliness** is the heart and soul of Christian character, and the aim of Christian living (cf. 1 Tim. 2:2; 2 Peter 3:11).

Spiritual self-discipline is the key to godly living. In 1 Corinthians 9:24–27 Paul wrote,

> Do you not know that those who run in a race all run, but only one receives the prize? Run in such a way that you may win. And everyone who

> competes in the games exercises self-control in all things. They then do it to receive a perishable wreath, but we an imperishable. Therefore I run in such a way, as not without aim; I box in such a way, as not beating the air; but I buffet my body and make it my slave, lest possibly, after I have preached to others, I myself should be disqualified.

In 2 Corinthians 7:1 he exhorted us to "cleanse ourselves from all defilement of flesh and spirit, perfecting holiness in the fear of God." In 2 Timothy 2:3–5 Paul commanded Timothy to

> Suffer hardship with me, as a good soldier of Christ Jesus. No soldier in active service entangles himself in the affairs of everyday life, so that he may please the one who enlisted him as a soldier. And also if anyone competes as an athlete, he does not win the prize unless he competes according to the rules.

Here Paul likens spiritual discipline to that required of a soldier and an athlete. Such discipline is necessary for victory in war, or in the games. The lack of spiritual discipline is the primary reason so many spiritual leaders fall into sin. They fail to spend time cultivating the means of grace, in the Word, in prayer, and in self-sacrificial service. An excellent minister is to pursue godliness, not success (cf. 1 Tim. 1:5; 2:8; 3:2, 10; 6:11; 2 Tim. 2:1, 21–22). He will one day hear from the Lord, "Well done, good and faithful slave" (Matt. 25:21).

In Paul's day, as in our own, there was a great emphasis on **bodily discipline.** While helpful, such **discipline is only of little profit.** Paul is showing that it is limited both in extent and duration. **Bodily discipline** affects only the physical body during this earthly life. On the other hand, **godliness is profitable for all things, since it holds promise for the present life and also for the life to come.** Unlike **bodily discipline, godliness is profitable** for the soul as well as the body. Its positive effects are also not limited to this life, because **it holds promise for the present life and also for the life to come.** Cultivating godliness will bring benefits in the present life (cf. Prov. 3:7–8), but it will primarily bring blessedness for all eternity.

So axiomatic is the truth of verse 8 that Paul calls it **a trustworthy statement deserving full acceptance.** As noted in chapter 3 of this volume, a **trustworthy statement** is a self-evident, obvious statement. It is something so patently clear that everyone acknowledges it. This affirmation refers back to verse 8, not ahead to the comment in verse 10. Verse 8 is much more of a proverbial, axiomatic statement than verse 10. A proverbial statement would not begin with a reference to laboring and striving, as does verse 10. Finally, the Greek phrase *eis* *touto gar* that begins verse 10 shows that verse 10 is not the trustworthy statement, but supports it. Verse 10, then, follows up the truth of verse 8.

It is axiomatic that believers are to be disciplining themselves for godliness because of its eternal value. Godliness, not fame, popularity, or reputation, is the pursuit of the excellent minister, who must be an example of spiritual virtue to his flock. He must apply all the means of grace as he endeavors to be able to say, as did Paul, "Be imitators of me, just as I also am of Christ " (1 Cor. 11:1).

An Excellent Minister Is Committed to Hard Work

For it is for this we labor and strive, because we have fixed our hope on the living God, who is the Savior of all men, especially of believers. (4:10)

The ministry of excellence is not only a heavenly pursuit demanding divine power, but also an earthly task, demanding hard work. As already noted, **for this** connects verse 10 with verse 8. The goal of laboring and striving is godliness, with its eternal implications. *Kopiaō* (**labor**) means "to work to the point of weariness and exhaustion." *Agōnizomai* (**strive**) is the source of our English word "agony." It means "to engage in a struggle." In 2 Corinthians 5:9–11, Paul gives two reasons such hard work is necessary: believers will appear before the judgment seat of Christ (v. 10), and unbelievers will face God's eternal judgment (v. 11; cf. Col. 1:28–29).

The knowledge of this demand for diligent labor spurs the excellent minister on to serious efforts. No wonder Henry Martyn, the missionary to India, exclaimed, "Now let me burn out for God." Because of his diligent, hard work as a missionary to the American Indians, David Brainerd was dead before he reached thirty. Ministers of God are engaged in an eternal work, with the destiny of men's souls at stake. The urgency of that work drives them on, through weariness, loneliness, and struggle. J. Oswald Sanders wrote, "If he is unwilling to pay the price of fatigue for his leadership, it will always be mediocre. . . . True leadership always exacts a heavy toll on the whole man, and the more effective the leadership is, the higher the price to be paid" (*Spiritual Leadership,* 175, 169). Paul affirmed to the Galatians that through the cross of Christ "the world has been crucified to me, and I to the world" (Gal. 6:14). To the Corinthians he wrote,

> For if I preach the gospel, I have nothing to boast of, for I am under compulsion; for woe is me if I do not preach the gospel. For if I do this

> voluntarily, I have a reward; but if against my will, I have a stewardship entrusted to me. . . . Therefore I run in such a way, as not without aim; I box in such a way, as not beating the air; but I buffet my body and make it my slave, lest possibly, after I have preached to others, I myself should be disqualified. (1 Cor. 9:16–17, 26–27)

Both those passages speak of Paul's commitment to hard work and privation, a commitment evidenced by his suffering recorded in 2 Corinthians 11.

An excellent minister lives with hope and is not motivated by instant gratification or immediate fulfillment. He has **fixed** his **hope on the living God.** The perfect tense of the verb indicates something done in the past with continuing results in the present. He constantly labors in the light of eternity. As he was saved in hope (Rom. 8:24), so he lives and ministers in that hope. His concerns do not relate to the temporal world or earthly fulfillment, but to the realm of eternity and the invisible kingdom.

As noted in chapter 12 of this volume, the phrase **the living God** is used frequently in the Old Testament in contrast with dead idols (cf. 1 Sam. 17:26; 2 Kings 19:4, 16; Pss. 42:2; 84:2). Excellent ministers do not serve dead idols for earthly rewards, but the eternally living and true God for results and rewards that will only be known in heaven.

In what sense God **is the Savior of all men, especially of believers** has been much disputed. Some, wanting to eliminate the Scriptural teaching of an eternal hell, argue that Paul here teaches universalism, that all men will be saved. That view violates the basic hermeneutical principle known as *analogia Scriptura.* According to that principle, the Bible never contradicts itself. It will never teach something in one passage that violates what it teaches elsewhere.

The Bible clearly teaches that those who reject God will be sentenced to hell (Revelation 20:11–15). Matthew 25:41 and 46 state that the duration of that punishment will be eternal. Second Thessalonians 1:8–9 says that those who do not know God and refuse to obey the gospel will suffer eternal punishment away from God's presence. Jesus repeatedly spoke of the danger of hell (Matt. 8:12; 13:41–42, 49–50; 22:13; 24:51; 25:30; Luke 13:28). He solemnly warned those who rejected Him that they would die in their sins (John 8:24). Universalism is undeniably contrary to Scripture, since the same words in the original that describe hell as eternal also describe God and heaven as eternal.

A second view might be dubbed the potential/actual view. According to this view, Christ is potentially the savior of all men, but actually only of those who believe. It is true that Christ's death was powerful enough to have redeemed the whole human race and to satisfy the justice of God and remove the barrier between God and all men. Therefore, all can be called to salvation and justly damned if they refuse that call.

By means of Christ's death, God made provision for the sins of the world (cf. the discussion of 1 Tim. 2:6 in chapter 6 of this volume).

That such is not the teaching of this verse, however, is revealed by the use of the adverb *malista* (**especially**), which must mean that all men will enjoy to some extent the same kind of salvation as believers enjoy. The adverb is not adversative or contrastive, it cannot be saying that **all men** are saved in one sense, but **believers** in another. The difference is one of degree, not kind.

It seems best to understand this verse to be teaching that God is really the Savior of all men, who actually does save them—but only in the temporal sense, while believers He saves in the eternal sense. In both cases, He is their Savior and there is a saving that He does on their behalf. In this life, all men experience to some degree the protecting, delivering, sustaining power of God. Believers will experience that to the fullest degree for time and for all eternity.

The word **Savior** is not always in Scripture limited to salvation from sin. In the Septuagint, the Greek translation of the Old Testament, *sotēr* (**Savior**) is sometimes used in the lesser sense of "deliverer" (cf. Judg. 3:9; 6:14; 2 Sam. 3:18; 2 Kings 13:5; Neh. 9:27; Obad. 21). Words in the same word group occasionally have that sense in the New Testament as well (cf. Luke 1:71; Acts 7:25; 27:34; Phil. 1:19; Heb. 11:7). A related word, *sōzō* ("to save") is used in the Gospels to refer to physical healing (Matt. 9:21–22; Mark 5:23; Luke 8:36, 50; John 11:12; cf. Acts 4:9). God **is the Savior of all men** in that He withholds the death and judgment all sinners should receive because of sin (cf. Ezek. 18:4, 32; Rom. 6:23). The reality that God delivers men from instant damnation and does "good and [gives them] rains from heaven and fruitful seasons, satisfying [their] hearts with food and gladness" (Acts 14:17) shows He is the Savior of all. He graciously gives "to all life and breath and all things" (Acts 17:25), and "causes His sun to rise on the evil and the good, and sends rain on the righteous and the unrighteous" (Matt. 5:45). He gives common grace to all men. Unbelievers experience God's goodness and mercy in that they are not instantly killed for their sin. Nor does He give them constant pain and permanent deprivation. They experience His temporal blessings in this life.

That principle is illustrated in Isaiah 63:8–10:

> For He said, "Surely, they are My people, sons who will not deal falsely." So He became their Savior. In all their affliction He was afflicted, and the angel of His presence saved them; in His love and in His mercy He redeemed them; And He lifted them and carried them all the days of old. But they rebelled and grieved His Holy Spirit; therefore, He turned Himself to become their enemy, He fought against them.

Verse 8 says God became Israel's Savior. He brought the nation out of Egypt, and cared for them. He provided food, water, and deliverance from their enemies. That He was not the Savior in a spiritual sense of every Israelite is clear from verse 10, which says He became their enemy and fought against them. That passage is analogous to Paul's thought in 4:10. God **is the Savior of all men** in the temporal sense, and **especially of believers** in the spiritual sense that they are delivered from sin's penalty forever!

So the excellent minister has no trouble working hard proclaiming the saving glory and work of God in Christ, knowing he serves the living God, who is by nature the Savior both in time and for eternity. That eternal aspect of God's saving was what motivated Paul to endure what he suffered in the course of his gospel ministry.

It is said that a minister named Thomas Cochrane was asked during an interview for the mission field, "To what portion of the field do you feel yourself especially called?" He replied, "I only know I should wish it to be the hardest you could offer me."

Richard Baxter, the godly seventeenth-century English Puritan, wrote,

> The ministerial work must be carried on diligently and laboriously, as being of such unspeakable consequence to ourselves and others. We are seeking to uphold the world, to save it from the curse of God, to perfect the creation, to attain the ends of Christ's death, to save ourselves and others from damnation, to overcome the devil, and demolish his kingdom, to set up the kingdom of Christ, and to attain and help others to the kingdom of glory. And are these works to be done with a careless mind, or a lazy hand? O see, then, that this work be done with all your might! Study hard, for the well is deep, and our brains are shallow. (*The Reformed Pastor* [Edinburgh: Banner of Truth, 1979], 112)

The excellent minister's labor must not be done in the power of the flesh, but of the Spirit. Paul strikes that balance in Colossians 1:28–29: "And we proclaim Him, admonishing every man and teaching every man with all wisdom, that we may present every man complete in Christ. And for this purpose also I labor, striving according to His power, which mightily works within me." Hard work in the ministry must be energized by God's power at work in the minister.

An Excellent Minister Teaches with Authority

Prescribe and teach these things. (4:11)

Paul's command to Timothy contrasts sharply with much contemporary preaching. Preaching in our day is often intriguing, but seldom commanding; often entertaining, but seldom convicting; often popular, but seldom powerful; often interesting, but less often transforming. Paul does not ask Timothy to share or make suggestions to his congregation. Rather, he is to **prescribe** the truth to them. *Parangellō* (**prescribe**), means "to command," or "to order" as in a mandate—a call to obedience by one in authority. **Teach** has the idea of passing on truth. **These things** are Paul's teaching in 4:6–10, and more. Everything God commanded Timothy to be he was to command others to be. The excellent minister's preaching is to be authoritative, done in a command mode. Such preaching imitates God Himself, of whom Paul wrote in Acts 17:30, "God is now declaring to men that all everywhere should repent." Jesus commanded His hearers to repent and believe, as John the Baptist had done. The Father commanded all to hear His Son and obey. Every call to believe the gospel with repentance is a command. Every call to saints to obey the Word is a command that is to come with authority. To Titus Paul wrote, "These things speak and exhort and reprove with all authority. Let no one disregard you" (Titus 2:15).

A faithful servant of our Lord is bold. He confronts sin, unbelief, and disobedience without vacillating. Paul instructed Timothy repeatedly to do just that. In 1 Timothy 1:3, Timothy was to "instruct certain men not to teach strange doctrines." Paul commanded him to "prescribe these things as well, so that they may be above reproach" (1 Tim. 5:7). In 1 Timothy 6:17 he was to give instructions to the rich. The excellent minister's boldness is tempered with gentleness, and never causes him to be abusive or ungracious. Nevertheless, every sermon should have an unmistakable tone of authority. He is, in Richard Baxter's words, to "screw the truth into men's minds" (cited in Thomas, *A Puritan Golden Treasury,* 222).

That authority is built upon a fourfold foundation. First, a strong commitment to the authority of God's Word. A man who is unsure if the Bible is God's Word will lack authority in his preaching. Second, proper interpretation of Scripture. The man who is not sure what the Bible means will also lack authority in his preaching. Third, a concern that the truth of God's Word be upheld and enforced by church discipline (cf. Matt. 18:15ff.; 1 Cor. 5:1–13; 2 Thess. 3:14–15). Fourth, the knowledge that the preacher does not need to say what might please men and not offend them, but he must say what pleases God or be guilty of prostituting the ministry.

An excellent minister teaches with authority. His preaching is marked by commands based on the authority of Scripture, not mere sentimental pleadings. He is not afraid to boldly proclaim the Word of God and let it do its perfect work.

Qualities of an Excellent Minister—part 2

15

Let no one look down on your youthfulness, but rather in speech, conduct, love, faith and purity, show yourself an example of those who believe. Until I come, give attention to the public reading of Scripture, to exhortation and teaching. Do not neglect the spiritual gift within you, which was bestowed upon you through prophetic utterance with the laying on of hands by the presbytery. Take pains with these things; be absorbed in them, so that your progress may be evident to all. Pay close attention to yourself and to your teaching; persevere in these things; for as you do this you will insure salvation both for yourself and for those who hear you. (4:12–16)

Having discussed the personal qualifications of those in the ministry in chapter 3, Paul turns in 4:6–16 to the standards of excellence relating to the ministry itself. He gives eleven rules by which an excellent minister must be measured. They are based not on his personal life, but on how he functions in the ministry. As noted in chapter 14, the first six convey that an excellent minister warns his people of error, is an expert student of Scripture, avoids the influence of unholy teaching, disciplines himself for godliness, is committed to hard work, and teaches with authority.

An Excellent Minister Is a Model of Spiritual Virtue

Let no one look down on your youthfulness, but rather in speech, conduct, love, faith and purity, show yourself an example of those who believe. (4:12)

The single greatest tool of leadership is the power of an exemplary life. The Puritan Thomas Brooks said, "Example is the most powerful rhetoric" (cited in I. D. E. Thomas, *A Puritan Golden Treasury* [Edinburgh: Banner of Truth, 1977], 96). Setting an example of godly living that others can follow is the *sine qua non* of excellence in ministry. When a manifest pattern of godliness is missing, the power is drained out of preaching, leaving it a hollow, empty shell. A minister's life is his most powerful message, and must reinforce what he says or he may as well not say it. Authoritative preaching is undermined if there is not a virtuous life backing it up.

The New Testament has much to say about the crucial role of example. To the Corinthians Paul wrote, "I exhort you therefore, be imitators of me" (1 Cor. 4:16; cf. 11:1). In Philippians 3:17 he said, "Brethren, join in following my example, and observe those who walk according to the pattern you have in us," while Philippians 4:9 says, "The things you have learned and received and heard and seen in me, practice these things; and the God of peace shall be with you." He reminded the Thessalonians that

> our gospel did not come to you in word only, but also in power and in the Holy Spirit and with full conviction; just as you know what kind of men we proved to be among you for your sake. You also became imitators of us and of the Lord, having received the word in much tribulation with the joy of the Holy Spirit. (1 Thess. 1:5–6; cf. 2 Thess. 3:7–9)

The writer of Hebrews exhorted his readers to "remember those who led you, who spoke the word of God to you; and considering the result of their conduct, imitate their faith" (Heb. 13:7).

By cautioning Timothy not to allow anyone to **look down on** his **youthfulness,** Paul warned him that because he had no long record to establish credibility, he would have to earn the respect of his people. The Greeks, as did most cultures, subordinated youth to age. If a man did not have age, he would have to earn respect.

Paul refers to Timothy as young, although it was now some fifteen years since they first met on the apostle's second missionary journey. Timothy was probably in his early twenties at that time. Although he was now in his late thirties, he was thirty years the junior of the aged apostle (Philem. 9) and still considered young by the standards of Greek culture. Luke describes Paul as a young man in Acts 7:58, though he must have been over thirty. *Neotēs* (**youthfulness**) was used to describe anyone under the age of forty. To offset that **youthfulness,** Paul exhorted Timothy to be **an example of those who believe.** *Tupos* (**example**) means "pattern," or "model." By so doing, he would gain the respect of his people. Paul lists five areas in which Timothy was to make every effort to be an example to the church.

First, Timothy was to be an example in **speech.** The conversation of an excellent minister must be exemplary. In Matthew 12:34–37, Jesus warned,

> For the mouth speaks out of that which fills the heart. The good man out of his good treasure brings forth what is good; and the evil man out of his evil treasure brings forth what is evil. And I say to you, that every careless word that men shall speak, they shall render account for it in the day of judgment. For by your words you shall be justified, and by your words you shall be condemned.

A man's speech reflects what is in his heart.

All types of sinful speech must be avoided by a man of God. That includes any deviation from truthfulness, as Paul makes clear in Ephesians 4:25 when he says, "Therefore, laying aside falsehood, speak truth, each one of you, with his neighbor." Nothing more surely reveals a sinful soul and more swiftly destroys a leader's credibility than lies. Absolute honesty is essential for one who speaks on behalf of the "God who cannot lie" (Titus 1:2; Heb. 6:18), and who hates lying (Prov. 6:16–17; 12:22). Ephesians 4:26 forbids angry speech, verse 29 impure speech, and verse 31 slanderous words. Such speech reflects an impure heart. To be called an excellent minister, one's speech must be "good for edification according to the need of the moment, that it may give grace to those who hear" (Eph. 4:29).

Second, Timothy was to be an example in **conduct.** An excellent minister is required to be a model of righteous living who manifests his biblical convictions in every area of his life. A biblical message paired with an ungodly lifestyle is nothing but blatant hypocrisy. Worse, people will tend to follow how the man lives, not what he teaches. On the other hand, a godly life brings power and authority to a man's message.

Scripture is replete with exhortations to godly living. James writes, "Who among you is wise and understanding? Let him show by his good behavior his deeds in the gentleness of wisdom" (James 3:13). Peter had much to say on the subject: "Like the Holy One who called you, be holy yourselves also in all your behavior" (1 Peter 1:15); "Keep your behavior excellent among the Gentiles, so that in the thing in which they slander you as evildoers, they may on account of your good deeds, as they observe them, glorify God in the day of visitation" (1 Peter 2:12); "Keep a good conscience so that in the thing in which you are slandered, those who revile your good behavior in Christ may be put to shame" (1 Peter 3:16).

Third, Timothy was to be an example in **love.** Biblical **love** is far different from the emotion our culture calls love. It involves self-sacrificing service on behalf of others regardless of how one feels. In John 15:13 our Lord said, "Greater love has no one than this, that one lay down his life for his friends." That verse sums up the essence of ministry as self-sacrificial love. The excellent minister gives his time and energy to the people he is called to serve, devoting his whole life to seeing them strengthened and built up in the Lord.

No personal sacrifice is too great, as Paul noted in Philippians 2:17: "But even if I am being poured out as a drink offering upon the sacrifice and service of your faith, I rejoice and share my joy with you all." He could readily say, "I rejoice in my sufferings for your sake, and in my flesh I do my share on behalf of His body (which is the church) in filling up that which is lacking in Christ's afflictions" (Col. 1:24). His love was so great for those he served that he was willing to love even if that love was not returned. He reminded the Corinthians of his love for them (2 Cor. 2:4; 11:11) and even adds, "I will most gladly spend and be expended for your souls. If I love you the more, am I to be loved the less" (2 Cor. 12:15)? His love for the church made him feel the pains of suffering all the time (cf. 2 Cor. 1:5–11; 6:4–10; 11:23–29; 12:7–10).

Paul reminded the Thessalonians that

> we proved to be gentle among you, as a nursing mother tenderly cares for her own children. Having thus a fond affection for you, we were well-pleased to impart to you not only the gospel of God but also our own lives, because you had become very dear to us. For you recall, brethren, our labor and hardship, how working night and day so as not to be a burden to any of you, we proclaimed to you the gospel of God. You are witnesses, and so is God, how devoutly and uprightly and blamelessly we behaved toward you believers; just as you know how we were exhorting and encouraging and imploring each one of you as a father would his own children, so that you may walk in a manner

worthy of the God who calls you into His own kingdom and glory. (1 Thess. 2:7–12)

In Philippians 2:25–30, Paul commended Epaphroditus, who, like the apostle himself, had nearly died from his strenuous service in the cause of Christ. And since an excellent minister works with eternity in view, he sees the sacrifices of love he makes as small.

Fourth, Timothy was to be an example in **faith. Faith** here does not refer to belief, but to faithfulness or unswerving commitment. An excellent minister is consistently faithful. He does not swerve off the track; he does not deviate from his course. "It is required of stewards," Paul wrote in 1 Corinthians 4:2, "that one be found trustworthy." This essential virtue of loyalty separates those who succeed in having a powerful influence from those who do not.

Finally, Timothy was to be an example in **purity.** *Hagneia* (**purity**) refers primarily to purity in the area of sexuality, both in actions and in the intentions of the heart. Nothing so ravages a ministry as sexual impurity. That is certainly evident in the list of standards for an overseer who is "above reproach." Heading that list is the requirement that he be a "one-woman man" (1 Tim. 3:2). Leaders are especially vulnerable in that area, since it is a priority area of qualification, and thus a common avenue of attack by Satan. An excellent minister must heed Paul's admonishment to Timothy to "flee from youthful lusts" (2 Tim. 2:22).

Anyone who is not able to set a pattern of godly virtue in those areas does not belong in church leadership. Since a leader's life sets the standard for others to follow, an unqualified leader inevitably lowers the standard of godliness in the church.

An Excellent Minister Has a Thoroughly Biblical Ministry

Until I come, give attention to the public reading of Scripture, to exhortation and teaching. (4:13)

Scripture is the material with which an excellent minister builds his ministry. The phrase **until I come** shows Paul intended to return to Ephesus (cf. 3:14). Until Paul arrived, Timothy was to continue to build with the revelation of God. His task was to **give attention to the public reading of Scripture, to exhortation and teaching. Give attention to** is the present active indicative form of *prosechō.* Timothy was to continually give his attention to those things; it was to be his way of life. Donald Guthrie writes that the verb "implies previous preparation in private" (*The Pastoral Epistles,* rev. ed. [Grand Rapids: Eerdmans, 1990],

109). It encompasses not just the act of teaching, but all the commitment, study, and preparation associated with it.

An excellent minister is to focus on the **public reading of Scripture, to exhortation and teaching.** Although the word **public** does not appear in the Greek text, it is implied by the use of the definite article. The **reading** was done in the public worship service of the church. Due in part to a lack of manuscripts, the practice of the synagogue had carried over into the early church. Part of every worship service in a synagogue was the reading and explanation of the Old Testament Scriptures (cf. Luke 4:16ff.; Acts 15:21). That custom dates back to the practice of the exiles who returned from the Babylonian captivity (cf. Neh. 8:1–8). To the reading of the Old Testament, the early church added the reading and explanation of the apostles' doctrine (cf. Acts 2:42; Col. 4:16; 1 Thess. 5:27). As New Testament letters were written and circulated during the early years, they took their place in the public reading.

The reading of the Scriptures was accompanied by an exposition of the passage read so that the hearers could understand it (cf. Neh. 8:1–8; Luke 4:16ff.). Anything that needed to be clarified would be explained. In our day, when we are culturally, geographically, linguistically, philosophically, and historically far removed from biblical times, exposition is essential.

Exhortation challenges people to apply the truths they have been taught. It warns people to obey, in light of the blessing to come on them if they do, and the judgment if they do not. **Exhortation** may take the form of rebuke, warning, counsel, or comfort, but always involves a binding of the conscience.

Didaskalia (**teaching**) appears fifteen times in the Pastoral Epistles. It involves the systematic explanation of the Word of God. It could embody developing a means of teaching people individually, or in small groups meeting in homes. The point is that an excellent minister is to disseminate sound teaching to all people at all times through all means. That is the heart and soul of the ministry, since the Word is the only source of life and truth. It is no surprise, then, that an elder was required to be able to teach (1 Tim. 3:2; cf. Titus 1:9).

From its earliest years, the church has been committed to the teaching of God's Word. Writing in the middle of the second century, the apologist Justin Martyr described a typical worship service of his day:

> On the day called Sunday there is a meeting in one place of those who live in cities or the country, and the memoirs of the apostles or the writings of the prophets are read as long as time permits. When the reader has finished, the president in a discourse urges and invites us to the

> imitation of these noble things. Then we all stand up together and offer prayers. And, as said before, when we have finished the prayer, bread is brought, and wine and water, and the president similarly sends up prayers and thanksgivings to the best of his ability, and the congregation assents, saying the Amen. (Cited in Cyril C. Richardson, ed., *Early Christian Fathers* [New York: MacMillan, 1978], 287)

The reading and explanation of the Word was central to the worship service.

The fourth-century bishop of Constantinople John Chrysostom was nicknamed "golden-mouthed." Of him John R. W. Stott writes,

> He is generally and justly regarded as the greatest pulpit orator of the Greek church. Nor has he any superior or equal among the Latin Fathers. He remains to this day a model for preachers in large cities.
>
> Four chief characteristics of his preaching may be mentioned. First, he was biblical. Not only did he preach systematically through several books, but his sermons are full of biblical quotations and allusions. Secondly, his interpretation of the Scriptures was simple and straightforward. He followed the Antiochene school of "literal" exegesis, in contrast to fanciful Alexandrian allegorizations. Thirdly, his moral applications were down to earth. Reading his sermons today, one can imagine without difficulty the pomp of the imperial court, the luxuries of the aristocracy, the wild races of the hippodrome, in fact the whole life of an oriental city at the end of the fourth century. Fourthly, he was fearless in his condemnations. In fact, "he was a martyr of the pulpit, for it was chiefly his faithful preaching that caused his exile." (Cited in John R. W. Stott, *Between Two Worlds* [Grand Rapids: Eerdmans, 1982], 21)

His simple, direct exposition of Scripture, coupled with moral application, is a model for all preachers to imitate.

The Reformers were deeply committed to the exposition of Scripture. Luther often preached four times on Sundays. Every quarter of the year he would teach a two-week series on doctrine using a catechism. Over 2,000 of his sermons are extant. Calvin ministered in Geneva from 1541 until his death in 1564. He preached twice each Sunday, and every other week preached each weeknight. His Sunday sermons covered the New Testament, his weeknight sermons the Old Testament. Those sermons were recorded by a stenographer, and became the basis of his commentaries. He produced commentaries on Genesis, Deuteronomy, Judges, Job, Psalms, 1 and 2 Samuel, 1 Kings, all the major and minor prophets, a harmony of the Gospels, Acts, 1 and 2 Corinthians, Galatians, Ephesians, 1 and 2 Thessalonians, and the Pastoral Epistles.

The nineteenth century saw great preachers like Joseph Parker and Alexander Maclaren, both of whom produced expositions of the entire Bible. They devoted a lifetime of study to the Word of God. They knew the truth expressed by John Huxtable, that a man "does not qualify to be a preacher of the Word by making weekly sallies into the good book to discover some peg on which to hang some scattered observations about men and affairs" (cited in Stott, *Between Two Worlds,* 182). The harder a man works at teaching the Word, the more honorable he is (cf. 1 Tim. 5:17). Such diligence is necessary because, as John Flavel notes, "It is not with us [preachers], as with other labourers: they find their work as they leave it, so do not we. Sin and Satan unravel almost all we do, the impressions we make on our people's souls in one sermon, vanish before the next" (cited in Thomas, *A Puritan Golden Treasury,* 193).

Preaching and teaching is the highest calling of a minister. It is tragic that so many in our day have been diverted from that. They spend their time on nonessentials, and their people end up spiritually impoverished.

An Excellent Minister Fulfills His Calling

Do not neglect the spiritual gift within you, which was bestowed upon you through prophetic utterance with the laying on of hands by the presbytery. (4:14)

Not all those who enter the ministry stay the course. Some leave because they did not belong in the ministry to begin with. Others, however, defect from the place God intended them to be.

Timothy was not beyond the temptation to do just that. The imperative form of the verb *ameleō* (**do not neglect**) indicates Timothy could actually be in danger of abandoning the ministry. In fact, he may have already been feeling such temptation.

In 2 Timothy 1:3–8, 12–15, Paul gives us an insight into the pressures Timothy faced at Ephesus:

> I thank God, whom I serve with a clear conscience the way my forefathers did, as I constantly remember you in my prayers night and day, longing to see you, even as I recall your tears, so that I may be filled with joy. For I am mindful of the sincere faith within you, which first dwelt in your grandmother Lois, and your mother Eunice, and I am sure that it is in you as well. And for this reason I remind you to kindle afresh the gift of God which is in you through the laying on of my hands. For God has not given us a spirit of timidity, but of power and

love and discipline. Therefore do not be ashamed of the testimony of our Lord, or of me His prisoner; but join with me in suffering for the gospel according to the power of God. . . . For this reason I also suffer these things, but I am not ashamed; for I know whom I have believed and I am convinced that He is able to guard what I have entrusted to Him until that day. Retain the standard of sound words which you have heard from me, in the faith and love which are in Christ Jesus. Guard, through the Holy Spirit who dwells in us, the treasure which has been entrusted to you. You are aware of the fact that all who are in Asia turned away from me, among whom are Phygelus and Hermogenes.

As already noted, Timothy was a young man in the reckoning of his culture. He faced some formidable foes in the Ephesian errorists. Paul reminded Timothy of his constant prayers on his behalf, as he remembered Timothy's tears. About three years after writing this first epistle to him, Paul had to exhort Timothy to rekindle his spiritual gift. He reminded him that power, not fear, came from God. And it is even possible that Timothy had felt temptation to be ashamed of Paul, or even of the Lord Himself. Paul urges him not to succumb to such evil alluring and turn away, as so many others had.

Apart from such external pressures were the internal temptations to lack of diligence and lust. Accordingly, Paul gave him the following exhortations in 2 Timothy 2:1, 3–6, 22:

You therefore, my son, be strong in the grace that is in Christ Jesus. . . . Suffer hardship with me, as a good soldier of Christ Jesus. No soldier in active service entangles himself in the affairs of everyday life, so that he may please the one who enlisted him as a soldier. And also if anyone competes as an athlete, he does not win the prize unless he competes according to the rules. The hard-working farmer ought to be the first to receive his share of the crops. . . . Now flee from youthful lusts, and pursue righteousness, faith, love and peace, with those who call on the Lord from a pure heart.

To encourage Timothy to remain faithful, Paul gave him three motives for not abandoning the ministry. First, he reminded him of **the spiritual gift within** him. *Charisma* (**spiritual gift**) refers to the gift given all believers at salvation (Rom. 12:4–8; 1 Cor. 12:1–31; 1 Peter 4:10–11). Each believer's gift is a God-designed blend of spiritual capabilities, which acts as a channel through which the Spirit of God ministers to others. Timothy's gift included evangelism, preaching, teaching, and leadership (cf. 4:6, 11, 13, 16; 6:2; 2 Tim. 2:24–25; 4:2, 5).

Second, Timothy's subjective gift was confirmed objectively. Paul reminded Timothy that his gift **was bestowed upon** him **through pro-**

phetic utterance. There was a public affirmation of his gift through direct revelation from God (cf. 1:18), though the circumstances of that **utterance** are not given in Scripture. It likely took place, however, shortly after Timothy met Paul on the apostle's second missionary journey (Acts 16:1–3). Timothy's prophetic call was reminiscent of that of Paul himself (cf. Acts 13:2).

In our day, God's call comes not through special revelation, but through providence. If God wants a man in the ministry, He will give him that desire and open a door of opportunity for him.

Finally, Timothy's gift was confirmed through **the laying on of hands by the presbytery.** That likely took place at the same time the prophecy was made about Timothy. Timothy's call to the ministry was thus confirmed subjectively, by means of his spiritual gift, objectively, through his prophetic call, and collectively, through the affirmation of the church. For Timothy to bail out of the ministry would be to fly in the face of that clear consensus. Paul urges him to remain faithful to his calling.

An Excellent Minister Is Totally Absorbed in His Work

Take pains with these things; be absorbed in them, (4:15a)

A man of God must have a single-minded, consuming devotion to his calling. He is not to be like the double-minded man James characterized as "unstable in all his ways" (James 1:8). *Meletaō* (**take pains with**) carries the idea of thinking through beforehand, planning, strategizing, or premeditating. When not involved in ministry, the excellent minister is preparing, praying, or planning for it. **Absorbed** is not in the Greek text, which literally reads **be in them,** a phrase emphasizing being totally engulfed. An excellent minister is consumed by his work.

In 2 Timothy 4:2, Paul commanded Timothy to "preach the word; be ready in season and out of season," when it is convenient, and when it is not. The servant of Jesus Christ is never off duty.

An Excellent Minister Is Progressing in Spiritual Growth

so that your progress may be evident to all. (4:15b)

Lest anyone think that a man must be flawless to be a servant of God, Paul mentions the necessity of spiritual **progress.** No minister is yet all that he should be. He is both blameless and growing. A spiritual leader must not try to hide his flaws from his people, but rather allow them to see his progress in spiritual knowledge, wisdom, and maturity. Even the apostle Paul admitted his need to grow in grace:

> Not that I have already obtained it, or have already become perfect, but I press on in order that I may lay hold of that for which also I was laid hold of by Christ Jesus. Brethren, I do not regard myself as having laid hold of it yet; but one thing I do: forgetting what lies behind and reaching forward to what lies ahead, I press on toward the goal for the prize of the upward call of God in Christ Jesus. (Phil. 3:12–14)

Prokopē (**progress**) was used in military terms to speak of an advancing force. The Stoics used the word to speak of advancing in learning, understanding, or knowledge. It could also refer to the strenuous effort of a pioneer blazing a trail to a new location. An excellent minister is to be advancing to Christlikeness, and his people should be able to mark his progress.

The Concluding Exhortation

Pay close attention to yourself and to your teaching; persevere in these things; for as you do this you will insure salvation both for yourself and for those who hear you. (4:16)

Paul wraps up his charge to Timothy regarding the qualities of a noble servant by commanding him to **pay close attention to** himself **and** his **teaching.** Each of the eleven characteristics of an excellent minister found in verses 6–16 fit into one of these two categories. A true man of God will concentrate totally on personal holiness and public instruction. The benefit of so doing is twofold: it will **insure salvation both** for the minister himself, **and for those who hear** him. It will bring about salvation for him in the sense that final salvation, deliverance from sin and entrance into eternal glory, demands perseverance. It is the unmistakable teaching of Scripture that persevering in the faith is a mark of genuine salvation. Jesus said in John 8:31, "If you abide in My word, then you are truly disciples of Mine" (cf. Matt. 10:22; 24:13; Acts 13:43; 14:22; Rom. 2:7; Col. 1:23; Heb. 3:14). Such perseverance is the result of giving careful heed and holding on to one's own devotion to spiritual virtue. While the perseverance of the saints can only be accomplished by the power of God, it is nonetheless the responsibility of each believer.

An excellent minister's perseverance will also bring salvation **for those who hear** his message. He, of course, is not the source of their salvation, but is merely the agent of it. God's glory is not at all forfeited or diminished because He uses human instruments in the divine work of saving souls. Rather, it is enhanced by His making useful those who are so weak, and ennobling them who are so ignoble. His godly life and faithful teaching of the Word will have a saving impact on those who hear him. The result, which is the true goal of all eleven marks of a godly minister, is that some will be saved. That is the church's highest calling, and the sole reason she remains in the world. It is the goal of all the noble servant does in the ministry.

Confronting Sin in the Spiritual Family

16

Do not sharply rebuke an older man, but rather appeal to him as a father, to the younger men as brothers, the older women as mothers, and the younger women as sisters, in all purity. (5:1–2)

The church is described in the New Testament by many metaphors and analogies. First Peter 2:9 calls it a holy nation, emphasizing believers' common citizenship in the heavenly realm. Revelation 5:10 calls the church a kingdom, emphasizing believers' common submission to the King of kings and Lord of lords. Peter calls the church a priesthood (1 Peter 2:5, 9), emphasizing the privilege all believers have of direct access to God. Our Lord calls the church a vine (John 15:5), emphasizing believers' common connection to the life of God that enables us to bear fruit. The apostle Paul calls the church a temple (Eph. 2:20–22), built upon the solid foundation of the apostles' doctrine, with Jesus Christ as the chief cornerstone. First Corinthians 12:12 calls the church a body, emphasizing believers' common life and dependence on their Head, the Lord Jesus Christ. Hebrews 12:23 calls the church an assembly, emphasizing believers' common calling to be gathered into the eternal presence of God. First Peter 5:2–3 calls the church a flock, emphasizing believers' common need to be led and fed by the Great Shepherd.

There is one more metaphor of the church, one that fits the context of this passage. That is the metaphor of the church as a family (cf. Eph. 2:19; 3:15; Gal. 6:10). The word "family" speaks of intimacy, care, openness, and love. Jesus said in John 13:34–35, "A new commandment I give to you, that you love one another, even as I have loved you, that you also love one another. By this all men will know that you are My disciples, if you have love for one another." Love is the backbone of the family, and of the church.

Within the framework of believers' love for each other is a very necessary and often overlooked element: confrontation of sin. In the church, as in the family, disobedience must be dealt with. That is a mark of a loving family. True love cares that others enjoy the blessing of God and prosper spiritually. Because of that, it does not hesitate to confront sin. In this brief passage, Paul covers the important issue of how that is to be done in the Lord's family.

Timothy was part of the spiritual family located in Ephesus. Some sinning members of that church had abandoned truth and godliness (1:5–6; 2:8). Others had shipwrecked their faith (1:19). Some women had abandoned their proper role and were trying to usurp the function of the men (2:9–15). Some of the men aspiring to leadership were not qualified, so Paul gave the qualifications necessary for elders and deacons (3:1–13; cf. 5:19–22). Others were teaching demonic false doctrines (4:1–5; 6:3–5). Some of the older widows were living impure lives (5:6–7), as were some of the younger ones (5:11–13).

Obviously, the condition of the spiritual family in Ephesus called for some correction. Sin needed to be dealt with because it disrupts the intimacy in a family. Further, that intimacy allows sin to spread through the members of a family like the disease that it is. As Paul cautioned the Corinthians in dealing with their sinning members,

> Do you not know that a little leaven leavens the whole lump of dough? Clean out the old leaven, that you may be a new lump. . . . I wrote to you in my letter not to associate with immoral people; I did not mean with the immoral people of this world . . . but . . . with any so-called brother if he should be an immoral person, or covetous, or an idolater, or a reviler, or a drunkard, or a swindler. . . . Remove the wicked man from among yourselves. (1 Cor. 5:6–7, 9–10, 11, 13)

Timothy already knew the importance of discipline, so Paul does not stress it in this passage. In 2 Samuel 7:14 God said of David's descendant, "I will be a father to him and he will be a son to Me; when he commits iniquity, I will correct him with the rod of men and the strokes of the sons of men." Job 5:17 says of God's discipline, "Behold, how happy is the man whom God reproves, so do not despise the discipline of the Almighty." Proverbs says much about discipline. It leads to understanding (Prov. 15:32), knowledge (19:25), wisdom (15:31; 29:15), honor (13:18), and a happy life (6:23). God laments to Israel in Jeremiah 44:4–5, "I sent you all My servants the prophets, again and again, saying, 'Oh, do not do this abominable thing which I hate.' But they did not listen or incline their ears to turn from their wickedness, so as not to burn sacrifices to other gods."

Perhaps the most definitive passage on the importance of discipline in the church family is found in Matthew 18:15–18:

> And if your brother sins, go and reprove him in private; if he listens to you, you have won your brother. But if he does not listen to you, take one or two more with you, so that by the mouth of two or three witnesses every fact may be confirmed. And if he refuses to listen to them, tell it to the church; and if he refuses to listen even to the church, let him be to you as a Gentile and a tax-gatherer.

It was part of Timothy's role as a leader in the church to confront sin.

Sin should be confronted fearlessly. Ezekiel 2:3–6 says,

> Then He said to me, "Son of man, I am sending you to the sons of Israel, to a rebellious people who have rebelled against Me; they and their fathers have transgressed against Me to this very day. And I am sending you to them who are stubborn and obstinate children; and you shall say to them, 'Thus says the Lord God.' As for them, whether they listen or not—for they are a rebellious house—they will know that a prophet has been among them. And you, son of man, neither fear them nor fear their words, though thistles and thorns are with you and you sit on scorpions; neither fear their words nor be dismayed at their presence, for they are a rebellious house."

Sin should also be confronted authoritatively. In Titus 2:15 Paul commanded Titus, "These things speak and exhort and reprove with all authority. Let no one disregard you." Such rebukes may need to be severe (Titus 1:13). Finally, rebuking of sin must be done with "great patience" (2 Tim. 4:2).

Confronting in Love

Do not sharply rebuke . . . but rather appeal (5:1a)

Two verbs govern this passage. The first, *epiplēssō* (**sharply rebuke**), is a strong term. It refers to harsh or violent rebuke. It appears only here in the New Testament, though a related word appears in 3:3, where it describes an elder as one not given to physical violence. Here verbal rather than physical violence is prohibited. A sinning Christian is not to be hammered with harsh words. That is foreign to family love. *Parakaleō* (**appeal**) can mean "to encourage, admonish, entreat, or appeal." It could perhaps best be translated "strengthen," and has the idea of coming alongside to hold up one who is weak. The related word *paraklētos* is a title of the Holy Spirit (cf. John 14:16, 26; 15:26; 16:7). The Scriptures are also a source of strength (cf. Rom. 15:4). As the Word of God and the Spirit of God strengthen believers, so must we come to their aid when they sin. Galatians 6:1–2 addresses this duty by saying, "Brethren, even if a man is caught in any trespass, you who are spiritual, restore such a one in a spirit of gentleness; each one looking to yourself, lest you too be tempted. Bear one another's burdens, and thus fulfill the law of Christ."

Confronting sin in the church is not to be done by violently attacking fallen brothers and sisters. Rather, sinning saints must be lovingly confronted, strengthened, and encouraged toward holy living. It is to be a restorative, redemptive, remedial confrontation, one that must be done with an attitude of gentleness (cf. 2 Tim. 2:24–25).

Having set forth in general the principle for dealing with sin in the family, Paul applies it to four groups: older men, younger men, older women, and younger women.

Confronting Older Men

an older man . . . as a father, (5:1b)

An older man is to be treated with respect by being appealed to **as a father.** *Presbuteros* (**older man**) is not used here to speak of the office of elder (as in 5:17 and 19). The context indicates that Paul has in mind the general category of older men. As a young man, Timothy was to confront sinning older men with the same respect and deference he would show his own father.

The Bible makes it quite clear that older men are to be treated with respect. Leviticus 19:32 commands, "You shall rise up before the grayheaded, and honor the aged." Proverbs 16:31 says that "a gray head is a crown of glory" (cf. Prov. 20:29; Job 32:4, 6). Respect for one's father is also commanded in Scripture. Proverbs 4:1–4 reads,

> Hear, O sons, the instruction of a father, and give attention that you may gain understanding, for I give you sound teaching; do not abandon my instruction. When I was a son to my father, tender and the only son in the sight of my mother, then he taught me and said to me, "Let your heart hold fast my words; keep my commandments and live."

Proverbs 30:17 warns in graphic terms of the consequences of not showing that respect: "The eye that mocks a father, and scorns a mother, the ravens of the valley will pick it out, and the young eagles will eat it." Disobedience to one's father in the Old Testament could even result in death: "He who curses his father or his mother shall surely be put to death" (Ex. 21:17). The same respect shown to one's **father** must be shown when rebuking any **older man.**

Although not involving a family situation, Daniel's rebuke of Nebuchadnezzar is a model of how to approach a sinning older man. In Daniel 4:27, Daniel showed great respect when confronting Nebuchadnezzar's sin: "Therefore, O king, may my advice be pleasing to you: break away now from your sins by doing righteousness, and from your iniquities by showing mercy to the poor, in case there may be a prolonging of your prosperity."

Another illustration is found in Paul's rebuke of Peter in Galatians 2:11–14:

> But when Cephas came to Antioch, I opposed him to his face, because he stood condemned. For prior to the coming of certain men from James, he used to eat with the Gentiles; but when they came, he began to withdraw and hold himself aloof, fearing the party of the circumcision. And the rest of the Jews joined him in hypocrisy, with the result that even Barnabas was carried away by their hypocrisy. But when I saw that they were not straightforward about the truth of the gospel, I said to Cephas in the presence of all, "If you, being a Jew, live like the Gentiles and not like the Jews, how is it that you compel the Gentiles to live like Jews?"

While he confronted Peter for his wrongdoing, Paul nevertheless did so with respect and deference. He didn't make an accusatory declaration, but gently asked him a question.

Confronting anyone in sin with gentleness is the responsibility of every believer. When that sinning brother is an older man, however, it must be done with special respect.

Confronting Younger Men

to the younger men as brothers, (5:1c)

The key word for confronting **younger men** is to treat them **as brothers.** Viewing them as **brothers** assumes no air of superiority; that term implies the absence of any hierarchy. In the Old Testament, the Israelites were forbidden to hate their brothers. Leviticus 19:17 says, "You shall not hate your fellow countryman in your heart; you may surely reprove your neighbor, but shall not incur sin because of him." Such love and humility was exhibited in Joseph's attitude toward his brothers despite their evil treatment of him (cf. Gen. 45:4ff.; 50:15ff.).

The New Testament also commands believers to love each other as brothers. The apostle John wrote,

> The one who says he is in the light and yet hates his brother is in the darkness until now. The one who loves his brother abides in the light and there is no cause for stumbling in him. But the one who hates his brother is in the darkness and walks in the darkness, and does not know where he is going because the darkness has blinded his eyes. (1 John 2:9–11; cf. 3:11–15)

Peter exhorted believers to "love the brotherhood" (1 Peter 2:17), as did Paul: "Be devoted to one another in brotherly love" (Rom. 12:10). The writer of Hebrews also commands believers to love each other: "Let love of the brethren continue" (Heb. 13:1).

Such love does not preclude confrontation for sin. As already noted, our Lord commanded such rebukes in Matthew 18:15: "And if your brother sins, go and reprove him." In Luke 17:3 He said, "If your brother sins, rebuke him; and if he repents, forgive him." As noted earlier, Paul wrote in Galatians 6:1 concerning Christian brothers caught in a trespass. To the Thessalonians he wrote,

> Now we command you, brethren, in the name of our Lord Jesus Christ, that you keep aloof from every brother who leads an unruly life and not according to the tradition which you received from us. . . . And if anyone does not obey our instruction in this letter, take special note of that man and do not associate with him, so that he may be put to shame. And yet do not regard him as an enemy, but admonish him as a brother. (2 Thess. 3:6, 14–15)

As the above verses indicate, brotherly confrontations are to be done in humility and love. That is the spirit to be present when confronting a younger man.

Confronting Older Women

the older women as mothers, (5:2a)

Older women are to be treated gently, **as mothers.** The Bible commands respect for mothers. Exodus 20:12 says, "Honor your father and your mother, that your days may be prolonged in the land which the Lord your God gives you" (cf. Deut. 5:16). Proverbs also stresses the importance of honoring mothers: "Hear, my son, your father's instruction, and do not forsake your mother's teaching" (1:8); "My son, observe the commandment of your father, and do not forsake the teaching of your mother" (6:20); "Listen to your father who begot you, and do not despise your mother when she is old" (23:22).

The apostle Paul furnishes us with an example of how to treat **older women.** In Philippians 4:1–3, he gave advice on how to deal with two women who were causing trouble at Philippi:

> Therefore, my beloved brethren whom I long to see, my joy and crown, so stand firm in the Lord, my beloved. I urge Euodia and I urge Syntyche to live in harmony in the Lord. Indeed, true comrade, I ask you also to help these women who have shared my struggle in the cause of the gospel, together with Clement also, and the rest of my fellow workers, whose names are in the book of life.

Even though those two women were harming the cause of Christ in Philippi, Paul nevertheless responded to their harm in a gracious, gentle manner. While rebuking them, he included them among the brethren that he loved. He also noted their service to him in the cause of the gospel. Paul lovingly treated them as he would his own mother.

Confronting Younger Women

the younger women as sisters, in all purity. (5:2b)

Scripture is clear that the **purity** of **younger women** is to be protected. Incest was strictly forbidden by the Old Testament law (cf. Lev. 18:9–18; 20:17–19; Deut. 27:22). By commanding Timothy to treat **the younger women as sisters,** Paul stresses that he must be indifferent to them in terms of lust. There are few things as evil as a pastor who sins mentally or physically with a young woman he had been helping spiritually. That is nothing less than incest in the spiritual family. For that reason, Paul adds the phrase **in all purity.**

Nothing so easily makes or breaks a young pastor as his conduct with women. Thoughtlessness or indiscretion, as well as outright immorality, violate his calling to lead the flock to purity. Younger women must be confronted with their sin and encouraged to godliness. They must, however, never be led into sin, but be treated as beloved spiritual sisters whose purity is the highest consideration.

The book of Proverbs gives some very practical advice on how to maintain **purity** in relationships with **younger women.**

First, avoid the look. Proverbs 6:25 says, "Do not . . . let her catch you with her eyelids." Our commitment must be that of Job: "I have made a covenant with my eyes; how then could I gaze at a virgin" (Job 31:1)?

Second, avoid the flattery. Proverbs 5:3 warns, "For the lips of an adulteress drip honey, and smoother than oil is her speech" (cf. 2:16; 6:24; 22:14).

Third, avoid the thoughts. Proverbs 6:25 says, "Do not desire her beauty in your heart."

Fourth, avoid the rendezvous. Proverbs 7 gives the following account of the naive youth:

> I saw among the naive, I discerned among the youths, a young man lacking sense, passing through the street near her corner; and he takes the way to her house, in the twilight, in the evening, in the middle of the night and in the darkness. And behold, a woman comes to meet him, dressed as a harlot and cunning of heart. She is boisterous and rebellious; her feet do not remain at home; she is now in the streets, now in the squares, and lurks by every corner. (vv. 7–12)

Great care must be taken when meeting with younger women.

Fifth, avoid the house. Proverbs 7:25–27 warns "Do not let your heart turn aside to her ways, do not stray into her paths. For many are the victims she has cast down, and numerous are all her slain. Her house is the way to Sheol, descending to the chambers of death" (cf. Prov. 5:8).

Finally, avoid the touch. Proverbs 7:13 records the result of the naive youth's failure to avoid the rendezvous: "So she seizes him and kisses him." That was the next step in a process that culminated in immorality.

It is a necessary part of ministry to deal with the sins of older men, younger men, older women, and younger women. In the corrective process, each of those groups must be treated in the proper way. Paul's instructions to Timothy send a clear message to all believers on how to confront sin in the spiritual family.

17 The Care of Widows in the Church—part 1 The Ministry of the Church to Widows

Honor widows who are widows indeed; but if any widow has children or grandchildren, let them first learn to practice piety in regard to their own family, and to make some return to their parents; for this is acceptable in the sight of God. Now she who is a widow indeed, and who has been left alone has fixed her hope on God, and continues in entreaties and prayers night and day. But she who gives herself to wanton pleasure is dead even while she lives. Prescribe these things as well, so that they may be above reproach. But if anyone does not provide for his own, and especially for those of his household, he has denied the faith, and is worse than an unbeliever. (5:3–8)

God has always designed that women be the special objects of care. They are to be under the umbrella of male protection, provision, authority, and direction. Anyone who believes that women, like men, are to support themselves needs to recognize the obvious fact that this whole section is concerned only with helping women in need. It assumes the divine design that calls men to support themselves and their wives, and a woman to love and serve the one who supports her. When that support is gone, she is still to be cared for. That is obvious through this entire text. Because of that, God takes a special interest in the plight of women who have lost their husbands. Psalm 68:5 describes God as "a father of the fatherless and a judge for the widows." Exodus 22:22–24 gives the following stern warning about the treatment of widows: "You shall not afflict any widow or orphan. If you afflict him at all, and if he does cry out to Me, I will surely hear his cry; and My anger will be kindled, and I will kill you with the sword; and your wives shall become widows and your children fatherless." Deuteronomy 27:19 adds, "Cursed is he who distorts the justice due an alien, orphan, and widow." In Isaiah 1:17 God says, "Learn to do good; seek justice, reprove the ruthless; defend the orphan, plead for the widow." Psalm 146:9 reads, "The Lord protects the strangers; He supports the fatherless and the widow." God's people must treat widows with the same special care that He does.

Ideally, the Old Testament indicates, widows were to remarry. Where remarriage was delayed or impossible, they were to remain in their father's house (Gen. 38:11), or even the home of their mother-in-law (Ruth 1:16). Further, under the levirate marriage provision of the law, a widow's unmarried brother-in-law was to marry her. If he were already married, the duty devolved to the next nearest kin (cf. Deut. 25:5–10). An example of that principle in action was the marriage of Boaz to Ruth (Ruth 3:12; 4:1–10).

In the New Testament, our Lord Jesus Christ reveals the compassionate heart of God toward widows. In Mark 12:41–44, He commended the poor widow who gave out of her poverty:

> And He sat down opposite the treasury, and began observing how the multitude were putting money into the treasury; and many rich people were putting in large sums. And a poor widow came and put in two small copper coins, which amount to a cent. And calling His disciples to Him, He said to them, "Truly I say to you, this poor widow put in more than all the contributors to the treasury; for they all put in out of their surplus, but she, out of her poverty, put in all she owned, all she had to live on."

That passage gives an insight into the status of widows in first-century Jewish culture. They were usually poor, and often destitute, without any means of earning a living since women were barred from employment outside the home. The hardship faced by widows is illustrated by our Lord's parable of the widow and the judge (Luke 18:1ff.; cf. Luke 20:47).

It fell upon the local synagogues to relieve the plight of widows. Customarily, a group from each synagogue would make the rounds on Friday mornings, collecting goods and money to be distributed to the needy widows later in the afternoon. In spite of those efforts, however, many widows were still impoverished, as the above passage indicates.

Luke 7:11–17 is another text which demonstrates God's loving concern for widows:

> And it came about soon afterwards, that He went to a city called Nain; and His disciples were going along with Him, accompanied by a large multitude. Now as He approached the gate of the city, behold, a dead man was being carried out, the only son of his mother, and she was a widow; and a sizeable crowd from the city was with her. And when the Lord saw her, He felt compassion for her, and said to her, "Do not weep." And He came up and touched the coffin; and the bearers came to a halt. And He said, "Young man, I say to you, arise!" And the dead man sat up, and began to speak. And Jesus gave him back to his mother. And fear gripped them all, and they began glorifying God, saying, "A great prophet has arisen among us!" and, "God has visited His people!" And this report concerning Him went out all over Judea, and in all the surrounding district.

This widow's situation was desperate, since the dead man was her only son. Without him, she had no means of support. Our Lord was so moved with compassion over her plight that He raised her son from the dead.

It is not surprising that the first ministry to develop in the early church involved the care of widows. The early Christians continued in the tradition of the Jewish synagogue, motivated in their efforts by the love of Christ. A conflict over the fairness of the treatment of Hellenistic Jewish widows caused the apostles to organize what had been a spontaneous ministry. Accordingly, they chose seven godly men to oversee it.

Acts 9:36–41 gives further insight into the early church's ministry to widows:

> Now in Joppa there was a certain disciple named Tabitha (which translated in Greek is called Dorcas); this woman was abounding with deeds of kindness and charity, which she continually did. And it came about at that time that she fell sick and died; and when they had washed her body, they laid it in an upper room. And since Lydda was near Joppa, the disciples, having heard that Peter was there, sent two men to him, entreating him, "Do not delay to come to us." And Peter arose and went with them. And when he had come, they brought him into the upper room; and all the widows stood beside him weeping, and showing all the tunics and garments that Dorcas used to make while she was with them. But Peter sent them all out and knelt down and prayed, and turning to the body, he said, "Tabitha, arise." And she

> opened her eyes, and when she saw Peter, she sat up. And he gave her his hand and raised her up; and calling the saints and widows, he presented her alive.

Dorcas was a godly Christian woman who gave of her time and resources to support widows. That shows once again the destitution of widows in that culture, and the compassionate heart of believers toward them. This is the second resurrection in the New Testament specifically to benefit widows.

The church still has the responsibility to care for widows. James 1:27 defines true religion as visiting "orphans and widows in their distress." To help Timothy lead the church at Ephesus to understand their responsibility to widows, Paul gives five principles to guide that service. This was a corrective passage for the Ephesian church, which undoubtedly was not handling this important duty appropriately. So Paul is compelled by the Holy Spirit to write instructions on the whole range of issues relating to widows.

The Obligation of the Church to Support Widows

Honor widows who are widows indeed; (5:3)

The English word *widow* describes a woman whose husband is dead. The Greek word *chēra* ("widow") includes that meaning, but is not limited to it. It is an adjective used as a noun, and means "bereft," "robbed," "having suffered loss," or "left alone." The word does not speak of how a woman was left alone, it merely describes the situation. It is broad enough to encompass those who lost their husbands through death, desertion, divorce, or imprisonment. It could even encompass those cases where a polygamist came to Christ and sent away his extra wives (William Barclay, *The Letters to Timothy, Titus, and Philemon* [Philadelphia: Westminster, 1975], 105).

The responsibility of the church thus extends to all qualifying women who have lost their husbands. With divorce and desertion rampant in our society, we face an even greater challenge than the Ephesian church.

The treatment of widows tests the spiritual character of the Christian community. Believers' devotion to Christ can be seen in how they treat those without resources. Through the care it provides, the church manifests Christ's love to the needy and gives witness of Christlike love to the watching world. Such care has been a part of the church's life throughout its history. The welfare system of Western nations is a direct legacy of the church's influence.

Honor is from *timaō* and means "to show respect or care," "to support," or "to treat graciously." It encompasses meeting needs, including financial ones (cf. Matt. 27:9, where it is used of pricing something; and 1 Tim. 5:17).

Matthew 15:1–6 further supports the use of *timaō* in reference to financial support:

> Then some Pharisees and scribes came to Jesus from Jerusalem, saying, "Why do Your disciples transgress the tradition of the elders? For they do not wash their hands when they eat bread." And He answered and said to them, "And why do you yourselves transgress the commandment of God for the sake of your tradition? For God said, 'Honor your father and mother,' and, 'He who speaks evil of father or mother, let him be put to death.' But you say, 'Whoever shall say to his father or mother, "Anything of mine you might have been helped by has been given to God,"' he is not to honor his father or his mother. And thus you invalidated the word of God for the sake of your tradition."

First-century Judaism had developed an intricate system of extrabiblical regulations, some of which contradicted Scripture. Jesus rebuked them because of one of those most wicked traditions. They thought that a person could avoid his responsibility to support his parents if he had devoted that money to God. As our Lord points out, however, that selfish and hypocritical tradition directly contradicts the Old Testament command to honor one's parents. In so saying, Jesus equates honoring parents with providing them financial support. Paul borrows the thought of Exodus 20:12, as interpreted by our Lord. He has in mind here not mere respect, but also money.

The church is not obligated to support all widows, only those who are **widows indeed.** Not all widows are truly alone and without means. Some have resources left them by their husbands or through their remaining family or friends. They do, however, need the spiritual comfort and care of the church. Financial support is to go to those completely alone and without necessary resources for daily life.

It is a sad commentary on our society that the number of bereft women in need of support is rising. The disintegration of the family not only creates more such women, but destroys the network of family support they depend on. The loss of that support will increase the burden on the church in the years ahead. That does not, however, alter the church's responsibility. Churches will have to look honestly and carefully at how much money they are spending on activities that have no biblical mandate. Such activities spend money that is then not available for widows.

THE OBLIGATION OF THE CHURCH TO EVALUATE THE NEEDS OF WIDOWS

but if any widow has children or grandchildren, let them first learn to practice piety in regard to their own family, and to make some return to their parents; for this is acceptable in the sight of God. Now she who is a widow indeed, and who has been left alone has fixed her hope on God, and continues in entreaties and prayers night and day. But she who gives herself to wanton pleasure is dead even while she lives. Prescribe these things as well, so that they may be above reproach. But if anyone does not provide for his own, and especially for those of his household, he has denied the faith, and is worse than an unbeliever. (5:4–8)

The church cannot indiscriminately support all widows who ask for assistance (cf. v. 3). Paul lists the criteria for determining what widows the church should support in verses 4–8. These verses define **a widow indeed.**

Widows with **children or grandchildren** are to receive support from them, not the church. The family has the primary responsibility for its own widows. A widow's relatives must **first learn to practice piety in regard to their own family.** The adverb *prōton* (**first**) means first in time or priority. **Piety,** or godliness, begins in one's **own family,** since the family is the context in which genuine godliness is manifested (cf. 3:4, 5, 12; 5:8).

Supporting widows is not only a mark of godliness, but of obedience. Believers are commanded **to make some return to their parents.** They owe a debt to those who brought them into the world, clothed them, fed them, housed them, supported them, and loved and nurtured them. Caring for a mother in the time of her need is but a small return for all she has done. **This,** Paul writes, **is acceptable in the sight of God** (cf. Ex. 20:12). The phrase carries a heavy responsibility, since it makes it obvious that this is a matter of priority for every child of God. No one can ever question what God requires in this area.

The principle that children must support their parents was generally accepted even in the pagan world. William Barclay writes a very interesting section on this historical perspective:

> It was Greek law from the time of Solon that sons and daughters were, not only morally, but also legally bound to support their parents. Any-

> one who refused that duty lost his civil rights. Aeschines, the Athenian orator, says in one of his speeches: "And whom did our law-giver (Solon) condemn to silence in the Assembly of the people? And where does he make this clear? 'Let there be,' he says, 'a scrutiny of public speakers, in case there be any speaker in the Assembly of the people who is a striker of his father or mother, or who neglects to maintain them or to give them a home.'" Demosthenes says: "I regard the man who neglects his parents as unbelieving in and hateful to the gods, as well as to men." Philo, writing of the commandment to honour parents, says: "When old storks become unable to fly, they remain in their nests and are fed by their children, who go to endless exertions to provide their food because of their piety." To Philo it was clear that even the animal creation acknowledged its obligations to aged parents, and how much more must men? Aristotle in the *Nichomachean Ethics* lays it down: "It would be thought in the matter of food we should help our parents before all others, since we owe our nourishment to them, and it is more honourable to help in this respect the authors of our being, even before ourselves." As Aristotle saw it, a man must himself starve before he would see his parents starve. Plato in *The Laws* has the same conviction of the debt that is owed parents: "Next comes the honour of loving parents, to whom, as is meet, we have to pay the first and greatest and oldest of debts, considering that all which a man has belongs to those who gave him birth and brought him up, and that he must do all that he can to minister to them; first, in his property; secondly, in his person; and thirdly, in his soul; paying the debts due to them for their care and travail which they bestowed upon him of old in the days of his infancy, and which he is now able to pay back to them, when they are old and in the extremity of their need." (*The Letters to Timothy, Titus, and Philemon* [Philadelphia: Westminster, 1975], 106–7)

Joseph is an illustration of a man who honored his parents in obedience to the law of God. In Genesis 45:9–11 he said,

> Hurry and go up to my father, and say to him, "Thus says your son Joseph, 'God has made me lord of all Egypt; come down to me, do not delay. And you shall live in the land of Goshen, and you shall be near me, you and your children and your children's children and your flocks and your herds and all that you have. There I will also provide for you, for there are still five years of famine to come, lest you and your household and all that you have be impoverished.'"

Jacob came to Egypt as invited and Joseph cared for him and all those with him (Gen. 46:26ff.). Such honor and care is what God expects of every believer.

Paul returns to the term **widow indeed** to further define **she who** is such. There are several features to consider. The first criterion for determining true widowhood is whether she has family. A widow **who has been left alone** meets that requirement. **Has been left alone** is from *monoō.* Our English word "mono," which means "single," derives from it. The perfect tense of the participle indicates a permanent state or condition of being forsaken and without resources. Obviously she is one who has no supporting family and the church has an obligation to such.

A second criterion is that a widow be a believer. She must be one who **has fixed her hope on God.** The perfect tense of the verb *elpizō* (**hope**) again indicates a continual state or condition. Her settled attitude is one of hope in God. That demonstrates the genuineness of her faith.

The specific contents of her **hope** include God's promises to care for widows. She looks to God for her help and thus obeys the command of Jeremiah 49:11: "Let your widows trust in Me." She trusts that God will provide her needs as He did for the widow of Zarephath in 1 Kings 17:8–16:

> Then the word of the Lord came to him, saying, "Arise, go to Zarephath, which belongs to Sidon, and stay there; behold, I have commanded a widow there to provide for you." So he arose and went to Zarephath, and when he came to the gate of the city, behold, a widow was there gathering sticks; and he called to her and said, "Please get me a little water in a jar, that I may drink." And as she was going to get it, he called to her and said, "Please bring me a piece of bread in your hand." But she said, "As the Lord your God lives, I have no bread, only a handful of flour in the bowl and a little oil in the jar; and behold, I am gathering a few sticks that I may go in and prepare for me and my son, that we may eat it and die." Then Elijah said to her, "Do not fear; go, do as you have said, but make me a little bread cake from it first, and bring it out to me, and afterward you may make one for yourself and for your son. For thus says the Lord God of Israel, 'The bowl of flour shall not be exhausted, nor shall the jar of oil be empty, until the day that the Lord sends rain on the face of the earth.'" So she went and did according to the word of Elijah, and she and he and her household ate for many days. The bowl of flour was not exhausted nor did the jar of oil become empty, according to the word of the Lord which He spoke through Elijah.

Only to such women does the church have a responsibility. Believers may choose to help non-Christian widows (cf. Gal. 6:10), but the church is obligated by heaven's command to help believing ones.

A third criterion is that a widow be a godly believer. She must be one who **continues in entreaties and prayers night and day.** Such devotion to communion with the Lord is a mark of a committed Christian. *Deēsis* (**entreaties**) refers to any manner or kind of requests, and could include the pleas for personal needs. Such praying shows her total dependence on God to supply her needs. *Proseuchē* (**prayers**) is a more general term. It refers to communion with God, which includes worship and praise. She not only makes requests of God, but also worships and communes with Him. **Night and day** is a Jewish idiomatic expression that means "constantly," or "all the time" (cf. Acts 20:31; 1 Thess. 2:9; 3:10; 2 Thess. 3:8). Throughout the day and night she lifts her heart to God in prayer and praise (cf. 1 Thess. 5:17; Eph. 6:18).

Such a widow was the prophetess Anna:

> And there was a prophetess, Anna the daughter of Phanuel, of the tribe of Asher. She was advanced in years, having lived with a husband seven years after her marriage, and then as a widow to the age of eighty-four. And she never left the temple, serving night and day with fastings and prayers. (Luke 2:36–37)

She was devoted to the service of the Lord, having never remarried. To her was given the privilege of seeing the Messiah. She is a model for the godly widows who receive care from the church.

On the other hand, a widow **who gives herself to wanton pleasure** does not qualify. *Spatalaō* (**gives herself to wanton pleasure**) appears only one other time in the New Testament (cf. James 5:5). The Septuagint, the Greek translation of the Old Testament, uses the term in Ezekiel 16:49. It is translated there "careless ease." The word describes the person who leads a life of pleasure with no thought of what is right or wrong. Such a widow, Paul declares, **is dead even while she lives.** Although she may be alive physically, she is dead spiritually. While she was no doubt involved in the church when her husband was around, she is clearly unregenerate (**dead;** cf. Eph. 2:1). Far from being supported by the church, such women need to be abandoned to the consequences of their sin. Their desperate situation may then lead them to repentance. In the meantime, kingdom resources must not be used to support a sinful lifestyle. The truth that such widows are not to be supported is so obvious that Paul does not bother to command it.

Paul then instructs Timothy to **prescribe** (command) **these things as well, so that they may be above reproach. These things** gathers up everything the apostle has said since verse 3. The goal of Paul's teaching is that all involved, widows, families, and the church,

be above reproach so that no one can find fault with their conduct in this matter. The church's reputation, and that of her Lord, are at stake. By supporting those widows who are deserving, and refusing to support those who are not, the church, as well as its pastors (cf. 3:2), will be above criticism and God will be honored.

Verse 8 states negatively the truth expressed positively in verse 4. In verse 4, Paul commanded that children take care of their parents. Here he states that those who fail to do so are worse than unbelievers, who naturally do so. The repetition of the principle implies there were many violations of it in the church at Ephesus. The phrase **but if anyone does not provide for his own, and especially for those of his household** is a first-class conditional statement in the original. It could be translated, "When any of you does not provide," or, "Since some of you are not providing." **Provide** is from *pronoeō,* which means "to plan before." It describes the forethought necessary to provide care for the widows in one's family.

The phrase **for his own** is purposely vague. It refers to anyone within the circle of family relationships, surely even servants or close friends. A believing man who is head of a house has a mandated responsibility to provide **for those of his household.** The latter group is more narrow than the phrase **his own.** It focuses on those in the immediate family, where his responsibility begins.

Failing to provide for those in either the narrow or the wide circle makes a believer guilty of two things. First, **he has denied the faith.** That does not refer to the loss of his personal salvation. Paul here is not judging the soul but the actions. Rather, it means that such a person has denied the principle of compassionate love that is at the heart of the Christian **faith** (cf. John 13:35; Rom. 5:5; 1 Thess. 4:9). There must be no dichotomy between faith and conduct.

Second, his failure makes him in practice **worse than an unbeliever.** As already noted, even the pagans knew the importance of and felt the duty of providing for their parents. For believers to fail to measure up to that standard is inexcusable. They are under greater condemnation because they have the commandment of God to love, and the power of God to enable them to do so.

The supreme example of loving care for the widows in one's family can be seen in our Lord Jesus Christ. On the cross, nearing death, He nevertheless arranged the care of His widowed mother. John 19:26–27 relates the story: "When Jesus therefore saw His mother, and the disciple whom He loved standing nearby, He said to His mother, 'Woman, behold, your son!' Then He said to the disciple, 'Behold, your mother!' And from that hour the disciple took her into his own household." That shows the importance of the issue of caring for widows. Jesus spoke from the cross to only two individuals. He forgave the dying thief, and arranged for the care of His widowed mother. Nothing so clearly reveals the heart of God as that. While bearing the burden of the world's sins, Jesus' mind was concerned with the salvation of one sinner, and the care of one widow.

The care of widows begins with each believer. The church cannot do collectively what it will not do individually. It is a responsibility that cannot be avoided.

The Care of Widows in the Church—part 2 The Ministry of Widows to the Church

18

Let a widow be put on the list only if she is not less than sixty years old, having been the wife of one man, having a reputation for good works; and if she has brought up children, if she has shown hospitality to strangers, if she has washed the saints' feet, if she has assisted those in distress, and if she has devoted herself to every good work. But refuse to put younger widows on the list, for when they feel sensual desires in disregard of Christ, they want to get married, thus incurring condemnation, because they have set aside their previous pledge. And at the same time they also learn to be idle, as they go around from house to house; and not merely idle, but also gossips and busybodies, talking about things not proper to mention. Therefore, I want younger widows to get married, bear children, keep house, and give the enemy no occasion for reproach; for some have already turned aside to follow Satan. If any woman who is a believer has dependent widows, let her assist them, and let not the church be burdened, so that it may assist those who are widows indeed. (5:9–16)

The church has an obligation to support those widows in its midst who are in need. Doing so reflects the compassionate heart of God toward those women bereft of their husbands.

Far from being a liability for the church, however, the older widows are a valuable asset. They have a wealth of wisdom and experience to share with younger women. They also have the time to participate in a wide range of ministries. Having discussed the church's ministry toward true widows in verses 3–8, Paul gives guidelines in verses 9–16 for the widows' ministry to the church.

The Obligation of the Church to Maintain High Standards for Widows Who Serve in the Church

Let a widow be put on the list only if she is not less than sixty years old, having been the wife of one man, having a reputation for good works; and if she has brought up children, if she has shown hospitality to strangers, if she has washed the saints' feet, if she has assisted those in distress, and if she has devoted herself to every good work. (5:9–10)

In the early church there were groups of widows who served in some officially recognized capacity. The requirements for being **put on the list,** reminiscent of those for church leaders given in chapter 3, make that evident. This godly group of women had a spiritual and practical ministry directly to the women and children of the church. They also ministered indirectly to the men by virtue of their influence on the women. They fulfilled Paul's injunction in Titus 2:3–5 that

> older women likewise are to be reverent in their behavior, not malicious gossips, nor enslaved to much wine, teaching what is good, that they may encourage the young women to love their husbands, to love their children, to be sensible, pure, workers at home, kind, being subject to their own husbands, that the word of God may not be dishonored.

Their duties surely included helping with the baptism of women, visiting the sick, visiting prisoners, teaching and discipling younger women, helping younger women rear and nurture their children, and providing hospitality for visitors and strangers. They may have also assisted in placing orphans into proper Christian homes. That was a very important ministry in the Roman world, since orphaned or abandoned children wound up as slaves, and often as prostitutes or gladiators. With their own husbands gone and their children grown, those widows had the time to pursue such essential ministries.

That such a group of widows existed in the early church is known from extrabiblical sources. In the late first and early second centuries, Ignatius and Polycarp wrote of such an order. Tertullian, who lived in the latter part of the second and early part of the third centuries, also mentioned it. The third-century document known as the *Didascalia,* and the fourth-century *Apostolic Constitutions* also refer to an order of widows.

There is no evidence that all the widows **on the list** were supported by the church. Some no doubt were, while others had resources of their own. The issue of support stops at verse 8, and Paul moves to a new topic in verse 9. **The list** Paul refers to was not, as some have argued, the list of those widows eligible for support. Rather, it was the list of those eligible for ministry. In verses 9–10 Paul gives the requirements for being **on the list.**

First, a widow had to be **not less than sixty years old.** That requirement offers further proof that the list of widows was not a list of those eligible to receive support. Paul had just stated in verses 3–8 that the church is to support all its widows who are without other means of support. No age requirement was given there.

Sixty was the age in that culture for people to retire from their activities to a life of contemplation. It was at that age that men and women should become priests and priestesses, according to Plato (William Barclay, *The Letters to Timothy, Titus, and Philemon* [Philadelphia: Westminster, 1975], 109). It was acknowledged that sexual passion began to wane at age sixty. Thus, the age requirement ensures that those widows would not be driven by desire. An older woman would have the time, maturity, character, reputation, and compassion to serve the Lord and the church. Unlike a younger woman, she would not be tempted to abandon her commitment to the Lord and remarry.

Second, a widow must have **been the wife of one man.** The Greek text literally reads "a one-man woman," a construction parallel to that of 3:2 and 12. That does not exclude women who have been married more than once. Paul himself commands younger widows to remarry (v. 14; cf. 1 Cor. 7:39), so that cannot be his intent here. A "one-man woman" is a woman who was totally devoted to her husband. It speaks of purity in action and attitude, as in the case of the overseer in 3:2, who is to be a "one-woman man"; it does not refer to marital status. Such a woman lived in complete fidelity to her husband in a chaste, pure, unspotted marriage relationship. A widow who did not measure up to this standard would not be a proper role model for the younger women to emulate.

Third, a widow had to have **a reputation for good works.** Her excellent character was to be common knowledge. Like the elders (3:2) and deacons (3:10), she had to be above reproach. Her good works would attest to the kind of woman she was. They would manifest outwardly the quality of her spiritual character.

Paul goes on to further define the nature of **a reputation for good works.** The five qualities he lists show the type of **good works** required of any woman. All women should seek to be of such spiritual virtue as to be **put on the list** to serve the church should they become widows.

First, **she** must be one who **has brought up children.** *Teknotropheō* (**brought up children**) appears only here in the New Testament. It means to nourish children. This quality views the godly widow as a Christian mother, rearing children in a godly home to follow the Lord. To do so is a woman's greatest privilege and responsibility (cf. 2:15).

Paul does not here depreciate women who were unable to have children, or who had the gift of singleness. Such fulfill different roles in the life of the family of God. Since having children was the norm, however, he gives this as a general principle. A woman with no natural children of her own could manifest this quality by rearing orphans. Only a woman with such experience could instruct younger women on how to rear godly children (cf. Titus 2:3–5).

Second, **she** must be one who **has shown hospitality to strangers.** Like the elders, she must be devoted to hospitality (cf. 3:2). Her home must be open to strangers, as well as friends and relatives. She must show sacrificial devotion to the needs of people she does not know. There were no motels or hotels in the ancient world, and inns were often filthy and dangerous. Christians away from home depended on the hospitality of other believers. Paul commended Phoebe as a "helper of many, and of myself as well" (Rom. 16:2). No doubt one of the ways she helped others was by opening her home to those in need of shelter and food.

This offers further evidence that the list Paul speaks of was not one of destitute widows in need of support. Such women would hardly have been able to open their homes to provide for others.

Third, **she** must be one who **has washed the saints' feet.** That menial task was the duty of slaves. Since the roads were either dusty or muddy, guests entering a house had their feet washed. Paul does not necessarily mean that she actually did that herself each time. The menial task of washing the feet spoke metaphorically of humility (cf. John 13:5–17). The requirement, then, stresses that a widow have a humble, servant's heart. She gives her life in lowly service to those in need and never seeks to exalt herself.

Fourth, **she** must be one who **has assisted those in distress. Those in distress** is from *thlibō,* and could be translated "those under pressure." She devotes her life to helping those under any sort of pressure, whether physical, mental, or emotional. *Eparkeō* (**has assisted**) appears only here and in verse 16. In the latter verse, it clearly refers to financial assistance. A godly widow also assists others with her financial resources.

Fifth, **she** must be one who **has devoted herself to every good work.** *Epakoloutheō* (**has devoted herself to**) is a strong verb. It describes the widow who has energetically and diligently given herself to the pursuit of good deeds (cf. Acts 9:36).

Because all those qualities describe the character of a widow qualified to serve the church, they must also be recognized as the standards for every Christian woman to follow in her life. Should the day come when she is considered for service in the church, she will then be qualified. In the mean time, she will gain a reputation as a woman of excellence (cf. Prov. 31:10–31).

The qualities Paul gives illustrate God's design for women. They are a woman's highest priorities. By following them, she can make a profound impact on the world. That truth is illustrated in a story told by the Scottish preacher Ian MacClaren of a woman in his church.

As they were talking, she began to wipe her eyes with the corner of her apron, so Dr. MacClaren said, "What's disturbing you?"

"Oh," she said, "Sometimes I feel I have done so little and when I think about it it makes my heart heavy, because really I've done so little for Jesus."

"When I was a wee girl the Lord spoke to my heart and I surrendered to Him. And I wanted to live for Him, oh so much. But I feel I haven't done anything."

"What have you done with your life?" he asked.

"Oh nothing," she said, "just nothing. I've washed dishes, cooked three meals a day, taken care of my children, mopped the floor, mended the clothes, you know, everything a mother does, that's all I've done."

MacClaren sat back in his chair and asked, "Where are your boys?"

"Oh, she spoke, "You know I named them all for the gospels, Matthew, Mark, Luke, and John. You know them all and you know where Mark is. You ordained him. He went to China. He's learned the language and now he is able to minister to the people in the name of the Lord."

"Where's Luke?" MacClaren said.

"You know well enough where he is because you sent him out and I had a letter from him the other day. He is in Africa and says a revival has broken out at his mission station."

"And Matthew?" he queried.

"He's with his brother in China and they are working together. And John, who's nineteen, came to me last night to say God has laid Africa on his heart. He said, 'I'm going to Africa, but don't worry about it, Mother, because the Lord has shown me that I am to stay with you until you go home to glory, and then I'll go. Until then I have to take care of you.'"

MacClaren looked at that elderly saint and said, "Your life has been wasted, you say?"

"Yes, it has been wasted."

"You have been cooking and mopping and washing—but I would like to see the reward when you are called home!"

The Obligation of the Church to Instruct Younger Widows to Remarry

But refuse to put younger widows on the list, for when they feel sensual desires in disregard of Christ, they want to get married, thus incurring condemnation, because they have set aside their previous pledge. And at the same time they also learn to be idle, as they go around from house to house; and not merely idle, but also gossips and busybodies, talking about things not proper to mention. Therefore, I want younger widows to get married, bear children, keep house, and give the enemy no occasion for reproach; for some have already turned aside to follow Satan. (5:11–15)

While qualified older widows are to permanently devote themselves to the service of the church, the plan for younger widows is very different. They are **to get married,** and the church has an obligation to encourage them to do just that. While they must be given aid if it is needed until they remarry, Paul commands Timothy to **refuse to put younger widows on the list** of those who serve the church. They are not to be admitted to the order of widows Paul mentions in verses 9–10.

Paraiteomai (**refuse**) is a strong word, expressing adamancy. It is used in 4:7 to speak of rejecting false teaching. Paul gives two reasons for his prohibition against putting younger widows on the list:

First, their service to the church would not be single minded and their loyalty could waver because **when they feel sensual desires in disregard of Christ, they want to get married.** Paul's concern is that a young widow, out of sorrow for the loss of her husband and gratitude to the church for its support, will make a vow she cannot keep. She will devote herself to remain single and to serve the Lord. According to Numbers 30:9, she will be obligated to keep that vow. Unlike the older women, however, she might eventually begin to **feel sensual desires.** She would then find it difficult to keep the vow she made during the emotional trauma of the loss of her husband. In keeping with those **sensual desires,** which include not merely sexual passion but all that is embodied in the marriage relationship, she would **want to get married.**

Breaking her vow would place her in disregard of Christ. *Katastrēniaō* (**feel sensual desires in disregard of**) appears only here in the New Testament. In extrabiblical literature, it is used to describe an ox trying to escape from its yoke. There is danger that a young widow might desire to escape from her vow of singular devotion to serve only the Lord.

The disastrous consequences of a woman on the list of widows being in that position are readily apparent. While ostensibly a model of spiritual virtue, she could actually become resentful, even hostile toward God. At best, she would be unfulfilled, unhappy, miserable, and unable to teach other women godly virtue. Worse still, her strong desire for a husband would leave her vulnerable. That vulnerability would only be heightened by her ministry to the church's families. She might even be tempted to go after someone else's husband. To Paul it was unthinkable that such a dangerous situation should be allowed to occur.

Such unfaithfulness to a vow has serious repercussions. Younger widows risk **incurring condemnation.** God will chasten them **because they have set aside their previous pledge.** *Pistis* (**pledge**) is the normal New Testament word for faith. In classical Greek, however, it can mean **pledge.** If understood in the sense of faith, Paul would be saying they have abandoned their original commitment to Christ. That commitment, made at salvation, was to love, obey, and serve Him. If translated **pledge,** it would be referring to the specific covenant made when placed on the list of widows. That **pledge** would have been to devote her life to the service of the Lord.

A second reason younger widows are not to be on the list is their lack of maturity: **At the same time they also learn to be idle.** The Greek idiom means "they qualify as idlers." Visits once carried out for the purpose of ministry are now occasions for idleness, **as they go around from house to house.** Nothing constructive takes place and, at best, trivial activity occupies her.

Worse, the potential is present for destructive behavior to take place. These women may become **not merely idle, but also gossips and busybodies, talking about things not proper to mention. Gossips** speak nonsense, talk idly, make empty charges, or accuse with malicious words. **Busybodies** is from *periergos,* which literally means "one who moves around." The implication is one who sticks his nose into other peoples' business. Such people pry into things that do not concern them. In the only other New Testament use of *periergos,* the word refers to practicing magic. People who do that are also guilty of prying into things that do not concern them.

The bottom of the downward spiral is **talking about things not proper to mention.** Proverbs warns against doing that: "He who goes about as a talebearer reveals secrets, but he who is trustworthy conceals a matter" (Prov. 11:13). "For lack of wood the fire goes out, and where there is no whisperer, contention quiets down" (Prov. 26:20). "A perverse man spreads strife, and a slanderer separates intimate friends" (Prov. 16:28). "He who goes about as a slanderer reveals secrets, therefore do not associate with a gossip" (Prov. 20:19). Those widows doing that were guilty of spreading slander instead of the gospel of Jesus Christ. Some may have even been spreading false teaching (cf. 2:11–13).

It takes serious-minded, mature, godly women to minister in homes to women and families. The secrets and problems of those families would be safe with them. For those reasons, as well as the danger that they will abandon their commitments to Christ, Paul forbids younger women to be put on the list.

Therefore, Paul writes, **I want younger widows to get married.** *Boulomai* (**I want**) is the will of desire springing from reason, not emotion. In this passage, it carries the force of a command. Jewish custom encouraged women who lost their husbands legitimately to remarry. The Scriptures also teach that a woman whose husband has died, or who is the innocent party in a divorce, has the right to remarry. Paul wrote in Romans 7:3, "So then if, while her husband is living, she is joined to another man, she shall be called an adulteress; but if her husband dies, she is free from the law, so that she is not an adulteress, though she is joined to another man." To the Corinthians he wrote, "If the unbelieving one leaves, let him leave; the brother or the sister is not under bondage in such cases, but God has called us to peace" (1 Cor. 7:15), and, "A wife is bound as long as her husband lives; but if her husband is dead, she is free to be married to whom she wishes, only in the Lord" (1 Cor. 7:39).

In Matthew 5:31–32 our Lord said, "And it was said, 'Whoever divorces his wife, let him give her a certificate of dismissal'; but I say to you that everyone who divorces his wife, except for the cause of unchastity, makes her commit adultery; and whoever marries a divorced woman commits adultery" (cf. Matt. 19:7–9). Paul is not giving a concession, but a command. Those who argue against remarriage will find no support in this passage. It is God's design for young women who lose their husbands to remarry. That protects them from living a life of singleness, their strong desire for marriage and longing to raise children make them ill suited for. It also protects them from seeking solace in improper relationships. But most importantly, it recognizes that a woman's highest calling is to the home. To argue that the Bible permits divorce but not remarriage raises some difficult questions. What will these women do, if they are barred from their God-designed roles as wives and mothers? Certainly all of them would not have the gift of singleness. How could the church possibly care for all of them? That would be a burden God never intended the church to bear. How could they fulfill the requirements for being included on the list? How could they prove to be one-man women if they had no husband? Younger widows, then, are to get married.

Paul describes the responsibilities of a widow who remarries as to **bear children** and **keep house.** *Teknogoneō* (**bear children**) means to have babies (cf. 2:15), indicating the widows Paul refers to were generally of childbearing age. The contemporary view that children are an inconvenience that cramp one's lifestyle is repulsive to the Lord. On the contrary, the Bible calls children "a gift of the Lord" (Ps. 127:3), and declares "How blessed is the man whose quiver is full of them" (Ps. 127:5). Although a young widow may have lost her husband, she still has the high calling and blessed privilege of bearing children. To do that requires her to remarry.

Keep house is from *oikodespoteō.* It goes beyond raising the children to include all aspects of managing the household. The man provides the resources through his labor, and the woman manages them for the care of her husband and children.

By remarrying and resuming her role in the home, she would **give the enemy no occasion for reproach. The enemy** is not Satan specifically, but encompasses any opponent of the Word of God. Satan, though the ultimate enemy, attacks through human agents. *Aphormē* (**occasion**) refers to a launching point for an attack, or a base of operations. By remarrying and raising a family, a young widow will avoid bringing **reproach** on the cause of Christ. She will avoid falling into some sexual sin or some perversion of God's intended role for women consistent with her calling as described in verse 10. On the other hand, those who violate God's purposes give ammunition to the enemies of the church.

Paul's warning to the Ephesian church was timely, since, tragically, **some** had **already turned aside to follow Satan.** Some of the younger widows had abandoned their vows to Christ. Having forsaken their true calling to have children and manage the home, they had given themselves to various sins (cf. 2 Tim. 3:6). Some were no doubt following false teachers, and even helping to spread false doctrine themselves. Some may have married unbelievers, and thus brought shame to the church. They were no longer serving Christ, but **Satan.** For that reason, Paul's command that the younger widows remarry was all the more urgent.

The Obligation of the Church to Make Sure That Capable Women Support Their Widows

If any woman who is a believer has dependent widows, let her assist them, and let not the church be burdened, so that it may assist those who are widows indeed. (5:16)

Paul brings his argument full circle and restates the truth he has already taught in verses 4 and 8. When no men are available, **any woman who is a believer** must care for her **dependent widows.** She must not ignore their needs, but must **assist them** if she is able. A widow's children and grandchildren have the primary responsibility for her care. Then come her male relatives, and after that her female relatives. Only when such people are unavailable or unable to help does the task fall to the church.

When families take care of their needy widows, **the church** is not **burdened.** It is then free to **assist those who are widows indeed.** Once again, Paul brings his argument full circle (cf. v. 3). Only those widows with no other means of support should be cared for by the church at large.

Helping widows brings the promise of blessing from God. Deuteronomy 14:29 says, "the alien, the orphan and the widow who are in your town, shall come and eat and be satisfied, in order that the Lord your God may bless you in all the work of your hand which you do." On the other hand, failing to do so brings judgment: "Cursed is he who distorts the justice due an alien, orphan, and widow" (Deut. 27:19). God's special love and care for widows must be reflected in the actions of His people.

Restoring Biblical Eldership

19

Let the elders who rule well be considered worthy of double honor, especially those who work hard at preaching and teaching. For the Scripture says, "You shall not muzzle the ox while he is threshing," and "The laborer is worthy of his wages." Do not receive an accusation against an elder except on the basis of two or three witnesses. Those who continue in sin, rebuke in the presence of all, so that the rest also may be fearful of sinning. I solemnly charge you in the presence of God and of Christ Jesus and of His chosen angels, to maintain these principles without bias, doing nothing in a spirit of partiality. Do not lay hands upon anyone too hastily and thus share responsibility for the sins of others; keep yourself free from sin. No longer drink water exclusively, but use a little wine for the sake of your stomach and your frequent ailments. The sins of some men are quite evident, going before them to judgment; for others, their sins follow after. Likewise also, deeds that are good are quite evident, and those which are otherwise cannot be concealed. (5:17–25)

During His life on earth, our Lord Jesus Christ founded only one organization: His church. That is also the only institution He specifically promised to bless (Matt. 16:18). The church was designed and chosen by the Father in eternity past, redeemed by the work of the Son on the cross, and begotten by the power of the Spirit. The church is the chosen channel through which God's saving truth flows to the world. It has temporarily replaced Israel in that capacity, because of the latter's apostasy (cf. Rom. 11:1–24).

The church is to maintain a purity and power that can penetrate the kingdom of darkness with the glorious light of the gospel. By so doing, it will rescue men and women from Satan's control and draw them into the kingdom of light. The church is the body of Christ, the visible form of Christ in the world. It's purpose is to reveal His glory and thus draw men savingly to Himself. The church is also to model godly virtue in an ungodly world by living according to God's commands.

Peter summed all that up when he wrote, "You are a chosen race, a royal priesthood, a holy nation, a people for God's own possession, that you may proclaim the excellencies of Him who has called you out of darkness into His marvelous light" (1 Peter 2:9).

The church's ability to fulfill its calling is humanly dependent on one crucial factor: the quality of its leadership. Hosea's statement, "like people, like priest" (Hos. 4:9) applies today. Churches do not rise higher than the level of their leadership.

Our Lord's plan for assuring that the church would be all He desired it to be was the same one He used when Israel was His witness people. God called Israel to proclaim His character and commands. To lead the nation, He raised up kings, priests, prophets, and elders. Their task was to model godliness and virtue as they gave their lives in the service of the sovereign Jehovah. By so doing, they would lead Israel toward the holiness that would enable her to effectively reach the world with the truth of forgiveness of sin by God's mercy.

Tragically, the history of Israel is largely the history of the failure of its leadership. The story of Israel's leaders is one of decline, apostasy, and defection, which led to the defection of the people. That in turn caused God to temporarily set them aside and cut a new channel for His truth—the church born at Pentecost.

Sadly, the history of the church has often paralleled that of Israel. The same pattern of defection from biblical truth that marred Israel's leadership has too often marked the church's leadership. Paul's call in this text for a restoration of a biblical eldership is one the contemporary church desperately needs to heed since many, if not most, of the problems facing the church can be traced to the failures of its leadership.

The Scripture advocates a shared leadership. A plurality of godly men are to share in the leadership responsibility, though they may differ in their specific functions and giftedness. The Bible knows nothing of one-man rule by pastor-kings. Nor does it envision any authority beyond it to which the leadership of a local congregation must submit. God's plan for choosing leaders in His church is simple. From within each congregation, the Holy Spirit gifts and identifies through their faithfulness a plurality of godly men. After being confirmed by the people, they share the burden of leadership responsibilities together.

The Ephesian church in Timothy's day could trace most of its troubles back to ineffective leadership. In this passage Paul teaches Timothy, the Ephesians, and us how to restore a truly biblical eldership. He does not repeat the qualifications he has given in chapter 3; he is not concerned here with the character and qualification of the overseer, but how the church views him. In setting his thoughts on these features, Paul opens to us the obligation of the church to its pastors. In so doing, he notes four principles defining a biblical eldership: honoring elders, protecting elders, rebuking elders, and selecting elders. Where a biblical eldership has been abandoned, following the teaching of this crucial text can help restore it.

Honoring Elders

Let the elders who rule well be considered worthy of double honor, especially those who work hard at preaching and teaching. For the Scripture says, "You shall not muzzle the ox while he is threshing," and "The laborer is worthy of his wages." (5:17–18)

The first principle and the first step toward restoring biblical eldership involves giving proper honor to those elders who serve faithfully in the church—a concept not unique to this passage. First Thessalonians 5:12–13 exhorts to the same end, "But we request of you, brethren, that you appreciate those who diligently labor among you, and have charge over you in the Lord and give you instruction, and that you esteem them very highly in love because of their work." The writer of Hebrews admonishes his readers to

> remember those who led you, who spoke the word of God to you; and considering the result of their conduct, imitate their faith. . . . Obey your leaders, and submit to them; for they keep watch over your souls, as those who will give an account. Let them do this with joy and not with grief, for this would be unprofitable for you. (Heb. 13:7, 17)

Elders is a general term referring to those who are also called "overseers" in 3:1. That the titles elder, pastor, and overseer all describe the same person is made clear by the use of all three words to describe the same men in Acts 20:17, 28. The term "pastor" emphasizes their shepherding or feeding function, "overseer" their authority and leading function, and "elder" their spiritual maturity. This passage assumes such elders are qualified (cf. 3:2ff.).

Honor translates *timē,* which generally refers to "respect," or "regard" (cf. 6:1). As already noted in the discussion of 5:3, it can also refer to financial support (cf. Matt. 27:6, 9; Acts 4:34; 1 Cor. 6:20 where it is translated "price"; Prov. 3:9 [LXX], which speaks of giving an offering to God). That usage is similar to the English word "honorarium," which refers to money given someone to honor them.

Paul, as was his custom, does not refer to money directly (cf. 2 Cor. 8:6–7; 9:1, 12–13; Gal. 6:6; Phil 4:18). He prefers instead to deal with the heart attitude that will result in remuneration. Those who honor elders will not begrudge generosity in paying their support. All elders are entitled to financial support as well as respect. Though Paul chose to support himself in his evangelistic efforts in pagan cities, those who do not are in no sense inferior, and are to be supported by the church. The laborer is worthy of his pay, and those who live to preach should be paid for it. Paul defended that truth in the important text of 1 Corinthians 9:1–14:

> Am I not free? Am I not an apostle? Have I not seen Jesus our Lord? Are you not my work in the Lord? If to others I am not an apostle, at least I am to you; for you are the seal of my apostleship in the Lord. My defense to those who examine me is this: Do we not have a right to eat and drink? Do we not have a right to take along a believing wife, even as the rest of the apostles, and the brothers of the Lord, and Cephas? Or do only Barnabas and I not have a right to refrain from working? Who at any time serves as a soldier at his own expense? Who plants a vineyard, and does not eat the fruit of it? Or who tends a flock and does not use the milk of the flock? I am not speaking these things according to human judgment, am I? Or does not the Law also say these things? For it is written in the Law of Moses, "You shall not muzzle the ox while he is threshing." God is not concerned about oxen, is He? Or is He speaking altogether for our sake? Yes, for our sake it was written, because the plowman ought to plow in hope, and the thresher to thresh in hope of sharing the crops. If we sowed spiritual things in you, is it too much if we should reap material things from you? If others share the right over you, do we not more? Nevertheless, we did not use this right, but we endure all things, that we may cause no hindrance to the gospel of Christ. Do you not know that those who perform sacred services eat the food of the temple, and those who attend regularly to the altar have their share with the altar? So also the Lord directed those who proclaim the gospel to get their living from the gospel.

The apostle himself also gladly received support on occasion. In response to the generosity of the Philippians he wrote,

> But I rejoiced in the Lord greatly, that now at last you have revived your concern for me; indeed, you were concerned before, but you lacked opportunity. Not that I speak from want; for I have learned to be content in whatever circumstances I am. I know how to get along with humble means, and I also know how to live in prosperity; in any and every circumstance I have learned the secret of being filled and going hungry, both of having abundance and suffering need. I can do all things through Him who strengthens me. Nevertheless, you have done well to share with me in my affliction. And you yourselves also know, Philippians, that at the first preaching of the gospel, after I departed from Macedonia, no church shared with me in the matter of giving and receiving but you alone; for even in Thessalonica you sent a gift more than once for my needs. Not that I seek the gift itself, but I seek for the profit which increases to your account. But I have received everything in full, and have an abundance; I am amply supplied, having received from Epaphroditus what you have sent, a fragrant aroma, an acceptable sacrifice, well-pleasing to God. And my God shall supply all your needs according to His riches in glory in Christ Jesus. Now to our God and Father be the glory forever and ever. Amen. (Phil. 4:10–20)

While all **elders** are to be thus honored, Paul singles out some as being **worthy of double honor.** He differentiates between the general category of elders and those who serve with greater commitment, effort, and excellence. They are **worthy** of greater acknowledgment from the congregations they serve. Paul is not here saying they should receive exactly twice the pay a normal elder receives. Rather, they should receive ample, generous remuneration and respect beyond that of other elders whose labors are not as diligent.

Paul gives two qualifications that mark **elders** as **worthy of double honor.** First, they **rule well. Rule** is from *proistēmi,* which means "to stand first." Elders are first in terms of leadership. They have the oversight of the church (cf. 3:1; cf. 1 Peter 5:2), and are to care for it (3:5). Because they are in charge (1 Thess. 5:12), they have a great responsibility (Heb. 13:17). When that privileged duty is discharged with unusual excellence, they should be compensated accordingly. Paul's emphasis, however, is not on the verb, but on the adverb **well.** *Kalos* (**well**) could be translated "with excellence." Excellence in ministry can be illustrated by a rehearsal of the qualities in 4:6–16.

Paul is not here setting up two categories of elders, those who rule and those who preach and teach. Nor is he contrasting holy and sinning elders. The latter would be disqualified and not be elders at all.

Paul's contrast is among faithful and gifted elders, to point out those who surpass the others in the excellence of their ministry.

The verb *axioō* (**let . . . be considered worthy**) reflects an estimate reached by the thinking process. It is to evaluate some elders and consider them **worthy of double honor.** The idea is that the **double honor** is not a gift, but something they deserve.

Paul further describes such men as **especially those who work hard at preaching and teaching.** *Malista* (**especially**) means "chiefly," or "particularly." The assumption is that some elders will not work as hard at **preaching and teaching** as others. Their role may be less prominent in those areas. **Work hard** is from *kopiaō,* which means "to work to the point of fatigue or exhaustion." It does not stress the amount of work, but rather the effort. A man's reward from God is proportional to the excellence of his ministry and the effort he puts into it. Excellence combined with diligence mark a man worthy of the highest honor.

Mediocrity comes from unwillingness to make the effort required. J. Oswald Sanders comments, "Willingness to renounce personal preferences, to sacrifice legitimate and natural desires for the sake of His kingdom, will characterize those marked out by God for positions of influence in His work" (*Spiritual Leadership,* rev. ed. [Chicago: Moody, 1980], 170–71).

Preaching is from *logos* and literally means "speech." It looks at public proclamation of the truth that includes exhortation and admonition. **Teaching** translates *didaskalia.* It emphasizes the idea of instruction more than proclamation. **Preaching** calls for a heart response to God, while **teaching** is a necessary bulwark against heresy. Not all elders will have the same burden of preaching and teaching. Some may teach or preach infrequently, some constantly. Those whose ministry demands all their attention should be freed from any need to earn a living and be cared for and even rewarded for their singular devotion.

Paul supports his point by quoting from both the Old and New Testaments. **For the Scripture says** is his usual way of introducing a biblical reference. **You shall not muzzle the ox while he is threshing** is a quote of Deuteronomy 25:4 (cf. 1 Cor. 9:9). The Old Testament law provided that the oxen who threshed the grain were entitled to eat of it. They were not to be muzzled to prevent them from doing that. Paul's point is obvious. God required that animals who labored to provide physical food for others were to be fed. How much more would He want faithful pastors, who provide spiritual food to their needy flocks, to be provided for?

The second quote, **The laborer is worthy of his wages,** is from Luke 10:7. It is very noteworthy that Paul refers to Luke's writing as **Scripture.** Here is a case of one New Testament writer affirming the inspiration of another (cf. 2 Peter 3:15–16). The early church recognized the canonicity and authority of the New Testament Scriptures even before their writers had died. This verse and 1 Corinthians 11:24 are the only times Paul quotes from the gospels. Both quotes are from Luke, reflecting Paul's close association with him.

With the second quote, Paul moves up a level from an animal to a servant. The Bible insists that servants are to be paid (Deut. 24:14–15; cf. James 5:4). To refuse to support those who provide spiritual food is as unjust and heartless as muzzling an animal, or refusing to pay a hired man.

PROTECTING ELDERS

Do not receive an accusation against an elder except on the basis of two or three witnesses. (5:19)

There are always people eager to falsely accuse a man of God. They may do so because they resent his calling, reject his teaching, resist biblical authority, resent virtue, or are jealous of the Lord's blessing on his life. Ultimately, however, they demonstrate by making such accusations that they have become messengers of Satan. Such false accusations are one of his most dangerous weapons. Joseph, Moses, David, Jeremiah, Nehemiah, and our Lord Jesus Christ all suffered from false accusations. So did Paul, and he particularly addressed that issue in his second letter to the Corinthians. As the Puritan writer John Trapp put it, "Truth hath always a scratcht face" (cited in Geoffery B. Wilson, *The Pastoral Epistles* [Edinburgh: Banner of Truth, 1982], 78).

It is a sacred trust to be in the ministry. That trust is based upon a man's integrity, credibility, and the consistent purity of his life. If he can be successfully attacked at that point and discredited, his ministry will be destroyed. It is imperative that his people be able to distinguish gossip and lies from reality.

Because false accusation is a very real danger, Paul gives Timothy instructions on how to deal with allegations against elders. First, unsubstantiated ones are to be rejected. **Receive** is from *paradechomai.* It means "to entertain," or "to consider in your mind." Such allegations are not to be investigated, but ignored. The simple act of turning a deaf ear to them is one of the best ways of protecting elders. **Accusation** translates *katēgoria,* a compound word from *kata* ("against") and *agora* ("public meeting place"). Such a public accusation is not to be entertained.

Second, Paul gives the conditions under which an accusation against an elder is to be taken seriously. The church is not to do so **except on the basis of two or three witnesses.** The accusation may yet prove false, but it must at least be investigated. The intent of having **two or three witnesses** is to provide confirmation (cf. Deut. 19:15; Matt. 18:16). That is not meant to place elders beyond successful accusation, but beyond illegitimate accusation. They are never to be at the mercy of frivolous, evil accusers.

To attack someone in a position of authority is a very serious matter. After cutting off part of Saul's robe, "it came about afterward that David's conscience bothered him because he had cut off the edge of Saul's robe" (1 Sam. 24:5). The Amalekite who thought to ingratiate himself with David by claiming to have killed Saul was executed instead (2 Sam. 1:1–16). Psalm 105:15 warns, "Do not touch My anointed ones, and do My prophets no harm." Those who set out to falsely accuse God's servants are treading on dangerous ground.

Rebuking Elders

Those who continue in sin, rebuke in the presence of all, so that the rest also may be fearful of sinning. I solemnly charge you in the presence of God and of Christ Jesus and of His chosen angels, to maintain these principles without bias, doing nothing in a spirit of partiality. (5:20–21)

Elders are to be protected from false accusations, but are not to receive immunity from true ones. **Those** elders **who continue in sin** must bear the consequences. Paul does not mention here any specific kinds of **sin.** Any **sin** that caused an elder to violate the qualifications listed in 3:2–7 would be grounds for **rebuke in the presence of all.** There are no elaborate steps of discipline to be followed. An accusation is made and confirmed, then investigated. If found true, the elder is publicly rebuked. *Elenchō* (**rebuke**) means "to expose," "to bring to open conviction," "to correct," or "to reprove." There are no exegetical grounds for limiting **all** to the other elders. It means everyone, elders and congregation. A sinning elder has nowhere to hide.

The sins of a man in a leadership role are more serious, and are to be punished more severely (cf. James 3:1). Whether or not he repents is not the issue. Since his credibility is forfeited, he is disqualified from the ministry in either case. He must be publicly rebuked so the people understand why he is no longer in leadership. Attempts to hush things up and allow a sinning elder to leave quietly often create the chaos of misunderstanding in a congregation.

The ministry is thus a two-edged sword. Those who serve faithfully are to be honored and protected, but those who sin are to be removed and publicly rebuked. One of the purposes for that public rebuke is so **that the rest also may be fearful of sinning.** *Loipos* (**the rest**) refers to the others in the same class. The class in view here is that of elders. When one elder is publicly disgraced because of sin, that puts a healthy fear into the hearts of the others. It also puts that same fear into the hearts of the congregation (cf. Matt. 18:17). Fear, along with love, is a proper motive for avoiding sin and obeying God (Deut. 13:6–11; 17:12–13; 19:16–20; Acts 5:5–11). Proverbs 9:10 says, "The fear of the Lord is the beginning of wisdom." Second Corinthians 7:1 admonishes believers to "cleanse [themselves] from all defilement of flesh and spirit, perfecting holiness in the fear of God" (cf. Acts 9:31; Eph. 5:21; Heb. 12:28; 1 Peter 2:17). Such fear is not sheer terror, but rather a sense of the ominous reality of God's hatred of evil.

If churches everywhere maintained that high standard for elders, unqualified men would be barred from the pastorate. As the standard is being lowered in our day, it is too often true that when a sinning pastor is disgraced in one church, he finds a position of honor in another. The church needs to decide whether to protect men's reputations, or God's. To allow sinning elders to resume ministry before they have erased all vestiges of dishonor and distrust (not always possible; sexual sin is a reproach that never goes away according to Prov. 6:33) defies Scripture and implies that God tolerates sin. Those who repent are to be forgiven and accepted by the congregation. That does not mean, however, they are to automatically be restored to ministry. Depending on the severity of the sin, they may be permanently disqualified.

To publicly rebuke a sinning elder takes great courage. Lest he be tempted to shirk that responsibility, Paul commands Timothy in verse 21, **I solemnly charge you in the presence of God and of Christ Jesus and of His chosen angels, to maintain these principles without bias, doing nothing in a spirit of partiality.** Paul reminds Timothy that **God** the Father, **Christ Jesus,** and the **chosen angels** are watching. They are the ones to fear, not the reactions of men. All heaven is concerned with the purity of the church. The church that tolerates sinning elders to protect its reputation on earth will lose its reputation in heaven.

Our Lord in Matthew 18 also encouraged believers to confront sin. He assured them that when they deal with sin on earth, they are acting in accord with heaven. God the Father and the Lord Jesus Himself are in their midst, agreeing with such purging (vv. 18–20).

The church must **maintain these principles** regarding sinning elders **without bias, doing nothing in a spirit of partiality.** No one is to receive preferential treatment. The rebuke of sinning elders must be done with accuracy and integrity. There must be no effort to protect those who are famous, specially gifted, or popular, nor to expose those who are not. The attitude of those involved must be one of sorrow, not self-righteousness.

To rebuke sinning leaders is not easy. Yet God requires it because holiness in the church must be upheld. The question facing any church is whether it is more concerned about its reputation or God's holiness.

Selecting Elders

Do not lay hands upon anyone too hastily and thus share responsibility for the sins of others; keep yourself free from sin. No longer drink water exclusively, but use a little wine for the sake of your stomach and your frequent ailments. The sins of some men are quite evident, going before them to judgment; for others, their sins follow after. Likewise also, deeds that are good are quite evident, and those which are otherwise cannot be concealed. (5:22–25)

The best way to prevent unqualified elders from serving in the ministry is to **not lay hands upon anyone too hastily.** Some have argued that this phrase reflects an early church custom of restoring sinning elders to the church fellowship. That interpretation is improbable, however, for several reasons. First, there is no evidence that such a custom existed in the New Testament church. Second, laying on of hands in the New Testament usually is connected with ordination (cf. Acts 6:6; 13:3; 1 Tim. 4:14; 2 Tim. 1:6). Finally, this interpretation flies in the face of the New Testament teaching about forgiveness. The New Testament nowhere urges caution in restoring a penitent sinner. Rather, it teaches the opposite (cf. Matt. 18:21–22; Gal. 6:1–2).

To **lay hands upon** someone in this context was to affirm their suitability for and acceptance into public ministry. It expressed solidarity, union, and identification with them. The practice had its roots in the Old Testament (cf. Num. 8:10; 27:18–23; Deut. 34:9). It derived from the practice of laying hands on a sacrificial animal to identify with it (cf. Ex. 29:10, 15, 19; Lev. 4:15). Laying on of hands also symbolizes identification in the New Testament (cf. Matt. 19:15; Acts 8:17–18; 9:17; Heb. 6:2).

Ordination in the New Testament was done by three groups. First, the apostles ordained elders (Acts 14:23). So did close associates of the apostles, such as Timothy and Titus (Titus 1:5). In the third phase, the existing elders in a church ordained other elders (1 Tim. 4:14). Today, since the first two groups have passed from the scene, the responsibility falls upon the elders of the church.

To **lay hands upon** someone, then, is to set them apart for ministry. It must not be done **hastily** (cf. 3:10). Thorough investigation must precede ordination. To fail to do so leaves the church liable to **share responsibility for the sins of others. Share** translates *koinoneō,* the verb form of the common New Testament word for fellowship. Hasty ordination, without proper examination, makes those responsible culpable in the man's sin. God's chastening may be on a church not only for a leader's sins, but also for the sins of those who failed to properly evaluate him.

By exercising proper caution in the matter of choosing pastors, Timothy would **keep** himself **free from sin. Keep** is from *tēreō,* which means "to exercise watchful care." The NASB translates *hagnos* as **free from sin,** but it literally means "pure," or "honorable" (cf. 2 Cor. 7:11; Phil. 4:8; James 3:17). By not lifting up unqualified leaders, and thus avoiding participation in their sins, Timothy would remain pure.

Verse 23 is a personal note, a parenthetical aside to Timothy in which Paul clarifies his exhortation to purity in verse 22. By calling for Timothy to remain pure, Paul was not advocating a rigid asceticism. He did not want Timothy to injure his health, and so encouraged him to **no longer drink water exclusively, but use a little wine for the sake of your stomach and your frequent ailments.** Timothy had obviously committed himself to total abstinence from wine. He desired to be a model of spiritual virtue and never establish a pattern that could make someone assume a liberty that would destroy them (cf. Rom. 14:13–23; 1 Cor. 8:12–13). Paul instructed him not to let that commitment injure his health. **Water** in the ancient world was impure and the carrier of diseases such as dysentery. Paul's advice to **use a little wine** would help safeguard Timothy's health from the sickness-producing effects of polluted water. It was also in keeping with the medicinal use of wine in the ancient world. The Talmud, Hippocrates, Pliny, and Plutarch all spoke of the value of wine in countering **stomach ailments** caused by impure water (Gordon D. Fee, *New International Biblical Commentary: 1 and 2 Timothy, Titus* [Peabody, Mass.: Hendrickson, 1988], 135). By advocating the temporary, curative use of wine, Paul does not ask Timothy to alter his commitment to the highest standard of behavior for leaders (cf. Num. 6:1–4; Prov. 31:4).

After the aside, Paul returns to his main emphasis of selecting elders. He gives four principles concerning that selection process.

First, **the sins of some men are quite evident, going before them to judgment.** Some are obviously unfit to serve as elders and can be rejected out of hand. Their **sins are quite evident** to all, and precede **them to judgment.** They rush in before them like heralds announcing their guilt in advance. The **judgment** in view here is not the final judgment, or the believers' judgment. Rather, it refers to the church's assessment of a man's suitability to serve.

Second, **for others, their sins follow after.** Their sins are not evident beforehand, but come to light during the church's assessment process. As R. C. H. Lenski put it, "Their sins march right into the meeting behind them and refuse to be left outside" (*The Interpretation of St. Paul's Epistles to the Colossians, to the Thessalonians, to Timothy, to Titus, and to Philemon* [Minneapolis: Augsburg, 1964], 692).

Third, **deeds that are good are quite evident.** It is obvious from the quality of some men's character that they are qualified to serve. A long discussion of their qualifications is thus unnecessary.

Finally, **those which are otherwise cannot be concealed.** The good deeds of some are not readily apparent. They **cannot be concealed,** however, and will come to light during the examination process. Such men will also be found qualified to serve as elders.

The church desperately needs qualified men to serve as pastors and elders. Their lives must meet the standards of 3:2–7, and their ministries those of 4:6–16. The church's responsibility to them is to honor and protect them, rebuke those who sin, and, above all, to be very cautious in selecting them. If those four principles are implemented, the church will be well on its way to restoring a biblical eldership.

The Conscientious Christian Employee

20

Let all who are under the yoke as slaves regard their own masters as worthy of all honor so that the name of God and our doctrine may not be spoken against. And let those who have believers as their masters not be disrespectful to them because they are brethren, but let them serve them all the more, because those who partake of the benefit are believers and beloved. Teach and preach these principles. (6:1–2)

Ours is a society that does not place a high value on work. According to one survey, 70 percent of American workers do not like their jobs. Of those 70 percent, 90 percent said they did not feel like getting up in the morning to go to work. The average worker is consumed with creature comforts, leisure, and materialism. He views his job as a necessary evil to finance his indulgences. That mentality is summed up in the popular bumper sticker that reads, "I Owe, I Owe, So Off to Work I Go."

Unfortunately, some of those unhappy workers are Christians, who need to be reminded of their responsibilities as employees. The church today needs to rediscover a biblical theology of work.

That theology begins in Genesis 2:15: "Then the Lord God took the man and put him into the garden of Eden to cultivate it and keep it." In the garden, before the Fall, man was assigned work. Work, therefore, is not a result of the curse, but of God's creative design for the fulfillment of man. Work did, however, become more painful and difficult after the Fall.

For the believer, work is a sacred duty. A Christian sees everything he does in reference to his relationship to God. The Reformers stressed that point. There is no aspect of life or conduct, however apparently insignificant, which should not be directed to the glory of God. No one stressed the sacredness of all work more than Martin Luther:

> To call popes, bishops, priests, monks, and nuns, the religious class, but princes, lords, artizans [sic], and farm-workers the secular class, is a specious device. . . . For all Christians whatsoever really and truly belong to the religious class, and there is no difference among them except in so far as they do different work. . . . Hence we deduce that there is, at bottom, really no other difference between laymen, priests, princes, bishops, or, in Romanist terminology, between religious and secular, than that of office or occupation, and not that of Christian status. All have spiritual status, and all are truly priests, bishops, and popes. But Christians do not all follow the same occupation. . . . A shoemaker, a smith, a farmer, each has his manual occupation and work; and yet, at the same time, all are eligible to act as priests and bishops. Every one of them in his occupation or handicraft ought to be useful to his fellows, and serve them in such a way that the various trades are all directed to the best advantage of the community, and promote the well-being of body and soul, just as all the organs of the body serve each other. ("An Appeal to the Ruling Class," in John Dillenberger, ed. *Martin Luther: Selections from His Writings* [Garden City, N.Y.: Anchor Books, 1961], 407, 409, 410)

Every legitimate job has intrinsic value because it is the arena in which believers live out their Christian lives. Christianity is not a hothouse religion, but one that survives and triumphs in the real world. Believers most commonly interact with that world in the work place, as they live out their faith on their jobs. They are to be a "city set on a hill" (Matt. 5:14). Christians must be concerned that their conduct on the job shows others the power of Jesus Christ to transform a life. Believers' work performance will bring either praise or blasphemy to the name of God. All work, whether directly or indirectly, is to advance God's Kingdom. Even those early Christians who were slaves could glorify God by faithfully fulfilling their duties.

Apparently the congregation under Timothy's charge was struggling to sustain a biblical work ethic in the world of slavery. Paul writes this passage as a corrective for them in this vital area. To do so, he addresses two simple points: Serving a non-Christian master, and serving a Christian master. The instruction he gives is vital to any Christian employee in any social system.

Serving a Non-Christian Master

Let all who are under the yoke as slaves regard their own masters as worthy of all honor so that the name of God and our doctrine may not be spoken against. (6:1)

Slavery was an integral social component of the Greco-Roman world in the first century. Slaves were the employees who did the work for their wealthy masters. It was a widespread scheme of employment. In fact, the entire economic structure of the Roman Empire depended on it. To understand slavery, believers today must strip away their preconceived notions of it. Those notions are drawn largely from the racial slavery of the pre–Civil War American South, which bears only some resemblance to slavery in the first-century Roman Empire.

In the Ancient Near East, much of the seasonal field work and part-time project work was done by hired day laborers (cf. Matt. 20:1ff.). Permanently employed domestic slaves served as managers (cf. Luke 16:1ff.), cooks, artisans, and teachers, becoming a part of the household, almost like family. In many respects they resembled the indentured servants of the American colonial era.

Slaves were acquired in several different ways. Many were prisoners of war (Num. 31:7–35; Deut. 20:10–14). They could also be purchased (Ex. 21:7; Lev. 25:44–46). Some people sold themselves into slavery (Lev. 25:39ff.; Deut. 15:12–17), others were sold to pay debts (2 Kings 4:1; Neh. 5:1–8). **Slaves** could be received as gifts (Gen. 29:24), or inherited (Lev. 25:46). Still others were born to slaves and remained in that role.

The system was not perfect, but it was workable. Most of the abuses came from the evil hearts of men, not from the institution itself. Such abuses can be found in every system of employment, whether slavery, feudalism, communism, or capitalism.

The Old Testament never forbade slavery, but carefully guarded the rights of **slaves.** Jewish slaves could not be held for more than six years (Ex. 21:2), unless they voluntarily chose to remain (Ex. 21:5–6). Those who came into slavery with a wife and children could take them when they left. Those given a wife by their master, however, could not take her until her time was up. That was necessary to protect the rights of the masters. Slaves who were abused by their masters were to be set free (Ex. 21:26–27). Their religious rights, such as enjoying the Sabbath rest, were also protected (Ex. 20:10). Slaves also enjoyed civil rights. The murder of a slave brought punishment (Ex. 21:20). Foreign slaves seeking asylum in Israel were to be protected (Deut. 23:15–16). Slaves had economic rights, including the right to own other slaves (cf. 2 Sam. 9:9–10). The nation of Israel even had state slaves, similar to civil service employees (Josh. 16:10; Judg. 1:28; Ezra 8:20).

Jewish **slaves** in New Testament times were similarly protected. They were to be treated as equal to the eldest son in a family. So protected were they that an old Jewish saying went, "Whoever buys a Jewish slave buys himself a master."

Gentile **slaves** were not always so well treated, but on the whole were better off than day laborers. Slaves had their food, clothing, and housing provided, along with a small wage and security. Subtracting the costs of food, clothing and housing from a day laborer's wages often left him worse off than a slave. Slavery was thus a workable, if not ideal, system. As in the Old, the New Testament nowhere calls for its abolition. By the New Testament era, slavery was waning in the Roman Empire, though there was still an enormous number of slaves. For Jesus and the apostles to have called for slavery's abolition would have been to promote unemployment and social chaos. Further, the saving message of the gospel would have been swallowed up in the call for social reform. Eventually, the influence of Christianity helped bring an end to abusive forms of slavery in the Roman Empire. (For a further discussion of slavery, see *Colossians and Philemon,* MacArthur New Testament Commentary [Chicago: Moody, 1992], 152–53, 201–35.)

The phrase **under the yoke** need not designate an abusive relationship (cf. Matt. 11:28–30). It was a colloquial expression of submissive service under the authority of someone else. **Slaves** is the plural form of the familiar New Testament word *doulos,* which designates a person in submission to another person. It has no inherent negative connotation—in fact, it can be a noble designation, as when it describes our Lord serving the Father (Phil. 2:7), or believers serving God (1 Peter 2:16). The word, in both its noun and verb forms, is used about 150 times in the New Testament. It speaks of a believer's slavery to his Lord (cf. Rom. 1:1; Gal. 1:10; 2 Tim. 2:24; James 1:1; 2 Peter 1:1; Jude 1; Rev. 1:1), to non-Christians (1 Cor. 9:19), and to other believers (Gal. 5:13).

Two New Testament passages illustrate the meaning of *doulos.* In Matthew 8:9, the centurion said to Jesus, "For I, too, am a man under authority, with soldiers under me; and I say to this one, 'Go!' and he goes, and to another, 'Come!' and he comes, and to my slave, 'Do this!'

and he does it." A *doulos* was one obligated to obey orders. Luke 17:7–10 gives us further insight into the word's meaning:

> But which of you, having a slave plowing or tending sheep, will say to him when he has come in from the field, "Come immediately and sit down to eat"? But will he not say to him, "Prepare something for me to eat, and properly clothe yourself and serve me until I have eaten and drunk; and afterward you will eat and drink"? He does not thank the slave because he did the things which were commanded, does he? So you too, when you do all the things which are commanded you, say, "We are unworthy slaves; we have done only that which we ought to have done."

A slave was one required to perform duties assigned to him by another who was over him in authority.

Masters is from *despotēs,* from which our English word "despot" derives. Unlike the English word, however, the Greek term does not carry the connotation of harsh, cruel, and abusive. It merely refers to someone with absolute, unrestricted authority, and was even used of our Lord Jesus Christ (2 Tim. 2:21; 2 Peter 2:1; Jude 4). In Greek culture and terminology, *doulos* and *despotēs* went together.

Their, with the adjective *idios* (**own**), implies some form of personal bond (cf. Eph. 5:22). Clearly, these are non-Christian employers, as indicated by the qualifying remark in verse 2, "and let those who have believers as their masters." This applies to anyone who is an authority over the believer at work. There is no spiritual bond, but there is a bond of duty.

Believers were to **regard** these non-Christian masters **as worthy of all honor.** *Hēgeomai* (**regard**) refers to an estimate based on objective criteria, not internal feelings. Believers are to have respect and a correct assessment of the authority of their employers, regardless of how they feel about them.

A correct assessment will find one's employer **worthy of all honor.** Along with widows (5:3) and elders (5:17), employers are to receive **honor.** Here it does not include financial support, but respect and dutiful service. Even those employers who are harsh and unfair are to be honored because of their role as superiors in the work place. Peter wrote,

> Servants, be submissive to your masters with all respect, not only to those who are good and gentle, but also to those who are unreasonable. For this finds favor, if for the sake of conscience toward God a man bears up under sorrows when suffering unjustly. For what credit is

there if, when you sin and are harshly treated, you endure it with patience? But if when you do what is right and suffer for it you patiently endure it, this finds favor with God. (1 Peter 2:18–20)

The reason masters are to be so honored is **so that the name of God and our doctrine may not be spoken against.** Believers' attitudes and behavior in their daily relations at work affect how people perceive **God** and **our doctrine,** the latter no doubt a reference particularly to the gospel. Those who fail to honor their employers will cause God and Christian truth to **be spoken against.** Their employers would question what kind of a God they served, who would lead them to laziness, insubordination, or hostility. They would also question the gospel's power to transform a life. R. C. H. Lenski writes,

> If a Christian slave dishonored his master in any way by disobedience, by acting disrespectfully, by speaking shamefully of his master, the worst consequence would not be the beating he would receive but the curses he would cause his master to hurl at this miserable slave's God, his religion, and the teaching he had embraced: "So that is what this new religion teaches its converts!" Instead of bringing honor to the true God and the gospel of his high and holy Name, as every Christian should be anxious to do, this slave would bring about the very opposite, to the devil's delight. (*The Interpretation of St. Paul's Epistles to the Colossians, to the Thessalonians, to Timothy, to Titus, and to Philemon* [Minneapolis: Augsburg, 1964], 694–95)

Apostate Israel brought reproach on the Name of God by her insubordination and unwillingness to obey her Lord and Master. Paul writes of them in Romans 2:23–24, "You who boast in the Law, through your breaking the Law, do you dishonor God? For 'the name of God is blasphemed among the Gentiles because of you,' just as it is written" (cf. Isa. 52:5).

This was a recurring issue needing to be confronted by Paul, so he repeats these instructions in his letter to Titus: "Urge bondslaves to be subject to their own masters in everything, to be well-pleasing, not argumentative, not pilfering, but showing all good faith that they may adorn the doctrine of God our Savior in every respect" (Titus 2:9–10). The connection of godly living to evangelism is evident from verse 11–14:

> For the grace of God has appeared, bringing salvation to all men, instructing us to deny ungodliness and worldly desires and to live sensibly, righteously and godly in the present age, looking for the blessed hope and the appearing of the glory of our great God and Savior, Christ

> Jesus; who gave Himself for us, that He might redeem us from every lawless deed and purify for Himself a people for His own possession, zealous for good deeds.

Christians have a divinely commanded responsibility to live out their faith in the work place. Having a proper attitude of submission and respect, and performing quality work, are necessary prerequisites to proclaiming a believable gospel.

Serving a Christian Master

And let those who have believers as their masters not be disrespectful to them because they are brethren, but let them serve them all the more, because those who partake of the benefit are believers and beloved. Teach and preach these principles. (6:2)

The temptation for those with Christian masters was to expect special privileges because of their equality in Christ. It was certainly not uncommon for a mature believer to be employed by an immature one, or even for an elder of the church to work for one who was not in church leadership. This could lead to conflict if the employee did not follow God's design for them in the work place. Galatians 3:28 says, "There is neither Jew nor Greek, there is neither slave nor free man, there is neither male nor female; for you are all one in Christ Jesus." That verse, however, does not eliminate racial, social, or sexual distinctions. Jews and Greeks, slaves and free men, and men and women retain their distinctiveness despite their spiritual equality. The same is true for slaves and masters. That verse provides no license for **those who have believers as their masters** to fail to honor them. Those who are leaders in the church are to be followed by all in the church (Heb. 13:17), but that does not carry over to the work place.

Christians who work for other Christians must **not be disrespectful to them because they are brethren.** *Kataphroneō* (**be disrespectful**) literally means "to think down." Believers are not to undervalue the authority of their Christian employers by treating them as equals on the job. A submissive working attitude and behavior must be maintained. **Because** the believing employers **are brethren** does not justify presumption, or assuming special privileges. Nor may they presume on their spiritual relationship with their employer by being insubordinate, or giving less than an honest day's work.

Those with Christian employers should **serve them all the more, because those who partake of the benefit are believers**

and beloved. Those with unbelieving masters are to do their very best in serving them. How much **more** should those with believing masters **serve** them? In that case, **those who partake of the benefit are believers and beloved,** brothers in Christ. Believers are to "do good to all men, and especially to those who are of the household of the faith" (Gal. 6:10). The phrase **believers and beloved** aptly describes Christians. They are **believers** in God, and **beloved** by Him.

Two other passages in the Pauline writings deal with Christian employees:

> Slaves, be obedient to those who are your masters according to the flesh, with fear and trembling, in the sincerity of your heart, as to Christ; not by way of eyeservice, as men-pleasers, but as slaves of Christ, doing the will of God from the heart. With good will render service, as to the Lord, and not to men, knowing that whatever good thing each one does, this he will receive back from the Lord, whether slave or free. (Eph. 6:5–8)
>
> Slaves, in all things obey those who are your masters on earth, not with external service, as those who merely please men, but with sincerity of heart, fearing the Lord. Whatever you do, do your work heartily, as for the Lord rather than for men; knowing that from the Lord you will receive the reward of the inheritance. It is the Lord Christ whom you serve. For he who does wrong will receive the consequences of the wrong which he has done, and that without partiality. (Col. 3:22–25)

From those passages we can summarize several principles of conduct for believers on the job. (For a complete exposition of these passages, see *Ephesians,* MacArthur New Testament Commentary [Chicago: Moody, 1986], and *Colossians and Philemon,* MacArthur New Testament Commentary [Chicago: Moody, 1992].)

First, believers are to serve their employers obediently (Eph. 6:5; Col. 3:22). They must dutifully, submissively respond to their employer's orders.

Second, believers are to serve their employers completely (Eph. 6:5; Col. 3:22). They are to carry out whatever tasks are assigned them, unless so doing would violate God's law (cf. Acts 5:29).

Third, believers are to serve their employers respectfully (Eph. 6:5). They must honor those God has placed in authority over them.

Fourth, believers are to serve their employers eagerly, in "sincerity" of heart (Eph. 6:5; Col. 3:22). They should serve voluntarily, not grudgingly.

Fifth, believers are to serve their employers excellently, "as to Christ" (Eph. 6:5; cf. Col. 3:23). They must do their jobs to the best of their ability.

Sixth, believers are to serve their employers diligently, "not by way of eyeservice" (Eph. 6:6; cf. Col. 3:22). They must not put on a show for the boss by working hard only when he is watching.

Seventh, believers are to serve their employers humbly, not "as men-pleasers" (Eph. 6:6; cf. Col. 3:23). They are not to show off to ingratiate themselves with others.

Eighth, believers are to serve their employers spiritually, "doing the will of God from the heart" (Eph. 6:6). As already noted, all work is sacred and performed ultimately for the glory of God.

Finally, believers are to serve their employers eschatologically, "knowing that from the Lord you will receive the reward of the inheritance. . . . For he who does wrong will receive the consequences of the wrong which he has done, and that without partiality" (Col. 3:24–25). Believers' eternal rewards will be affected by their job performance.

Paul closes by exhorting Timothy to **teach and preach these principles** (cf. 4:11). The present-tense verbs indicate that was to be Timothy's constant practice, reflecting that **these principles** are foundational to Christian living and evangelism, and that they are not widely practiced. In the arena of the work place, as in all of life, believers must seek to glorify their Lord (1 Cor. 10:31).

Christians' social and economic status as slaves, masters, freemen, employers, or employees has no eternal relevance. All such roles pass away with the world, so we focus on what is eternal, not on the social system or our place in it. Paul writes,

> Were you called while a slave? Do not worry about it; but if you are able also to become free, rather do that. For he who was called in the Lord while a slave, is the Lord's freedman; likewise he who was called while free, is Christ's slave. . . . The form of this world is passing away. (1 Cor. 7:21–22, 31b)

It is not the church's role to undermine the foundations of social order by fostering rebellion. Rather, believers are to be compliant and obedient on their jobs, and thus to give witness that the grace of Jesus Christ has transformed their lives.

The Pathology of False Teachers

21

If anyone advocates a different doctrine, and does not agree with sound words, those of our Lord Jesus Christ, and with the doctrine conforming to godliness, he is conceited and understands nothing; but he has a morbid interest in controversial questions and disputes about words, out of which arise envy, strife, abusive language, evil suspicions, and constant friction between men of depraved mind and deprived of the truth, who suppose that godliness is a means of gain. (6:3–5)

Throughout history, deadly epidemics have ravaged mankind. In the fourteenth century, the infamous "Black Death" (an outbreak of bubonic plague) killed millions in Europe. Cholera, diphtheria, malaria, and other sicknesses have ravaged towns and cities. Our generation has witnessed the rapid spread of the fatal disease Acquired Immune Deficiency Syndrome (AIDS). More deadly than any of those diseases, however, is the plague of false teaching that has afflicted the church throughout its history. While illness may kill the body, false teaching damns the soul.

Like AIDS and the plague, false teaching has a definite, observable pathology. (Pathology is the study of the elements of abnormality that characterize a disease.) Scientists study the pathology of a disease to better equip themselves to recognize it and to combat it.

Every leader in the church should be a spiritual pathologist, able to discern deviations from spiritual health. Only then will he be equipped to diagnose the deadly disease of false teaching, and to do what is necessary to check its spread among his people. Paul warned of the subtle danger of satanic lies, describing their purveyors as

> false apostles, deceitful workers, disguising themselves as apostles of Christ. And no wonder, for even Satan disguises himself as an angel of light. Therefore it is not surprising if his servants also disguise themselves as servants of righteousness; whose end shall be according to their deeds. (2 Cor. 11:13–15)

It takes careful discernment to see that the light is really darkness.

Paul writes these verses to teach Timothy how to diagnose satanic darkness masquerading as divine light. He gives seven symptoms that identify those infected with the spiritual disease of false teaching: their mark, attitude, mentality, effects, cause, condition, and motive.

The Mark of False Teachers

If anyone advocates a different doctrine, and does not agree with sound words, those of our Lord Jesus Christ, and with the doctrine conforming to godliness, (6:3)

Physical diseases have symptoms, or marks, by which they may be diagnosed. The same is true of false teaching. Those infected by it will manifest certain characteristics. **If** introduces a first-class conditional clause and assumes reality. There were already some in Ephesus who were carriers of the disease of false teaching (cf. 1:3–4, 6–7, 20; 4:1–5). **Anyone** indicates Paul did not want to limit his warning to any specific teaching or teachers. He gives a generic warning embracing all false teaching. It includes everything Timothy faced, as well as all the false teaching the church would subsequently encounter.

The first mark, or symptom, of false teachers is what they affirm. A false teacher **advocates a different doctrine. Advocates a different doctrine** is from *heterodidaskaleō,* a compound word from *heteros* ("other") and *didaskaleō* ("to teach"). It describes any teaching that contradicts God's revelation in Scripture. Such teaching is heterodoxy rather than orthodoxy.

False teaching may take many forms. It may deny God's existence, or teach error about His nature and attributes. It may deny the Trinity. Error about Christ's Person and work is also common in false systems. Those who deny His virgin birth, sinless perfection, substitutionary death, bodily resurrection or future return show signs of a dangerous infection. False teachers also teach error about the nature, Person, and works of the Holy Spirit. Yet another strain of the disease of false teaching denies the authenticity, inspiration, authority, or inerrancy of Scripture. That strain is particularly virulent in the church today.

To spot the carriers of spiritual disease, believers must be well grounded in Scripture. Those who know the Word will easily spot teaching contrary to it. They will be spiritual young men, who have overcome the evil one because they are strong in the knowledge of God's Word (1 John 2:14). Since the evil one primarily operates in false systems of religion, this indicates a level of maturity where sound doctrine has been laid as a solid foundation. Spiritual young men, by knowing the Word which abides in them, overcome the lies of Satan. Those who have grown past being spiritual infants through their knowledge of sound doctrine can see error for what it is.

In his farewell address to the Ephesian elders, Paul reminded them of their responsibility to diagnose and deal with error:

> I did not shrink from declaring to you the whole purpose of God. Be on guard for yourselves and for all the flock, among which the Holy Spirit has made you overseers, to shepherd the church of God which He purchased with His own blood. I know that after my departure savage wolves will come in among you, not sparing the flock; and from among your own selves men will arise, speaking perverse things, to draw away the disciples after them. Therefore be on the alert, remembering that night and day for a period of three years I did not cease to admonish each one with tears. And now I commend you to God and to the word of His grace, which is able to build you up and to give you the inheritance among all those who are sanctified. (Acts 20:27–32)

After warning them of the threat of false teachers, Paul pointed out the only antidote, the "word of His grace." According to Ephesians 6:17, the Christian's offensive weapon against false teaching is the "the sword of the Spirit, which is the word of God." Paul defines a true spiritual leader as one "nourished on the words of the faith and . . . sound doctrine" (1 Tim. 4:6; cf. v. 16; 2 Tim. 1:13–14; 2:2). The primary function of a spiritual leader is to feed his people the Word. They will then avoid the noxious weeds of false doctrine and grow to maturity (cf. Eph. 4:11–15).

Another mark of false teachers is what they deny. Their teaching not only affirms error, but also **does not agree with sound words, those of our Lord Jesus Christ.** *Proserchomai* (**agree with**) is in the present tense, indicating false teachers are in a continuous state of not agreeing with **sound words. Sound** is from *hugiainō,* from which the English word "hygiene" derives. False teachers are not in agreement with spiritually wholesome and beneficial words. That believers need to pay attention to sound, healthy teaching is repeatedly emphasized in the Pastoral Epistles (cf. 1 Tim. 1:10; 2 Tim. 1:13; Titus 1:9; 2:1).

Paul further describes **sound words** as **those of our Lord Jesus Christ.** That phrase refers to more than the quotes of our Lord given in the gospel. It encompasses His message as revealed in Scripture, "the word of Christ" (Col. 3:16; cf. 1 Thess. 1:8; 2 Thess. 3:1). It is that Word that provides the healthy teaching by which believers grow. Peter wrote, "Like newborn babes, long for the pure milk of the word, that by it you may grow in respect to salvation" (1 Peter 2:2).

False teachers are not committed to Scripture. They may speak of Jesus and the Father, but the heart of their ministry will not be the Word of God. They will either add to it, take away from it, interpret it in some heretical fashion, add other "revelations" to it, or deny it altogether.

A third symptom of false teachers is their rejection of **the doctrine conforming to godliness.** The ultimate test of any teaching is whether it produces **godliness.** Teaching not based on Scripture will result in an unholy life. Godliness translates *eusebeia,* which means "piety," "reverence," or "likeness to God." Such behavior is the fruit of truth. In Matthew 7:15–20, Jesus warned,

> Beware of the false prophets, who come to you in sheep's clothing, but inwardly are ravenous wolves. You will know them by their fruits. Grapes are not gathered from thorn bushes, nor figs from thistles, are they? Even so, every good tree bears good fruit; but the bad tree bears bad fruit. A good tree cannot produce bad fruit, nor can a bad tree produce good fruit. Every tree that does not bear good fruit is cut down and thrown into the fire. So then, you will know them by their fruits.

Instead of **godliness,** the lives of false teachers will be characterized by sin. Peter graphically describes them as

> those who indulge the flesh in its corrupt desires and despise authority. Daring, self-willed, they do not tremble when they revile angelic majesties, whereas angels who are greater in might and power do not bring a reviling judgment against them before the Lord. But these, like unreasoning animals, born as creatures of instinct to be captured and killed, reviling where they have no knowledge, will in the destruction of those creatures also be destroyed, suffering wrong as the wages of

> doing wrong. They count it a pleasure to revel in the daytime. They are stains and blemishes, reveling in their deceptions, as they carouse with you, having eyes full of adultery and that never cease from sin, enticing unstable souls, having a heart trained in greed, accursed children; forsaking the right way they have gone astray, having followed the way of Balaam, the son of Beor, who loved the wages of unrighteousness, but he received a rebuke for his own transgression; for a dumb donkey, speaking with a voice of a man, restrained the madness of the prophet. These are springs without water, and mists driven by a storm, for whom the black darkness has been reserved. For speaking out arrogant words of vanity they entice by fleshly desires, by sensuality, those who barely escape from the ones who live in error, promising them freedom while they themselves are slaves of corruption; for by what a man is overcome, by this he is enslaved. For if after they have escaped the defilements of the world by the knowledge of the Lord and Savior Jesus Christ, they are again entangled in them and are overcome, the last state has become worse for them than the first. For it would be better for them not to have known the way of righteousness, than having known it, to turn away from the holy commandment delivered to them. It has happened to them according to the true proverb, "A dog returns to its own vomit," and, "A sow, after washing, returns to wallowing in the mire." (2 Peter 2:10–22; cf. Jude 4, 8–16)

Heresy has no power to produce genuine **godliness.**

The Attitude of False Teachers

he is conceited (6:4a)

The attitude of false teachers can be summed up in one word: pride. It takes an immense ego to place oneself as judge of the Bible. Such egotism blatantly usurps the place of God. **Conceited** is from *tuphoō,* the same word used in 3:6. As noted in the discussion of that passage in chapter 10 of this volume, it derives from a root word meaning "smoke." The verb means "to puff up like a cloud of smoke." In English slang, we would describe such a person as "blowing smoke," or "full of hot air."

The word also implies arrogance, an inevitable mark of false teachers. To set one's own teaching up as superior to the Word of God is the epitome of arrogance. False teachers speak "arrogant words of vanity" (2 Peter 2:18), useless talk that merely reveals their arrogant attitude. Such a man was Simon the sorcerer, who "[claimed] to be someone great" (Acts 8:9). Paul describes such a one as "inflated without cause by his fleshly mind" (Col. 2:18).

False teachers have an overinflated sense of their own importance, not hesitating to rebel against God and His Word. That merely confirms, however, that they are infected with a deadly spiritual disease.

The Mentality of False Teachers

and understands nothing; but he has a morbid interest in controversial questions and disputes about words, (6:4b)

Although a false teacher may be filled with pride over his supposed knowledge, in reality he **understands nothing.** All of his imagined intelligence, pretended scholarship, and supposed deeper insights amounts to mere foolishness to God (Rom. 1:22; 1 Cor. 2:9–16). Lacking insight into spiritual truth, his wisdom "is not that which comes down from above, but is earthly, natural, demonic" (James 3:15). Those who know and believe the Word of God have far more insight into spiritual reality than the most educated heretic.

Instead of focusing on the truth, false teachers have **a morbid interest in controversial questions and disputes about words.** Their disease involves a preoccupation with useless questions and fighting over words. **Questions** translates *zētēsis,* which refers to idle speculations. *Logomachia* (**disputes about words**) literally means "word battles." False teachers do little more than quibble over terminology. They indulge in pseudo-intellectual theorizing rather than in productive study of and submission to God's Word.

There are many examples of such specious theorizing. The Bible teaches that God created the universe in six literal twenty-four-hour days (Gen. 1:5, 8, 13, 19, 23, 31; cf. Ex. 20:11). Some, intimidated by the scientifically bankrupt theory of evolution, reject that clearly stated biblical truth. Instead, they opt for compromise positions such as theistic evolution or progressive creationism. By so doing, they hope to mollify the militant defenders of evolution.

Others, cowed by the "assured results of higher criticism," are disciples of the thoroughly discredited Documentary Hypothesis. That view carves up the Pentateuch and assigns its authorship to four (or more) imaginary sources, the J (Yahwist), E (Elohimist), D (Deuteronomist), and P (Priestly) sources. That theory is utterly lacking in manuscript support, and contrary to the words of our Lord, who affirmed the Mosaic authorship of the Pentateuch (cf. Mark 7:10; 12:26; Luke 24:44). Nevertheless, its devotees march on under the banner of "objective" scholarship and imagine that such denial of Scripture qualifies them as intellectuals. Instead of being humbled and fearful over such deviations, they are proud of their ignorance.

The New Testament also has been subjected to its share of word battles. Virtually every New Testament book has been attacked by critics who deny the traditional view of its authorship. Many refuse to accept the Gospels as straightforward historical accounts. They prefer instead to view them as a collection of myths invented by Christ's mistaken followers after His death.

Such fruitless speculations are ultimately doctrines of demons. To engage in them is a sign of spiritual sickness.

THE EFFECTS OF FALSE TEACHERS

out of which arise envy, strife, abusive language, evil suspicions, and constant friction (6:4c–5a)

As noted earlier, false teaching fails the test of truth because it fails to produce godliness. A second way it fails is in its inability to produce unity. The word battles of false teachers result in chaos and confusion. **Envy** is the inward discontent with the advantages or popularity enjoyed by others. It results in **strife,** which often manifests itself in the **abusive language** of slander and insult. That **abusive language** consists of **evil suspicions,** which means to ascribe evil motives to someone. The net result of false teaching is **constant friction.** False teachers constantly rub each other the wrong way. That helps spread their spiritual disease, much as sheep might rub together and infect each other. False teaching can never produce unity. Only the truth unifies.

THE CAUSE OF FALSE TEACHERS

between men of depraved mind (6:5b)

The external cause of false teaching is satanic deception (cf. 4:1). The internal cause, however, is the **depraved** or unregenerate **mind** of the false teacher. "The mind set on the flesh," writes Paul, "is hostile toward God" (Rom. 8:7). Such a mind does not function normally in the spiritual realm; it does not react normally to truth. Being natural men, false teachers cannot understand the things of God, which seem foolish to them (1 Cor. 2:14). As a result, "God gave them over to a depraved mind" (Rom. 1:28; cf. Eph. 2:1–3; 4:17–19).

Not having "the mind of Christ" (1 Cor. 2:16), false teachers can produce only error.

The Condition of False Teachers

and deprived of the truth, (6:5c)

The condition of false teachers is critical; they are in a state of apostasy. **Deprived** is from *apostereō,* which means "to steal," "rob," or "deprive." The passive voice of the participle indicates someone or something pulled them away from the truth. That does not imply they were saved, but that they had contact with the truth. Like those described in Hebrews 6:4–6, they were thoroughly exposed to it, but rejected it. As a result, they "have gone astray from the truth" (2 Tim. 2:18), and are "always learning and never able to come to the knowledge of the truth" (2 Tim. 3:7). In 2 Timothy 3:8 Paul writes of them, "these men also oppose the truth, men of depraved mind, rejected as regards the faith."

Unfortunately, their prognosis is not hopeful. Their spiritual condition is terminal. Those who are **deprived of the truth** are headed for judgment. Hebrews 6:6 solemnly warns of such men that "it is impossible to renew them again to repentance, since they again crucify to themselves the Son of God, and put Him to open shame." Peter says that they bring "swift destruction upon themselves" (2 Peter 2:1). He then illustrates that truth in verses 4–9:

> For if God did not spare angels when they sinned, but cast them into hell and committed them to pits of darkness, reserved for judgment; and did not spare the ancient world, but preserved Noah, a preacher of righteousness, with seven others, when He brought a flood upon the world of the ungodly; and if He condemned the cities of Sodom and Gomorrah to destruction by reducing them to ashes, having made them an example to those who would live ungodly thereafter; and if He rescued righteous Lot, oppressed by the sensual conduct of unprincipled men (for by what he saw and heard that righteous man, while living among them, felt his righteous soul tormented day after day with their lawless deeds), then the Lord knows how to rescue the godly from temptation, and to keep the unrighteous under punishment for the day of judgment.

Jude also warns of their impending doom:

> For certain persons have crept in unnoticed, those who were long beforehand marked out for this condemnation, ungodly persons who turn the grace of our God into licentiousness and deny our only Master and Lord, Jesus Christ. . . . [He will return] to execute judgment upon

> all, and to convict all the ungodly of all their ungodly deeds which they have done in an ungodly way, and of all the harsh things which ungodly sinners have spoken against Him. (Jude 4, 15)

The severest hell will be reserved for those who, having been exposed to the truth, turned away from it (cf. Heb. 10:26–31).

THE MOTIVE OF FALSE TEACHERS

who suppose that godliness is a means of gain. (6:5d)

False teachers have a simple motivation: money. They **suppose that godliness** (used sarcastically of their false piety) will bring them such **gain.** Unlike Paul, they cannot say, "I have coveted no one's silver or gold or clothes" (Acts 20:33). They are not "free from the love of money" (3:3). In the words of Peter, "forsaking the right way they have gone astray, having followed the way of Balaam, the son of Beor, who loved the wages of unrighteousness" (2 Peter 2:15). Simon the sorcerer was an example of a greedy false teacher. His foolish attempt to buy the power of the Spirit brought a stinging rebuke from Peter:

> Now when Simon saw that the Spirit was bestowed through the laying on of the apostles' hands, he offered them money, saying, "Give this authority to me as well, so that everyone on whom I lay my hands may receive the Holy Spirit." But Peter said to him, "May your silver perish with you, because you thought you could obtain the gift of God with money! You have no part or portion in this matter, for your heart is not right before God. Therefore repent of this wickedness of yours, and pray the Lord that if possible, the intention of your heart may be forgiven you. For I see that you are in the gall of bitterness and in the bondage of iniquity. (Acts 8:18–23)

Our day, too, has more than its share of Simons. Their greed betrays their impure motives and marks them as false teachers.

The pathology of false teachers is clear. They deny the truth, and their teaching does not produce godly living. They are arrogant and ignorant of spiritual truth. They spend their time in foolish speculations that lead only to chaos and division. Having forsaken the truth, they face eternal destruction. And they serve money, not God. The church must take extreme care not to allow these men to spread their deadly disease. The resulting epidemic would be tragic.

The Danger of Loving Money

22

But godliness actually is a means of great gain, when accompanied by contentment. For we have brought nothing into the world, so we cannot take anything out of it either. And if we have food and covering, with these we shall be content. But those who want to get rich fall into temptation and a snare and many foolish and harmful desires which plunge men into ruin and destruction. For the love of money is a root of all sorts of evil, and some by longing for it have wandered away from the faith, and pierced themselves with many a pang. (6:6–10)

The Bible is replete with warnings against loving money. Perhaps none is more pointed than the one given by our Lord in Matthew 6:21: "For where your treasure is, there will your heart be also." What believers do with their money is one of the truest measures of their spiritual maturity.

How should believers view money? First, they must realize that having money is not wrong in itself. First Samuel 2:7 says, "The Lord makes poor and rich" (cf. 1 Chron. 29:12). The Bible does not teach that being wealthy is a sin. Some of the great men of the Old Testament, such as Abraham, Job, and Solomon were extremely wealthy.

Second, they should recognize that money is a gift from God. Moses cautioned the Israelites not to forget that truth:

> Beware lest you forget the Lord your God by not keeping His commandments and His ordinances and His statutes which I am commanding you today; lest, when you have eaten and are satisfied, and have built good houses and lived in them, and when your herds and your flocks multiply, and your silver and gold multiply, and all that you have multiplies, then your heart becomes proud, and you forget the Lord your God who brought you out from the land of Egypt, out of the house of slavery. He led you through the great and terrible wilderness, with its fiery serpents and scorpions and thirsty ground where there was no water; He brought water for you out of the rock of flint. In the wilderness He fed you manna which your fathers did not know, that He might humble you and that He might test you, to do good for you in the end. Otherwise, you may say in your heart, "My power and the strength of my hand made me this wealth." But you shall remember the Lord your God, for it is He who is giving you power to make wealth, that He may confirm His covenant which He swore to your fathers, as it is this day. (Deut. 8:11–18)

All that believers have has come to them through God's providence.

Third, believers must be willing to part with their money if God so requires (cf. Matt. 19:27). Job understood that principle. In Job 1:21 he said, "The Lord gave and the Lord has taken away. Blessed be the name of the Lord."

Fourth, those who have money must not be given preferential treatment. James warned,

> My brethren, do not hold your faith in our glorious Lord Jesus Christ with an attitude of personal favoritism. For if a man comes into your assembly with a gold ring and dressed in fine clothes, and there also comes in a poor man in dirty clothes, and you pay special attention to the one who is wearing the fine clothes, and say, "You sit here in a good place," and you say to the poor man, "You stand over there, or sit down by my footstool," have you not made distinctions among yourselves, and become judges with evil motives? Listen, my beloved brethren: did not God choose the poor of this world to be rich in faith and heirs of the kingdom which He promised to those who love Him? But you have dishonored the poor man. Is it not the rich who oppress you and personally drag you into court? Do they not blaspheme the fair name by which you have been called? If, however, you are fulfilling the royal law, according to the Scripture, "You shall love your neighbor as yourself," you are doing well. But if you show partiality, you are committing sin and are convicted by the law as transgressors. For whoever

keeps the whole law and yet stumbles in one point, he has become guilty of all. (James 2:1–10)

Fifth, those with money must not be proud, nor seek security from it. In 1 Timothy 6:17 Paul instructed the rich "not to be conceited or to fix their hope on the uncertainty of riches, but on God, who richly supplies us with all things to enjoy." Proverbs 11:28 cautions that "he who trusts in his riches will fall, but the righteous will flourish like the green leaf."

Sixth, believers must never make the pursuit of money the highest goal of their lives. In Matthew 6:33 the Lord Jesus Christ commanded, "Seek first His kingdom and His righteousness; and all these things shall be added to you."

Seventh, money must be used for eternal purposes. Jesus said we are to use our money to make eternal friends; that is, to lead souls to the Lord (Luke 16:9).

Finally, money must not be loved—selfishly hoarded or indulgently spent. Proverbs 11:24–25 says, "There is one who scatters, yet increases all the more, and there is one who withholds what is justly due, but it results only in want. The generous man will be prosperous, and he who waters will himself be watered." Our Lord echoed that thought in Luke 6:38: "Give, and it will be given to you; good measure, pressed down, shaken together, running over, they will pour into your lap. For by your standard of measure it will be measured to you in return." Paul told the Corinthians that "he who sows sparingly shall also reap sparingly; and he who sows bountifully shall also reap bountifully. Let each one do just as he has purposed in his heart; not grudgingly or under compulsion; for God loves a cheerful giver" (2 Cor. 9:6–7). Sacrificial generosity should mark every believer, and the absence of such a perspective reveals that one loves money.

The principle concerning loving money is found in verse 10: **The love of money is a root of all sorts of evil.** That applies directly in this context to those who are teachers, but also applies to every believer as a general rule. True preachers must avoid the money love of false teachers, as must all Christians. Like a gun, there is nothing inherently wrong with money. But like a gun, money can be used for good and evil purposes. Thus, the issue is not money, but one's attitude toward it. The sin in view is the sin of greed.

What are the danger signs of loving money? First, those who love money are more concerned with making it than with honesty, or giving a quality effort. Believers must pursue truth and excellence, for which money may be the reward.

Second, those who love money never have enough. Like the leech's daughters of Proverbs 30:15, all they can say is "Give, Give." Such people stand in sharp contrast to Paul, who wrote to the Philippians, "I have learned to be content in whatever circumstances I am" (Phil. 4:11).

Third, those who love money tend to flaunt it. They derive an inordinate pleasure from wearing, driving, or living in what money buys.

Fourth, those who love money resent giving it. They want to use it all for their own selfish gratification.

Lastly, those who love money will often sin to get it. They will cheat on their income tax or their expense account, or pilfer from work. Those who compromise their principles for money betray a heart that loves it more than God, righteousness, and truth.

In the preceding passage, the apostle discussed false teachers (6:3–5) and their inordinate love for money. That issue leads to his discussion in verses 6–10. He wrote to counter the perverted notion that religious piety was a means to material gain (v. 5). Paul looks at the nature, effects, and illustrations of loving money.

The Nature of Money Love

But godliness actually is a means of great gain, when accompanied by contentment. For we have brought nothing into the world, so we cannot take anything out of it either. And if we have food and covering, with these we shall be content. (6:6–8)

Loving money is dangerous because of its very nature. Paul lists three features of money love that highlight that danger.

LOVING MONEY IGNORES THE TRUE GAIN

But godliness actually is a means of great gain, when accompanied by contentment. (6:6)

This verse is closely connected with verse 5. *De* (**but**) could also be translated "indeed." In that case, Paul would be saying in response to the false teachers who saw their religious activity as a way to get rich, "Indeed, godliness does provide great gain." The NASB translation reflects an adversative sense of the word. Paul's meaning then is "But as over against the false understanding of godliness displayed by the false teachers, true godliness does result in great gain." The apostle's point is that true godliness is profitable, but not as some think.

Godliness translates *eusebeia,* a familiar term in the Pastoral Epistles. It means "piety," "reverence," or "likeness to God," and here even "religion," in the true sense. As such, it describes true holiness, spirituality, and virtue. **When accompanied by contentment,** such religion or godliness **is a means of great gain.** *Autarkēia* (**contentment**) means "self-sufficiency," and was used by the Cynic and Stoic philosophers to describe the person who was unflappable, unmoved by outside circumstances, and who properly reacted to his environment (cf. Geoffrey B. Wilson, *The Pastoral Epistles* [Edinburgh: Banner of Truth, 1982], 85). To be content means to be satisfied and sufficient, and to seek nothing more than what one has.

For the Christian, unlike the Greek philosophers, contentment derives from God. Paul writes in 2 Corinthians 3:5, "Not that we are adequate in ourselves to consider anything as coming from ourselves, but our adequacy is from God." In 2 Corinthians 9:8 he adds, "God is able to make all grace abound to you, that always having all sufficiency in everything, you may have an abundance for every good deed." The apostle gave testimony to his own contentment in Philippians 4:11–13:

> I have learned to be content in whatever circumstances I am. I know how to get along with humble means, and I also know how to live in prosperity; in any and every circumstance I have learned the secret of being filled and going hungry, both of having abundance and suffering need. I can do all things through Him who strengthens me.

In verse 19 of the same chapter he adds, "My God shall supply all your needs according to His riches in glory in Christ Jesus." For the believer, then, contentment is more than a mere noble human virtue. It is based on the sufficiency provided by God the Father and Jesus Christ. Loving money deprives one of that contentment, thus ignoring the true gain provided by true godliness.

True **godliness** produces **contentment** and spiritual riches. People are truly rich when they are content with what they have. The richest person is the one who doesn't need anything else. When asked the secret of contentment, the Greek philosopher Epicurus replied, "Add not to a man's possessions but take away from his desires" (cited in William Barclay, *The Letters to Timothy, Titus, and Philemon* [Philadelphia: Westminster, 1975], 129). He is richest who desires the least. Proverbs 30:8–9 puts it this way: "Give me neither poverty nor riches; feed me with the food that is my portion, lest I be full and deny Thee and say, "Who is the Lord?" Or lest I be in want and steal, and profane the name of my God."

A godly person is motivated not by the love of money but by the love of God. He seeks the true riches of spiritual contentment that come from complete trust in an all-sufficient God. David said in Psalm 63:1–5,

> O God, Thou art my God; I shall seek Thee earnestly; my soul thirsts for Thee, my flesh yearns for Thee, in a dry and weary land where there is no water. Thus I have beheld Thee in the sanctuary, to see Thy power and Thy glory. Because Thy lovingkindness is better than life, my lips will praise Thee. So I will bless Thee as long as I live; I will lift up my hands in Thy name. My soul is satisfied as with marrow and fatness, and my mouth offers praises with joyful lips (cf. Ps. 107:9; Isa. 55:2; 58:11).

No amount of money will make up for a lack of contentment. John D. Rockefeller once said, "I have made many millions, but they have brought me no happiness." Cornelius Vanderbilt added, "The care of millions is too great a load . . . there is no pleasure in it." Millionaire John Jacob Astor described himself as "the most miserable man on earth." Despite his wealth, Henry Ford once remarked, "I was happier doing mechanic's work." And John D. Rockefeller commented, "The poorest man I know is the man who has nothing but money."

Love of money and contentment are mutually exclusive. As a Roman proverb put it, money is like sea water, the more you drink the thirstier you get (Barclay, *The Letters to Timothy, Titus, and Philemon,* 132). Ecclesiastes 5:10 sums it up, "He who loves money will not be satisfied with money."

LOVING MONEY FOCUSES ON THE TEMPORAL

For we have brought nothing into the world, so we cannot take anything out of it either. (6:7)

In the Greek text, the word **nothing** is placed first in the sentence for emphasis. **We** bring **nothing into the world** when we are born, and **we cannot take anything out of it either** when we die. In Job 1:21 Job said, "Naked I came from my mother's womb, and naked I shall return there." Ecclesiastes 5:15 adds, "As he had come naked from his mother's womb, so will he return as he came. He will take nothing from the fruit of his labor that he can carry in his hand." People whose lives are dominated by the love of money spend their time pursuing what is locked into time and space. They ignore the things that have eternal value. Proverbs 27:24 warns that "riches are not forever." As an old Spanish proverb put it, there are no pockets in a shroud. The modern equivalent of that saying is that hearses do not haul trailers.

Our Lord had much to say about the foolishness of pursuing temporal riches. In Matthew 6:19–20 He said, "Do not lay up for yourselves treasures upon earth, where moth and rust destroy, and where thieves break in and steal. But lay up for yourselves treasures in heaven, where neither moth nor rust destroys, and where thieves do not break in or steal." Mark 8:36 adds, "For what does it profit a man to gain the whole world, and forfeit his soul?" In Luke 12:15–21, Jesus gave a parable to illustrate that point:

> And He said to them, "Beware, and be on your guard against every form of greed; for not even when one has an abundance does his life consist of his possessions." And He told them a parable, saying, "The land of a certain rich man was very productive. And he began reasoning to himself, saying, 'What shall I do, since I have no place to store my crops?' And he said, 'This is what I will do: I will tear down my barns and build larger ones, and there I will store all my grain and my goods. And I will say to my soul, "Soul, you have many goods laid up for many years to come; take your ease, eat, drink and be merry."' But God said to him, 'You fool! This very night your soul is required of you; and now who will own what you have prepared?' So is the man who lays up treasure for himself, and is not rich toward God."

To be so focused on temporal possessions as to miss the eternal riches is the height of folly.

LOVING MONEY OBSCURES THE SIMPLICITY OF LIFE

And if we have food and covering, with these we shall be content. (6:8)

The more money and possessions one has, the more complex life becomes. The preacher in Ecclesiastes 5:11 mused, "When good things increase, those who consume them increase. So what is the advantage to their owners except to look on?" Material things demand time and energy that could be better spent on eternal realities. **Food and covering** (the basic necessities of life) should be enough to make Christians **content.** Paul does not condemn having possessions, if God graciously provides them. No vow of poverty is required. What he does condemn is a self-indulgent desire for money rising from discontent. The supreme goal of a believer's life must be to love and glorify God, not to amass material possessions. As we love and glorify God, He may choose to bless us with riches. In that case, we are to deal with them from the same motive of loving and glorifying Him.

Our society replaces people with things, conversation with entertainment. By so doing, we have lost the simple joys of life, which center on relationships, the essence of Christian fellowship. Material things can pull believers away from those vital relationships with God and others.

The clearest statement on living a simple life free from the love of material things comes from our Lord. In Matthew 6:24–33 He said,

> No one can serve two masters; for either he will hate the one and love the other, or he will hold to one and despise the other. You cannot serve God and mammon. For this reason I say to you, do not be anxious for your life, as to what you shall eat, or what you shall drink; nor for your body, as to what you shall put on. Is not life more than food, and the body than clothing? Look at the birds of the air, that they do not sow, neither do they reap, nor gather into barns, and yet your heavenly Father feeds them. Are you not worth much more than they? And which of you by being anxious can add a single cubit to his life's span? And why are you anxious about clothing? Observe how the lilies of the field grow; they do not toil nor do they spin, yet I say to you that even Solomon in all his glory did not clothe himself like one of these. But if God so arrays the grass of the field, which is alive today and tomorrow is thrown into the furnace, will He not much more do so for you, O men of little faith? Do not be anxious then, saying, "What shall we eat?" or "What shall we drink?" or "With what shall we clothe ourselves?" For all these things the Gentiles eagerly seek; for your heavenly Father knows that you need all these things. But seek first His kingdom and His righteousness; and all these things shall be added to you.

The simple life involves accepting what God provides and avoiding covetousness.

The following practical principles will help keep life free from the desire for more material possessions.

First, believers must consciously realize that the Lord owns everything they have. They are mere stewards of their possessions. Purchases should be evaluated as to how they would advance the kingdom, or make one's ministry more effective.

Second, believers must cultivate a thankful heart. Since God owes them nothing, anything they receive from Him should make them thankful.

Third, believers must learn to distinguish wants from needs. That principle, if followed, would greatly increase the amount of money available for the Lord's work.

Fourth, believers must discipline themselves to spend less than they make. The ease of buying things on credit has become a severe temptation. As a result, many people are so hopelessly mired in debt that they will never get out.

Finally, believers must give sacrificially to the Lord. Laying up treasure in heaven for the work of the kingdom should be their highest joy and source of greatest reward.

THE EFFECTS OF MONEY LOVE

But those who want to get rich fall into temptation and a snare and many foolish and harmful desires which plunge men into ruin and destruction. (6:9)

The sin of loving money is dangerous not only because of its nature, but also because of its effects.

LOVING MONEY RESULTS IN SINFUL ENTRAPMENT

But those who want to get rich fall into temptation and a snare (6:9a)

People **who want to get rich** are tempted strongly and often caught in painful, debilitating sin like an animal in a **snare.** *Boulomai* (**want**) refers to a settled desire, one born of reason, not emotion, and describes clearly those guilty of the sin of greed. The present tense of the verb *empiptō* (**fall**) indicates a continual falling into **temptation** and traps. Greedy people are continually entrapped by their consuming drive for more. Their pursuit of what they want is their passion. Their sinful behavior becomes compulsive and controls their lives.

The Bible cautions against becoming entrapped by material things. In Deuteronomy 7:25 Moses warned the Israelites, "The graven images of their gods you are to burn with fire; you shall not covet the silver or the gold that is on them, nor take it for yourselves, lest you be snared by it, for it is an abomination to the Lord your God." Love of money is a trap that needs to be carefully avoided.

LOVING MONEY RESULTS IN SUCCUMBING TO HARMFUL DESIRES

and many foolish and harmful desires (6:9b)

Loving money leads to the trap of crippling sin, which results in one being controlled by **foolish and harmful desires.** *Epithumia* (**desires**) usually speaks of evil desires. They are **foolish** because they are irrational, senseless, illogical. Those controlled by them thrash around like an animal in a trap, victims of their own evil lusts. When their **desires** are thwarted, they may even resort to violence (James 4:1–2). Their sinful **desires** are thus **harmful** to them. Those desires lead to the opposite of true happiness, because they have nothing whatsoever to do with the spiritual realm or the service of God. That alone is the source of true joy.

LOVING MONEY RESULTS IN ETERNAL JUDGMENT

which plunge men into ruin and destruction. (6:9c)

The wholehearted pursuit of material wealth ultimately ruins one's spiritual life. **Plunge** is from *buthizō,* which means "to sink," "submerge," or "drag to the bottom." The pursuit of riches ultimately drowns men. *Olethros* (**ruin**) is often used of the body, though it can have a more general meaning (cf. 1 Thess. 5:3). *Apōleia* (**destruction**) usually refers to the eternal ruin of the soul (cf. Rom. 9:22; 2 Thess. 2:3; Heb. 10:39; Rev. 17:8). The three terms together paint a picture of the total devastation of both body and soul. Love of money destroys people.

The Scriptures contain many tragic examples of those destroyed by money love. Achan's love for money brought defeat to Israel, and death to himself and his family (Josh. 7:1–26). Judas betrayed the Lord Jesus Christ for a paltry sum of money (Matt. 27:3–5). In Acts 8:20–23, Peter sternly rebuked Simon, who sought to buy the Spirit's power:

> But Peter said to him, "May your silver perish with you, because you thought you could obtain the gift of God with money! You have no part or portion in this matter, for your heart is not right before God. Therefore repent of this wickedness of yours, and pray the Lord that if possible, the intention of your heart may be forgiven you. For I see that you are in the gall of bitterness and in the bondage of iniquity."

James condemned in no uncertain terms those who love money:

> Come now, you rich, weep and howl for your miseries which are coming upon you. Your riches have rotted and your garments have become moth-eaten. Your gold and your silver have rusted; and their rust will be a witness against you and will consume your flesh like fire. It is in

> the last days that you have stored up your treasure! Behold, the pay of the laborers who mowed your fields, and which has been withheld by you, cries out against you; and the outcry of those who did the harvesting has reached the ears of the Lord of Sabaoth. You have lived luxuriously on the earth and led a life of wanton pleasure; you have fattened your hearts in a day of slaughter. (James 5:1–5)

"Neither their silver nor their gold," sums up Zephaniah 1:18, "will be able to deliver them on the day of the Lord's wrath."

The Illustrations of Money Love

For the love of money is a root of all sorts of evil, and some by longing for it have wandered away from the faith, and pierced themselves with many a pang. (6:10)

The phrase **the love of money is a root of all sorts of evil,** is the theme of this section. Everything else is an exposition of the significance of that statement. **Love of money** translates *philarguria,* a compound word that literally means "affection for silver." As already noted, money is not intrinsically evil. Paul condemns **the love of money,** not money itself. That love becomes the **root** from which develops **all sorts of evil.** It is hard to imagine a sin that has not been committed for **love of money.** Such love causes people to indulge themselves, show off, distort justice, take advantage of the poor, lie, cheat, steal, and murder.

Paul closes this passage by illustrating the danger of loving money. **Some by longing for it,** he warns, had **wandered away from the faith, and pierced themselves with many a pang.** Paul does not name names, but he would shortly have an example from his inner circle. Demas was perhaps even then turning aside to pursue the things of this world (cf. 2 Tim. 4:10). He, and others like him, **have wandered away from the faith.** Here, as in Jude 3, **the faith** refers to the body of Christian truth. For these apostates, gold replaced God.

Not only have they become apostates, but they have also **pierced themselves with many a pang.** Like an animal placed on a spit, they have skewered their own souls and brought themselves consuming grief. A condemning conscience, unfulfilled desires, dissatisfaction, and disillusionment are their lot. As Psalm 32:10 says, "Many are the sorrows of the wicked." The ultimate **pang** they will suffer may well be eternal torment in hell.

Believers must pursue God, not money. Like David, they should be able to say, "As for me, I shall behold Thy face in righteousness; I will be satisfied with Thy likeness when I awake" (Ps. 17:15).

C. T. Studd was one of nineteenth-century England's greatest cricket stars. After his conversion to Christ, he decided upon a missionary career. Before leaving for the mission field, he decided to give away his inheritance. His biographer picks up the story:

> So far as he could judge, his inheritance was £29,000. But in order to leave a margin for error, he decided to start by giving £25,000. One memorable day, Jan. 13, 1887, he sent off four cheques of £5,000 each, and five of £1,000. . . . This was no fool's plunge on his part. It was his public testimony before God and man that he believed God's Word to be the surest thing on earth, and that the hundredfold interest which God has promised in this life, not to speak of the next, is an actual reality for those who believe it and act on it.
>
> He sent £5,000 to Mr. [D. L.] Moody, expressing the hope that he would be able to start some Gospel Work at Tirhoot in North India, where his father had made his fortune. Moody hoped to carry this out, but was unable to, and instead used the money to start the famous Moody Bible Institute in Chicago. . .
>
> £5,000 he sent to Mr. George Müller, £4,000 to be used on missionary work, and £1,000 among the orphans; £5,000 to George Holland, in Whitechapel, "to be used for the Lord among His poor in London," . . . and £5,000 to Commissioner Booth Tucker for the Salvation Army in India. (Norman P. Grubb, *C. T. Studd: Cricketer and Pioneer* [London: Lutterworth Press, 1953], 65–66)

Various other organizations received the remainder of the £25,000. His actual inheritance turned out to be a few thousand pounds more than he originally figured. He gave some of that money to other organizations and the rest to his fiancee as a wedding present. Not to be outdone, she gave that money away. The couple then went to Africa as missionaries with nothing (Grubb, *C. T. Studd,* 66–67).

The Man of God —part 1 The Characteristics of a Spiritual Leader

23

But flee from these things, you man of God; and pursue righteousness, godliness, faith, love, perseverance and gentleness. Fight the good fight of faith; take hold of the eternal life to which you were called, and you made the good confession in the presence of many witnesses. I charge you in the presence of God, who gives life to all things, and of Christ Jesus, who testified the good confession before Pontius Pilate, that you keep the commandment without stain or reproach until the appearing of our Lord Jesus Christ, (6:11–14)

The title **man of God** is simple, yet immeasurably rich. It is a sacred privilege to be identified as God's personal possession, a privilege that carries with it a grave responsibility. Although the phrase **man of God** is commonly used in the Old Testament, it describes only Timothy in the New. Paul used that title to increase Timothy's sense of responsibility to discharge his ministry. How could the man who personally belonged to God do any less?

The phrase **man of God** first appears in Deuteronomy 33:1 where it describes Moses (cf. 1 Chron. 23:14; 2 Chron. 30:16; Ezra 3:2; Ps. 90:1), the great deliver of his people and author of the Pentateuch.

The Angel of the Lord, (the preincarnate Christ) who appeared to Samson's parents, is also called "a man of God" (Judg. 13:6, 8). In 1 Samuel 2:27, the term describes the prophet sent to pronounce judgment on the house of Eli, while in 1 Samuel 9:6ff. it describes Eli's successor, Samuel. The prophet Shemaiah, who rebuked King Rehoboam, also bears the title "the man of God" in 1 Kings 12:22, as do the prophets who rebuked Kings Jeroboam (1 Kings 13:1ff.) and Amaziah (2 Chron. 25:7), and the prophet Igdaliah, a contemporary of Jeremiah (Jer. 35:4). In addition, such great figures as Elijah (1 Kings 17:18, 24), Elisha (2 Kings 4:7ff.), and David (Neh. 12:24, 36) were also called men of God. Peter uses the plural phrase "men of God" to refer to those who wrote the Old Testament Scriptures (2 Peter 1:21 KJV).

All of the Old Testament uses point to an individual who represents God by proclaiming His Word. By calling his young protege a **man of God,** Paul places Timothy into that rich Old Testament tradition. He, like those before him, was called, ordained, and responsible to preach the Word of God.

The only other use of the singular phrase is in 2 Timothy 3:16–17. Although Timothy is the subject of those verses (cf. vv. 14–15), the term can include anyone in the proclamation ministry. At its widest point of interpretation, it can embrace any believer, since the Word does equip all Christians for good works. But the primary emphasis is on how the Word equips the preacher to be "adequate, equipped for every good work." As did Timothy, all men of God stand in the long line of historic spokesmen dating back to Moses. They are, in the words of John Bunyan, the King's champions (*The Pilgrim's Progress* [reprint; Grand Rapids: Zondervan, 1976], 120). Having been lifted above worldly aims, they are utterly devoted to proclaiming God's Word.

All of that was important for Timothy to consider. He faced a formidable task in Ephesus, as he attempted to restore truth and order to a church that had lost its way. Paul mentions the danger of false teachers three times in this epistle (1:3–7; 4:1–5; 6:3–10). The apostle follows each warning with a charge to Timothy to resist them in light of his call to the ministry (1:18–20; 4:14–16; 6:11–12). He was God's man, His champion in the war against false teaching, His voice.

How is such a man of God to conduct himself? In this passage Paul lists four characteristics that mark the loyal man of God: what he flees from, follows after, fights for, and is faithful to.

A Man of God Is Known by What He Flees From

But flee from these things, you man of God; (6:11a)

The adversative sense of *de* (**but**), coupled with the use of the personal pronoun *su* (**you**), sharply contrasts Timothy with the false teachers. They are money's men, he is God's man; they are sin's men, he is righteousness's man; they are the world's men, he is heaven's man. Although left untranslated by the NASB, the Greek text uses the interjection *ō* ("O"). The use of that interjection with the vocative case is rare in the New Testament, indicating the intensity of Paul's appeal.

A **man of God** realizes there are certain things to be avoided at all cost. **Flee** is from *pheugō,* from which our English word "fugitive" derives. God's man must flee from sexual sin (1 Cor. 6:18), idolatry (1 Cor. 10:14), and "youthful lusts" (2 Tim. 2:22). The present tense of the verb indicates the **man of God** is to constantly **flee from these things.** The direct antecedent of **these things** is the evils associated with loving money in vv. 9–10.

That is the cardinal sin of false teachers, who pervert the truth for personal gain. From Balaam, who sold himself to the highest bidder, through the greedy false prophets of Israel, to Judas and Demas in the New Testament, the hallmark of false teachers is greed.

Paul carefully avoided any appearance of loving money. In his farewell address to the Ephesian elders, he reminded them,

> I have coveted no one's silver or gold or clothes. You yourselves know that these hands ministered to my own needs and to the men who were with me. In everything I showed you that by working hard in this manner you must help the weak and remember the words of the Lord Jesus, that He Himself said, "It is more blessed to give than to receive." (Acts 20:33–35)

To the Thessalonians he wrote, "For you recall, brethren, our labor and hardship, how working night and day so as not to be a burden to any of you, we proclaimed to you the gospel of God" (1 Thess. 2:9). He reminded the Corinthians of his right to financial support, but then waived it so no one would question his motives (1 Cor. 9:1–15).

Although they may call themselves ministers of the gospel, those in it for the money are not God's men. They have prostituted the call of God for personal gain. Those who put a price on their ministry devalue it in God's sight to zero.

A Man of God Is Known by What He Follows After

and pursue righteousness, godliness, faith, love, perseverance and gentleness. (6:11b)

As fast as the man of God runs from the corrupting love of money he runs toward spiritual virtue. A man of God not only flees from sin, but also is to continually pursue holiness. The form here is parallel to 2 Timothy 2:22, where Paul commands Timothy not only to "flee from youthful lusts," but also to "pursue righteousness, faith, love and peace." If he stops, what is behind him (sin) will catch him, and he will miss his goal of holiness. In verse 11, Paul lists six virtues that every man of God must pursue to deserve that privileged title.

The first two are general virtues, one having to do with external behavior, the other with the internal attitude and motive. **Righteousness** translates the familiar New Testament term *dikaiosunē.* It means to do what is right, in relation to both God and man. The righteousness Paul describes here is not Christ's righteousness imputed to us at salvation, but holiness of life. God's man is known for doing what is right. His is a lifestyle marked by obedience to God's commands.

The internal counterpart to **righteousness** is **godliness.** While **righteousness** looks to the outward behavior, **godliness** has to do with the attitudes and motives. Right behavior flows from right motives. *Eusebeia* (**godliness**), a familiar term in the Pastorals (appearing ten times), refers to reverence for God flowing out of a worshiping heart. It could be translated "God-likeness." Godly people "offer to God an acceptable service with reverence and awe" (Heb. 12:28). They will one day receive praise from the Lord Himself (1 Cor. 4:1–5).

Those two virtues are central to a godly minister's power and usefulness. They form an essential part of what Spurgeon called "the minister's self-watch" (C. H. Spurgeon, *Lectures to My Students*, vol. 1 [Grand Rapids: Baker, 1980]). The Puritan Richard Baxter had much to say on that topic, devoting an entire section of his classic work *The Reformed Pastor* to it. He warned, "Many a tailor goes in rags, that maketh costly clothes for others; and many a cook scarcely licks his fingers, when he hath dressed for others the most costly dishes" (*The Reformed Pastor* [Edinburgh: Banner of Truth, 1979], 54).

Paul knew well the importance of the minister's watch over himself. In Acts 20:28 he exhorted the leaders of the Ephesian church to "be on guard for yourselves." In 1 Timothy 4:16, he commanded Timothy to "pay close attention to [himself]." Knowing his own sinfulness (cf. Rom. 7:14–25; 1 Tim. 1:12–15), Paul strenuously disciplined himself. To the Corinthians he wrote,

> Do you not know that those who run in a race all run, but only one receives the prize? Run in such a way that you may win. And everyone who competes in the games exercises self-control in all things. They then do it to receive a perishable wreath, but we an imperishable.

> Therefore I run in such a way, as not without aim; I box in such a way, as not beating the air; but I buffet my body and make it my slave, lest possibly, after I have preached to others, I myself should be disqualified. (1 Cor. 9:24–27)

The Puritan John Flavel pointedly observed, "Brethren, it is easier to declaim against a thousand sins of others, than to mortify one sin in ourselves" (cited in I. D. E. Thomas, *A Puritan Golden Treasury* [Edinburgh: Banner of Truth, 1977], 191).

John Owen added, "A minister may fill his pews, his communion roll, the mouths of the public, but what that minister is on his knees in secret before God Almighty, that he is and no more" (cited in Thomas, *A Puritan Golden Treasury,* 192).

The nineteenth-century English pastor Charles Bridges wrote,

> For if we should study the Bible more as Ministers than as Christians—more to find matter for the instruction of our people, than food for the nourishment of our own souls, we neglect then to place ourselves at the feet of our Divine Teacher, our communion with Him is cut off, and we become mere formalists in our sacred profession. . . . We cannot live by feeding others; or heal ourselves by the mere employment of healing our people; and therefore by this course of official service, our familiarity with the awful realities of death and eternity may be rather like that of the grave-digger, the physician, and the soldier, than the man of God, viewing eternity with deep seriousness and concern and bringing to his people the profitable fruit of his contemplations. It has well been remarked—that 'when once a man begins to view religion not as of personal, but merely of professional importance, he has an obstacle in his course, with which a private Christian is unacquainted.' It is indeed difficult to determine, whether our familiar intercourse with the things of God is more our temptation or our advantage. (*The Christian Ministry* [Edinburgh: Banner of Truth, 1980], 163)

The apostle next names the dominant internal virtues: **faith** and **love. Faith** is simply confident trust in God for everything. It involves loyalty to the Lord and unwavering confidence in His power, purpose, plan, provision, and promise. Faith is the atmosphere in which the man of God exists. He trusts God to keep and fulfill His Word.

As he often does in his writings, Paul couples **love** with **faith** (cf. 1 Thess. 3:6; 5:8; 1 Tim. 1:14; 2 Tim. 1:13). *Agapē* (**love**) is the love of volition and choice. It is unrestricted and unrestrained, encompassing love for God, other believers, and non-Christians. The man of God understands the significance of our Lord's words in Matthew 22:37–39: "'You shall love the Lord your God with all your heart, and with all your soul, and with all your mind.' This is the great and foremost commandment. The second is like it, 'You shall love your neighbor as yourself.'" Because he is a lover of God, the man of God loves those whom He loves (cf. 1 John 4:7–21). The love of God, "poured out within [his heart] through the Holy Spirit" (Rom. 5:5) flows out of him to others (cf. 2 Cor. 6:11–13; 12:15; Phil. 2:25ff.; Col. 1:27–28; 4:12).

Paul then mentions two external virtues, **perseverance and gentleness. Perseverance** translates *hupomonē,* which means "to remain under." It does not describe a passive, fatalistic resignation, but a victorious, triumphant, unswerving loyalty to the Lord in the midst of trials (cf. James 1:2–4). It is the **perseverance** of the martyr, who will lay down his life if necessary for the cause of Christ. Paul and most of the other apostles would exhibit that supreme measure of **perseverance. Perseverance** enables the man of God to stick with the task, no matter what the cost.

Gentleness translates *praupathia,* which means kindness or meekness, and appears only here in the New Testament. Although consumed with the greatest of causes, the man of God recognizes that in himself he makes no contribution to its success, and is marked by considerate humility. His is the attitude expressed by John Bunyan in *The Pilgrim's Progress*:

> He that is down needs fear no fall,
> He that is low no pride;
> He that is humble ever shall
> Have God to be his guide.
> (Bunyan, 219)

A Man of God Is Known by What He Fights For

Fight the good fight of faith; take hold of the eternal life to which you were called, and you made the good confession in the presence of many witnesses. (6:12)

Being a spokesman for God calls a man into warfare. It is a constant battle against the flesh, the devil, and the resistance of the fallen world that loves sin and error and hates truth and holiness. It is also a struggle against lethargic Christians and apathetic churches. Paul charged Timothy to "suffer hardship with me, as a good soldier of Christ Jesus" (2 Tim. 2:3). The apostle's own triumphant epitaph reads, "I have fought the good fight, I have finished the course, I have kept the faith" (2 Tim. 4:7).

Sadly, some do not even realize they are in a battle. Others seek positions of ease and comfort, in effect going AWOL from the spiritual battle. Paul was under no such delusions, however. He told the believers in Lystra, Iconium, and Antioch that "through many tribulations we must enter the kingdom of God" (Acts 14:22). In his second letter to Timothy he wrote, "Indeed, all who desire to live godly in Christ Jesus will be persecuted" (2 Tim. 3:12). Our Lord warned, "He who does not take his cross and follow after Me is not worthy of Me" (Matt. 10:38).

The verb **fight** is from *agonizomai,* from which our English word "agonize" derives. It was used in both military and athletic contexts to describe the concentration, discipline, conviction, and effort needed to win. The present imperative tense of the verb once again indicates the continuous nature of the battle. **Good** translates *kalos,* which could be translated "noble," or "excellent." The noun **fight** translates *agōn,* from the same root as the verb. It refers to the spiritual conflict with Satan's kingdom, in which the man of God must play his part.

Faith refers to the body of Christian truth, the contents of the Word of God, the "faith which was once for all delivered to the saints" (Jude 3). The **faith** is the supreme reality we all can fight for.

By commanding Timothy to **take hold of eternal life,** Paul obviously did not mean to imply that Timothy needed salvation. Instead, he admonished Timothy to "get a grip" on the reality of eternal life, so that he would live and minister in the light of eternity. Those who minister for what they can get in this world have a wrong perspective. The man of God "set[s his] mind on the things above, not on the things that are on earth" (Col. 3:2), knowing that his "citizenship is in heaven" (Phil. 3:20).

Called refers to the effectual sovereign call of God to salvation (cf. Rom. 8:30; 2 Tim. 1:9). Timothy had been called by God to salvation, to eternal glory; now he was to preach in the light of the reality that what is eternal is all that matters. He affirmed his calling to preach initially when he **made the good confession in the presence of many witnesses.** That refers to his public confession of faith in our Lord Jesus Christ. Timothy "confess[ed] with [his] mouth Jesus as Lord, and believe[d] in [his] heart that God raised Him from the dead" (Rom. 10:9; cf. Phil. 2:11). That confession was probably made at Timothy's baptism, and again at his ordination to the ministry (4:14; 2 Tim. 1:6).

The man of God, aware of God's effectual call to eternal salvation and his own public profession of faith in response to that call, maintains an eternal perspective. He does not engage in the petty, meaningless battles of this world, but focuses on the eternal things. He lives above the mundane and trivial matters of the passing world. He is consumed with what will never pass away—God's Word and the souls of men.

A Man of God Is Known by What He Is Faithful To

I charge you in the presence of God, who gives life to all things, and of Christ Jesus, who testified the good confession before Pontius Pilate, that you keep the commandment without stain or reproach until the appearing of our Lord Jesus Christ, (6:13–14)

The key to this section comes in verse 14, where Paul commands Timothy to **keep the commandment.** The rest of verses 13 and 14 explain that phrase. Verse 13 tells Timothy why he should **keep the commandment,** and the remainder of verse 14 tells him how he should keep it.

There is no limiting feature in the context that would narrow the definition of **the commandment.** It should therefore be understood in the broadest sense as the entire revealed Word of God, which Timothy is charged to preach (cf. Acts 20:20, 27; 2 Tim. 4:2). To **keep** the **commandment** is to guard it, not only by proclaiming it, but also by protecting it. Not surprisingly, Paul repeatedly encouraged Timothy to guard the truth that had been entrusted to him (cf. 1 Tim. 1:18–19; 4:6, 16; 6:20; 2 Tim. 1:13–14; 2:15–18). He was to do so "through the Holy Spirit" (2 Tim. 1:14). Only through His power can the man of God hold on to the truth and faithfully proclaim it.

To encourage Timothy to persevere no matter what the cost, Paul calls on two sovereign, supreme persons who will hold him accountable. **God, who gives life to all things,** is the first. It is in the Father's **presence** that the man of God lives and ministers. He is not to be a man-pleaser, but a God-pleaser (cf. Gal. 1:8–10). Knowledge of His omniscient and omnipresent scrutiny and perfect standard should motivate the man of God to diligence. *Zōogoneō* (**gives life to**) certainly refers to God as the One who alone has created all life and can and will preserve it until His sovereign purposes are accomplished. It can also refer to God's power to raise the dead (cf. Heb. 11:19). Paul's point is that God is in charge of all life, including Timothy's. Therefore, the preacher should not be concerned about the price of his faithful proclamation because the Lord will sustain him until he has finished his work. Even if the man of God is killed for his faithfulness to the Lord, God has the power and will resurrect him in glory.

The second witness is **Christ Jesus, who testified the good confession before Pontius Pilate.** Our Lord is the supreme earthly example of One who held fast to His confession, who remained faithful to the Word of God no matter what the cost. He did so because He trusted in God to deliver Him in life and death (cf. 1 Peter 2:21–23). When **Pontius Pilate** asked Him, "Are You the King of the Jews?" He fearlessly replied, "It is as you say" (Matt. 27:11). Our Lord boldly stood His ground, spoke the truth, and entrusted His life to God. Timothy, or any man of God, can do no less.

The apostle then told Timothy in what manner a man of God is to keep the commandment. First, he was to do so **without stain or reproach.** No blemish or legitimate accusation is to mar his testimony (cf. James 1:27). He was to be completely beyond reproach. He was also to be permanently faithful, **until the appearing of our Lord Jesus Christ.** *Epiphaneia* (**appearing**) is a reference to the return of the Lord. Timothy was to remain faithful all his life, until his death or His Savior's arrival. The expectation of his Lord's imminent return further motivates the man of God (cf. Acts 1:8–11; 1 Cor. 4:5; Rev. 22:12).

To proclaim God's Word as His own man is an immeasurable privilege. That privilege, however, carries with it a serious warning. James cautioned, "Let not many of you become teachers, my brethren, knowing that as such we shall incur a stricter judgment" (James 3:1). "From everyone who has been given much," Jesus warned, "shall much be required" (Luke 12:48).

One of the most sobering examples of a man of God who failed is found in 1 Kings 13:1–26:

> Now behold, there came a man of God from Judah to Bethel by the word of the Lord, while Jeroboam was standing by the altar to burn incense. And he cried against the altar by the word of the Lord, and said, "O altar, altar, thus says the Lord, 'Behold, a son shall be born to the house of David, Josiah by name; and on you he shall sacrifice the priests of the high places who burn incense on you, and human bones shall be burned on you.'" Then he gave a sign the same day, saying, "This is the sign which the Lord has spoken, 'Behold, the altar shall be split apart and the ashes which are on it shall be poured out.'" Now it came about when the king heard the saying of the man of God, which he cried against the altar in Bethel, that Jeroboam stretched out his hand from the altar, saying, "Seize him." But his hand which he stretched out against him dried up, so that he could not draw it back to himself. The altar also was split apart and the ashes were poured out from the altar, according to the sign which the man of God had given by the word of the Lord. And the king answered and said to the man of God, "Please entreat the Lord your God, and pray for me, that my hand may be restored to me." So the man of God entreated the Lord, and the king's hand was restored to him, and it became as it was before. Then the king said to the man of God, "Come home with me and refresh yourself, and I will give you a reward." But the man of God said to the king, "If you were to give me half your house I would not go with you, nor would I eat bread or drink water in this place. For so it was commanded me by the word of the Lord, saying, 'You shall eat no bread,

> nor drink water, nor return by the way which you came.'" So he went another way, and did not return by the way which he came to Bethel. Now an old prophet was living in Bethel; and his sons came and told him all the deeds which the man of God had done that day in Bethel; the words which he had spoken to the king, these also they related to their father. And their father said to them, "Which way did he go?" Now his sons had seen the way which the man of God who came from Judah had gone. Then he said to his sons, "Saddle the donkey for me." So they saddled the donkey for him and he rode away on it. So he went after the man of God and found him sitting under an oak; and he said to him, "Are you the man of God who came from Judah?" And he said, "I am." Then he said to him, "Come home with me and eat bread." And he said, "I cannot return with you, nor go with you, nor will I eat bread or drink water with you in this place. For a command came to me by the word of the Lord, 'You shall eat no bread, nor drink water there; do not return by going the way which you came.'" And he said to him, "I also am a prophet like you, and an angel spoke to me by the word of the Lord, saying, 'Bring him back with you to your house, that he may eat bread and drink water.'" But he lied to him. So he went back with him, and ate bread in his house and drank water. Now it came about, as they were sitting down at the table, that the word of the Lord came to the prophet who had brought him back; and he cried to the man of God who came from Judah, saying, "Thus says the Lord, 'Because you have disobeyed the command of the Lord, and have not observed the commandment which the Lord your God commanded you, but have returned and eaten bread and drunk water in the place of which He said to you, "Eat no bread and drink no water"; your body shall not come to the grave of your fathers.'" And it came about after he had eaten bread and after he had drunk, that he saddled the donkey for him, for the prophet whom he had brought back. Now when he had gone, a lion met him on the way and killed him, and his body was thrown on the road, with the donkey standing beside it; the lion also was standing beside the body. And behold, men passed by and saw the body thrown on the road, and the lion standing beside the body; so they came and told it in the city where the old prophet lived. Now when the prophet who brought him back from the way heard it, he said, "It is the man of God, who disobeyed the command of the Lord; therefore the Lord has given him to the lion, which has torn him and killed him, according to the word of the Lord which He spoke to him."

The unnamed prophet had the privilege of being used by God to rebuke King Jeroboam. By violating God's Word, however, he brought upon himself a terrible judgment. That is a warning every man of God should heed. Being a man of God is an elevated earthly privilege matched by an elevated heavenly accountability.

The Man of God —part 2 The Motivation of a Spiritual Leader

24

I charge you in the presence of God, who gives life to all things, and of Christ Jesus, who testified the good confession before Pontius Pilate, that you keep the commandment without stain or reproach until the appearing of our Lord Jesus Christ, which He will bring about at the proper time—He who is the blessed and only Sovereign, the King of kings and Lord of lords; who alone possesses immortality and dwells in unapproachable light; whom no man has seen or can see. To Him be honor and eternal dominion! Amen. (6:13–16)

First Timothy begins and ends with a doxology—a hymn of praise to the Lord (cf. 1:17). Therein lies the single greatest motivating factor for a man of God: the character of the God he serves. The apostle knew that theology proper (the doctrine of God) controls behavior. Put another way, how a person lives reflects what he really believes about God. J. B. Phillips decried the ineffectiveness of Christians by complaining, *Your God Is Too Small* (New York: Macmillan, 1961). A. W. Tozer stated the issue with great force and clarity in his classic work *The Knowledge of the Holy*: "What comes into our minds when we think about God is the most important thing about us" ([1961; reprint, New York: Harper & Row, 1975], 9). He went on to say,

> The history of mankind will probably show that no people has ever risen above its religion, and man's spiritual history will positively demonstrate that no religion has ever been greater than its idea of God. . . . For this reason the gravest question before the Church is always God Himself, and the most portentous fact about any man is not what he at a given time may say or do, but what he in his deep heart conceives God to be like. . . . Were we able to extract from any man a complete answer to the question, "What comes into your mind when you think about God?" we might predict with certainty the spiritual future of that man. (Tozer, 9)

Paul calls upon Timothy to fulfill his duty based upon who his God is. He himself was an example of one who "did not prove disobedient to the heavenly vision" (Acts 26:19).

In light of Timothy's prophetically confirmed call to the ministry (cf. 1:18; 4:14; 6:12), the question arises as to why he needed any further motivation. The answer lies in understanding the opposition he faced at Ephesus. He was an outsider, alone in confronting both opposition from false teachers and the sins of his people. He was looked down on for being young (4:12), and his battle with the lusts of youth (2 Tim. 2:22) was no doubt discouraging. His youthful zeal also tended to make him combative and overly argumentative (2 Tim. 2:24–26). His lack of experience put him at a further disadvantage when dealing with false doctrine.

Timothy was surely tempted to abandon his ministry there altogether. Paul had to remind him that "God has not given us a spirit of timidity, but of power and love and discipline" (2 Tim. 1:7), and urged him to "kindle afresh the gift of God which is in you through the laying on of my hands" (2 Tim. 1:6). Timothy was being pressured to become ashamed of Christ, and Paul (2 Tim. 1:8) because of the growing hostility toward the faith. Therefore, he had to be exhorted to hold fast to sound doctrine (2 Tim. 1:13–14). He was sorely in need of encouragement, fortitude, and strength to carry out his preaching and teaching.

There was and is only one source of strength for those in the ministry: God. Confidence in Him, and understanding of His character, lays the foundation that brings courage and strength to face any trial. That knowledge of the Almighty, more than anything else, also serves to motivate the man of God to fulfill his calling. So to encourage and stimulate his struggling young protege, Paul gives one of the most magnificent presentations of God's character found on the pages of Scripture.

Although the doxology does not come until verses 15–16, a review of verses 13–14 must be included, since they also give a glimpse of our magnificent God. In those four verses, six attributes of God can be discerned: the power of God, the invincibility of God, the blessedness of God, the sovereignty of God, the eternity of God, and the holiness of God.

The Power of God

I charge you in the presence of God, who gives life to all things, and of Christ Jesus, who testified the good confession before Pontius Pilate (6:13)

God's power is seen in His ability to give **life to all things.** There are four aspects of that ability.

First, the phrase refers to God as creator of all things. The first verse of the Bible states that "in the beginning God created the heavens and the earth" (Gen. 1:1). "Creator" is a frequent title of God (cf. Eccl. 12:1; Isa. 27:11; 40:28; 43:1, 15; Rom. 1:25; 1 Peter 4:19).

Second, God sustains all life. In Acts 17:28, Paul told the pagan Athenians, "In Him we live and move and exist." "O Lord," exclaimed the psalmist, "Thou preservest man and beast" (Ps. 36:6; cf. Neh. 9:6; Ps. 66:8–9; Heb. 1:3).

Third, God protects His own. David said in Psalm 37:28 that "the Lord . . . does not forsake His godly ones; they are preserved forever" (cf. Pss. 91:11–14; 140:7). Our Lord said in Matthew 10:29–31, "Are not two sparrows sold for a cent? And yet not one of them will fall to the ground apart from your Father. But the very hairs of your head are all numbered. Therefore do not fear; you are of more value than many sparrows." The triumphant cry of the believer is "In God I have put my trust; I shall not be afraid. What can mere man do to me" (Ps. 56:4; cf. 56:11; 118:6)?

The fourth principle is the most glorious feature in this realm. God's ability to give life to all is seen in His power to raise the dead to live eternally. Paul reminds Timothy that the worst men can do to him is to kill him. Even if they did so, that would merely usher Timothy into the Lord's presence. Paul put it this way to the Philippians: "For to me, to live is Christ, and to die is gain" (Phil. 1:21), since he had the "desire to depart and be with Christ, for that is very much better" (Phil. 1:23). Warned of persecution and imprisonment facing him when he returned to Jerusalem, the apostle replied,

> And now, behold, bound in spirit, I am on my way to Jerusalem, not knowing what will happen to me there, except that the Holy Spirit solemnly testifies to me in every city, saying that bonds and afflictions await me. But I do not consider my life of any account as dear to myself, in order that I may finish my course, and the ministry which I received from the Lord Jesus, to testify solemnly of the gospel of the grace of God. (Acts 20:22–24)

Paul understood the truth that "to be absent from the body" was to "be at home with the Lord" (2 Cor. 5:8), as did Abraham (Heb. 11:17–19), Job (Job 19:26), David (Ps. 16:10), the sons of Korah (Ps. 49:15), Isaiah (Isa. 26:19), Daniel (Dan. 12:2), and Hosea (Hos. 13:14).

The clearest indication that God's resurrection power is included in this passage comes from the mention of **Christ Jesus, who testified the good confession before Pontius Pilate.** The story of that confession is told in John 18:33–37:

> Pilate therefore entered again into the Praetorium, and summoned Jesus, and said to Him, "Are You the King of the Jews?" Jesus answered, "Are you saying this on your own initiative, or did others tell you about Me?" Pilate answered, "I am not a Jew, am I? Your own nation and the chief priests delivered You up to me; what have You done?" Jesus answered, "My kingdom is not of this world. If My kingdom were of this world, then My servants would be fighting, that I might not be delivered up to the Jews; but as it is, My kingdom is not of this realm." Pilate therefore said to Him, "So You are a king?" Jesus answered, "You say correctly that I am a king. For this I have been born, and for this I have come into the world, to bear witness to the truth. Everyone who is of the truth hears My voice."

Knowing that it would cost Him His life, Jesus confessed that He was indeed the King and Messiah. He never equivocated in the face of danger, having committed Himself to the God who raises the dead (cf. Col. 2:12). No wonder that Revelation calls Him "the faithful witness" (Rev. 1:5; cf. 3:14).

Understanding God's power to raise the dead allows the man of God to freely give away his life in sacrificial service. In the words of our Lord Jesus Christ, "For whoever wishes to save his life shall lose it, but whoever loses his life for My sake, he is the one who will save it" (Luke 9:24). Viewing his ministry in that light frees the man of God to pursue it fearlessly to the utmost.

THE INVINCIBILITY OF GOD

that you keep the commandment without stain or reproach until the appearing of our Lord Jesus Christ, which He will bring about at the proper time (6:14–15a)

The man of God understands that God's plan in history culminates in the **appearing of our Lord Jesus Christ.** As already noted, that is a general reference to the visible, glorious event when Christ comes to earth to judge and to set up His Kingdom. In Acts 1:11, the angels told the disciples that "This Jesus, who has been taken up from you into heaven, will come in just the same way as you have watched Him go into heaven." Our Lord described His return in vivid terms:

> For just as the lightning comes from the east, and flashes even to the west, so shall the coming of the Son of Man be. . . . But immediately after the tribulation of those days the sun will be darkened, and the moon will not give its light, and the stars will fall from the sky, and the powers of the heavens will be shaken, and then the sign of the Son of Man will appear in the sky, and then all the tribes of the earth will mourn, and they will see the Son of Man coming on the clouds of the sky with power and great glory. . . . But when the Son of Man comes in His glory, and all the angels with Him, then He will sit on His glorious throne. (Matt. 24:27, 29–30; 25:31)

That event is the culmination of human history and the vindication of Christ and those who are His. Prior to that judgment and the establishment of the kingdom on earth, the Lord will take His own saints to heaven (cf. John 14:1–4; 1 Thess. 4:13–18).

The man of God must keep a proper perspective on that coming reality. This life is "just a vapor that appears for a little while and then vanishes away" (James 4:14). It is the eternal realm into which he will enter and for which he labors. What kept Paul going through the rough times of his ministry was the certain knowledge that "in the future there is laid up for me the crown of righteousness, which the Lord, the righteous Judge, will award to me on that day" (2 Tim. 4:8). That crown of eternal righteousness is not only available to Paul, "but also to all who have loved His appearing" (2 Tim. 4:8).

As already noted, Christ's return vindicates Him by reversing the foolish judgment passed on Him by this world. His return also provides vindication for believers. "When Christ, who is our life, is revealed," wrote Paul, "then you also will be revealed with Him in glory" (Col. 3:4). Romans 8:19 reads, "For the anxious longing of the creation waits eagerly for the revealing of the sons of God," while 1 John 3:2 adds, "Beloved, now we are children of God, and it has not appeared as yet what we shall be. We know that, when He appears, we shall be like Him, because we shall see Him just as He is." The world may not know who believers are now, but one day their true character and position as sons of God will be manifested. Is it any wonder, then, that Paul could say, "I consider that the sufferings of this present time are not worthy to be compared with the glory that is to be revealed to us" (Rom. 8:18)?

God has provided an incredibly glorious future for believers. The man of God keeps his focus on that truth as he endures the trials of living and ministering in this present world. He is assured that the Lord will bring glorious victory in the day of Christ's return. He eagerly awaits the revelation of his Lord, **which He will bring about at the proper time.** He refers to God the Father, since the doxology that follows refers to Him. Despite the many futile attempts to set a date for the Second Coming, only the Father knows when it will be (Mark 13:32; Acts 1:7). We can trust Him to **bring** it **about at the proper time.**

The imminency of Christ's return further serves to motivate believers to service. The church must understand that

> the time has been shortened, so that from now on those who have wives should be as though they had none; and those who weep, as though they did not weep; and those who rejoice, as though they did not rejoice; and those who buy, as though they did not possess; and those who use the world, as though they did not make full use of it; for the form of this world is passing away. (1 Cor. 7:29–31)

For that reason, believers must focus on eternal realities. To the Corinthians Paul wrote, "Knowing the fear of the Lord, we persuade men" (2 Cor. 5:11). The reality that the wicked would one day stand before the Lord to be judged motivated the apostle's evangelistic efforts. The reality that he would one day be examined by the Lord further motivated his faithfulness as a steward of the mysteries of divine revelation (1 Cor. 4:1–5).

THE BLESSEDNESS OF GOD

He who is the blessed (6:15b)

Beginning with this phrase, Paul launches into one of the magnificent doxologies of Scripture. Each phrase in it expresses the transcendent, incomparable greatness of God. This first phrase of the doxology yields a third attribute of God, His blessedness. *Makarios* (**blessed**) means "happy," "content," or "fulfilled." When used in reference to God, it describes His lack of unhappiness, frustration, and anxiety. He is content, satisfied, at peace, fulfilled, and perfectly joyful. While some things please Him and other things do not, nothing alters His heavenly contentment. He controls everything to His own joyous ends.

Those who enter into a relationship with God enter into His calm. They can be unperturbed because He is unperturbed. The Psalmist wrote, "How blessed are all who take refuge in Him" (Ps. 2:12; cf. 34:8; 40:4; 84:12; 112:1; 128:1)! Scripture describes the blessed as those whom God chooses (Ps. 65:4), those who know Christ (Matt. 16:16–17), those who believe the Gospel (Gal. 3:9), those whose sins are forgiven (Rom. 4:7), those to whom God grants righteousness apart from works (Rom. 4:6–9), and those who obey the Word (James 1:25).

No matter what the opposition, no matter what trials or persecutions he faces, the man of God can be at peace. That peace is not based on external circumstances but on the knowledge that God is in control. Believers are blessed because they are in union with the God who is **blessed.**

The Sovereignty of God

and only Sovereign, the King of kings and Lord of lords; (6:15c)

God is the **only Sovereign** because He alone is God (Deut. 4:35, 39; 6:4; 32:39; 1 Sam. 2:2; 2 Sam. 7:22; 22:32; 1 Kings 8:23, 60; 2 Kings 19:15, 19; 2 Chron. 6:14; Neh. 9:6; Pss. 18:31; 86:10; Isa. 37:16, 20; 43:10; 44:6, 8; 45:5–6, 21–22; 46:9; Joel 2:27; 1 Cor. 8:4, 6). There is no one to vie with Him for control of the universe. "I act," says the Lord, "and who can reverse it" (Isa. 43:13)?

Isaiah understood that God is uniquely sovereign. He wrote,

> "To whom then will you liken Me that I should be his equal?" says the Holy One. Lift up your eyes on high and see who has created these stars, the One who leads forth their host by number, He calls them all by name; because of the greatness of His might and the strength of His power not one of them is missing. Why do you say, O Jacob, and assert, O Israel, "My way is hidden from the Lord, and the justice due me escapes the notice of my God"? Do you not know? Have you not heard? The Everlasting God, the Lord, the Creator of the ends of the earth does not become weary or tired. His understanding is inscrutable. He gives strength to the weary, and to him who lacks might He increases power.

> Though youths grow weary and tired, and vigorous young men stumble badly, yet those who wait for the Lord will gain new strength; they will mount up with wings like eagles, they will run and not get tired, they will walk and not become weary. (Isa. 40:25–31)

Dunastēs (**Sovereign**) comes from a word group whose basic meaning is "power." The adjective **only** shows that God's power to rule is inherent in Himself, not delegated from an outside source. God is absolutely sovereign and omnipotently rules everything everywhere. He has no rivals, certainly not Satan, whom He created, cast out of heaven, and sentenced to eternal hell.

God's sovereignty is further amplified by the title **King of kings and Lord of lords.** Such titles were given to God in the Old Testament (cf. Deut. 10:17; Ps. 136:2–3; Dan. 2:47). Although this title describes the Lord Jesus Christ in Rev. 17:14 and 19:16, it is here used in reference to the Father. The phrase "whom no man has seen or can see" clearly does not apply to Christ, "who was revealed in the flesh" (3:16).

It is likely that Paul intended this title as a conscious rebuttal to the cult of emperor worship. The deification of the emperor dates back to Augustus. It gradually assumed a central place in the empire, and became "the supreme cause of Roman persecution of Christians" (Bruce L. Shelley, *Church History in Plain Language* [Waco, Tex.: Word, 1982], 58). The Romans viewed emperor worship as the unifying factor that bound their diverse empire together. To refuse to worship Caesar was considered an act of treason. To counter that, Paul insists that God alone is the **Sovereign,** and He alone is to be worshiped.

The sovereignty of God is the most encouraging and comforting doctrine in all of Scripture. An understanding of it removes the anxiety from life. It also gives the man of God courage in spiritual duty and willingness to face any danger. God is never surprised, nor is His will ever frustrated. He says in Isaiah 46:11, "Truly I have spoken; truly I will bring it to pass. I have planned it, surely I will do it." Because He is in total control, there is no need to worry, to compromise, to equivocate, or to manipulate to achieve a goal.

The man of God knows that the success of his ministry does not depend on his ingenuity, wisdom, or talent. He is relieved of the intolerable burden of imagining that people's eternal destiny rests on the persuasiveness of his preaching or the cleverness of his invitation. He understands that no one comes to faith in Christ apart from God's gracious, sovereign choice. And he, too, is operating under the constant surveillance of and within the plan of the God who is in perfect control of everything. That frees him to focus on faithfully expounding the Word and fulfilling his calling with contentment.

The Eternity of God

who alone possesses immortality (6:16a)

Once again the apostle counters the cult of emperor worship. Although the Romans imagined the emperors to be immortal, Paul emphasizes that God **alone possesses immortality.** That phrase describes God's eternity. He **alone possesses immortality** in the sense that He is inherently immortal. Angels and men, having come into existence, will exist forever. Their immortality, however, derives from God. **Immortality** does not translate *aphtharsia,* which means "incorruptible," but *athanasia,* which means "deathless." God has an unending quality of life, and is incapable of dying. The psalmist wrote, "For with Thee is the fountain of life" (Ps. 36:9). Jesus said, "The Father has life in Himself" (John 5:26). Isaiah called Him "the Everlasting God" (Isa. 40:28), while Moses wrote in Psalm 90:2, "Before the mountains were born, or Thou didst give birth to the earth and the world, even from everlasting to everlasting, Thou art God" (cf. Hab. 1:12). Micah 5:2 describes the Lord Jesus Christ as eternal, offering further proof of His deity.

The man of God derives comfort from the knowledge that his God is above history and beyond time. No matter what happens during his brief span of time on this earth, the deathless, eternal One is available to support him. He shares the perspective of Paul, who told the Romans, "I consider that the sufferings of this present time are not worthy to be compared with the glory that is to be revealed to us" (Rom. 8:18; cf. 2 Cor. 4:17).

The Holiness of God

and dwells in unapproachable light; whom no man has seen or can see. (6:16b)

In this age of casual familiarity with God, it is well to remember His utter holiness. While God is our loving, gracious Father, He nevertheless **dwells in unapproachable light.** He is transcendent, totally beyond us. He is, in Martin Luther's words, *Deus absconditus,* the hidden God. Had he not revealed Himself and come out of His holy habitation, man could have had no knowledge of Him.

The psalmist wrote of Him, "O Lord my God, Thou art very great; Thou art clothed with splendor and majesty, covering Thyself with light as with a cloak" (Ps. 104:1–2). When Moses prayed for God to reveal His glory, the Lord replied,

> "I Myself will make all My goodness pass before you, and will proclaim the name of the Lord before you; and I will be gracious to whom I will be gracious, and will show compassion on whom I will show compassion." But He said, "You cannot see My face, for no man can see Me and live!" (Ex. 33:19–20)

The writer of Hebrews put it simply, "our God is a consuming fire" (Heb. 12:29).

The imagery of God as blazing light aptly expresses His holiness. He is totally separate from sin. Psalm 5:4 reads, "For Thou art not a God who takes pleasure in wickedness; no evil dwells with Thee." He is "majestic in holiness" (Ex. 15:11). "There is no one holy like the Lord" (1 Sam. 2:2).

Because of that holiness, God is inaccessible to man. He lives in an atmosphere of absolute purity, far too holy for mortals to ever enter. Such passages as Matthew 5:8, "Blessed are the pure in heart, for they shall see God," and 1 Corinthians 13:12, "Now we see in a mirror dimly, but then face to face," refer to only that much of a vision of God which glorified humanity can perceive.

How does God's absolute holiness fit into this doxology? Paul emphasizes God's inability to make any mistakes. He always does exactly what is right and just. That provides great comfort for the man of God as he pursues his ministry. Not only is God in total control, but He also never makes a misjudgment. Further, those who oppose and persecute him will one day be judged by the holy God. That knowledge equips the man of God to faithfully serve his Lord.

It is fitting that the doxology ends with a refrain of praise, **to Him be honor and eternal dominion! Amen.** Paul exclaims, "let God always be respected, and may his rule never end." That refrain takes its place alongside the other great hymns of praise to God in Scripture (cf. 1 Peter 4:11; 5:11; Jude 24–25).

Nothing motivates a man of God like a true understanding of the greatness of his God. Those who know their God can say with the writer to Hebrews, "The Lord is my helper, I will not be afraid. What shall man do to me" (Heb. 13:6)?

Handling Treasure

25

Instruct those who are rich in this present world not to be conceited or to fix their hope on the uncertainty of riches, but on God, who richly supplies us with all things to enjoy. Instruct them to do good, to be rich in good works, to be generous and ready to share, storing up for themselves the treasure of a good foundation for the future, so that they may take hold of that which is life indeed. (6:17–19)

As the apostle closes out his first epistle to his beloved son in the faith, two issues remain on his mind that relate to handling treasure. How believers handle those two treasures is a measure of their spiritual maturity and devotion to Christ. All believers are stewards, given the responsibility to protect and manage what the Lord has given them. In this passage Paul mentions the first of these vital areas in which believers are called to be stewards: material possessions.

The marvelous doxology of verses 15 and 16 was in reality a worshipful digression from which Paul now returns to his theme of duty. In so doing, he brings Timothy crashing down to earth from the glorious heights of God's exalted nature. The Christian life consists of both worship and duty. The highest form of worship is to do God's will (Rom.

12:1–2), while duty not springing from a worshipful heart is nothing but legalism. The Lord Jesus Christ joined worship and duty in Matthew 4:10: "You shall worship the Lord your God, and serve Him only." What He has joined together, man dares not separate.

Paul had already discussed the issue of earthly treasures as it relates to false teachers (6:5, 9–10). He pointed out the devastating consequences of loving and pursuing money. In verses 17–19 he covers the same topic from a different perspective. In verses 5, 9–10, the apostle spoke of those who desired to be rich. In verses 17–19, he counsels those who are already rich. Obviously, in the prosperous city of Ephesus there were some wealthy church members, so this passage provides an important balance to Paul's teaching earlier in the chapter. Had the apostle not added this further teaching, those in the congregation who were rich would have been left open to the charge of loving and pursuing money.

Paul does not condemn those whom God has enriched with material wealth, but does call upon them to exercise a proper stewardship of their God-given resources (cf. Deut. 8:18; 1 Sam. 2:7; 1 Chron. 29:12). It is not a sin to be rich. Such Old Testament saints as Abraham, Job, and Solomon were wealthy, as were such New Testament figures as Lydia, Dorcas, and Philemon. It is a sin, however, to love riches and fail to be a good steward of one's possessions.

While having money is not a sin, neither does it necessarily indicate God's blessing on a life. Many godly people are poor; even some faithful pastors can hardly afford to buy a new Bible when theirs wears out. On the other hand, many wicked men are very wealthy (cf. Ps. 73:3–12).

As Paul's delegate and the Lord's representative in prosperous Ephesus, Timothy was to **instruct those who are rich in this present world. Those who are rich** are not just those with the most expensive homes and the most extensive lands. To be **rich** is to have more than the mere essentials of food, clothing, and shelter. In today's terminology, it means to have discretionary dollars. Most Western Christians today fall into that category. **This present world** (literally, "the now age") is identified to indicate that earthly wealth is in view here, not spiritual riches.

Paul does not command the rich to divest themselves of their possessions and take a vow of poverty, but to have a proper perspective on handling their treasure. That includes realizing there is a danger to avoid, a duty to fulfill, and a development to consider.

The Danger to Avoid

Instruct those who are rich in this present world not to be conceited or to fix their hope on the uncertainty of riches, but on God, who richly supplies us with all things to enjoy. (6:17)

The first danger facing **those who are rich** is that they will become **conceited. Conceited** is from *hupsēlophroneō,* a compound verb meaning "to think lofty," "be haughty," or "have an exalted opinion of oneself." Looking down on those lower on the economic ladder is a distressing trait of fallen human nature. Rich people are constantly faced with the temptation to put on airs of superiority. Riches and pride are frequently found together, and the wealthier an individual is, the greater the temptation. It is exceedingly difficult to be wealthy and have a humble spirit. The temptation is to view others as mere servants, since wealthy people tend to hire others to do everything for them. Proverbs 18:23 describes what often transpires: "The poor man utters supplications, but the rich man answers roughly." That happens because "the rich man is wise in his own eyes" (Prov. 28:11).

The opposite of being **conceited** is having "humility of mind" (Phil. 2:3). That virtue was scorned by the haughty Greek culture, with its glorification of pride. Paul wants the rich in the Ephesian assembly to avoid that cultural iniquity and be humble.

Ezekiel 28:1–5 illustrates one who fell prey to pride due to his wealth:

> The word of the Lord came again to me saying, "Son of man, say to the leader of Tyre, 'Thus says the Lord God, "because your heart is lifted up and you have said," 'I am a god, I sit in the seat of gods, in the heart of the seas'; yet you are a man and not God, although you make your heart like the heart of God—behold, you are wiser than Daniel; there is no secret that is a match for you. By your wisdom and understanding you have acquired riches for yourself, and have acquired gold and silver for your treasuries. By your great wisdom, by your trade you have increased your riches, and your heart is lifted up because of your riches."'"

James warns against such an attitude in the church:

> My brethren, do not hold your faith in our glorious Lord Jesus Christ with an attitude of personal favoritism. For if a man comes into your assembly with a gold ring and dressed in fine clothes, and there also comes in a poor man in dirty clothes, and you pay special attention to the one who is wearing the fine clothes, and say, "You sit here in a good place," and you say to the poor man, "You stand over there, or sit down by my footstool," have you not made distinctions among yourselves, and become judges with evil motives? (2:1–4)

A second danger facing the rich is the temptation **to fix their hope on the uncertainty of riches.** To base **their hope on the un-**

certainty of riches, instead of God, is foolish. Proverbs 11:28 warns that "he who trusts in his riches will fall." Proverbs 23:4–5 adds, "Do not weary yourself to gain wealth, cease from your consideration of it. When you set your eyes on it, it is gone. For wealth certainly makes itself wings, like an eagle that flies toward the heavens." Once again, this is especially a temptation for the rich. Those who have a lot tend to trust in it, while those who have little can't trust in what they have, and so are more likely to turn to God in hope that He will supply.

In the parable of the rich fool, the Lord Jesus Christ warned of the foolishness of trusting riches (Luke 12:16–21):

> And He told them a parable, saying, "The land of a certain rich man was very productive. And he began reasoning to himself, saying, 'What shall I do, since I have no place to store my crops?' And he said, 'This is what I will do: I will tear down my barns and build larger ones, and there I will store all my grain and my goods. And I will say to my soul, "Soul, you have many goods laid up for many years to come; take your ease, eat, drink and be merry."' But God said to him, 'You fool! This very night your soul is required of you; and now who will own what you have prepared?' So is the man who lays up treasure for himself, and is not rich toward God."

Rather than trusting in riches, believers are to fix their hope **on God, who richly supplies us with all things to enjoy.** God provides far more security than any earthly investment. Psalm 50:10–12 describes His incalculable wealth: "Every beast of the forest is Mine, the cattle on a thousand hills. I know every bird of the mountains, and everything that moves in the field is Mine. If I were hungry, I would not tell you; for the world is Mine, and all it contains." God is not stingy; He **richly supplies** His children **with all things to enjoy.** Ecclesiastes 5:18–20 reads,

> Here is what I have seen to be good and fitting: to eat, to drink and enjoy oneself in all one's labor in which he toils under the sun during the few years of his life which God has given him; for this is his reward. Furthermore, as for every man to whom God has given riches and wealth, He has also empowered him to eat from them and to receive his reward and rejoice in his labor; this is the gift of God. For he will not often consider the years of his life, because God keeps him occupied with the gladness of his heart.

The highest form of joy for the believer is to bring glory to the Lord. True gladness, then, comes when believers give heed to Jesus' words in Matthew 6:19–21:

> Do not lay up for yourselves treasures upon earth, where moth and rust destroy, and where thieves break in and steal. But lay up for yourselves treasures in heaven, where neither moth nor rust destroys, and where thieves do not break in or steal; for where your treasure is, there will your heart be also.

The Duty to Fulfill

Instruct them to do good, to be rich in good works, to be generous and ready to share, (6:18)

The duty of all rich believers is to use their resources to meet the needs of others. The apostle gives four phrases that define that duty.

First, Timothy is to **instruct them to do good.** *Agathoergeō* (**do good**) appears only here in the New Testament. It means "to do what is inherently, intrinsically, and qualitatively good." The verb refers to doing what is noble and excellent, not what is only superficially good. It describes the most general aspect of the duty; the wealthy are to use their lives and their money to do genuinely good and noble things.

The second aspect narrows the duty of the rich further. They are **to be rich in good works.** God does not intend for material wealth to be hoarded or doled out sparingly. The key word is **rich,** meaning "abounding," or "abundantly furnished." Material wealth is to be used to perform **good works** on behalf of others. Believers' resources are to be used to support their own families (5:8), especially needy widows (5:4). The leaders of the church (5:17), and any believer in need (Acts 4:34–35), must also be provided for. And all such sharing is not to be minimal, but to fully cover the need and more.

A third phrase sharpens the apostle's focus still more as it zeros in on the motive. As they meet the needs of others, those with money must **be generous.** *Eumetadotos* (**generous**) means "liberal," or "bountiful." The duty of the rich involves meeting the needs of others beyond minimums, and that requires a generous, unselfish heart. Believers are to act toward others with the same generous love that moved God to act so richly toward them. Like the Macedonians commended by Paul in 2 Corinthians 8:1–4, they must give sacrificially from an open and unrestrained heart.

Such an attitude of generous giving is illustrated by the people of Israel. First Chronicles 29:1–17 records the story of their liberal giving to prepare for the building of Solomon's temple:

> Then King David said to the entire assembly, "My son Solomon, whom alone God has chosen, is still young and inexperienced and the work

is great; for the temple is not for man, but for the Lord God. Now with all my ability I have provided for the house of my God the gold for the things of gold, and the silver for the things of silver, and the bronze for the things of bronze, the iron for the things of iron, and wood for the things of wood, onyx stones and inlaid stones, stones of antimony, and stones of various colors, and all kinds of precious stones, and alabaster in abundance. And moreover, in my delight in the house of my God, the treasure I have of gold and silver, I give to the house of my God, over and above all that I have already provided for the holy temple, namely, 3,000 talents of gold, of the gold of Ophir, and 7,000 talents of refined silver, to overlay the walls of the buildings; of gold for the things of gold, and of silver for the things of silver, that is, for all the work done by the craftsmen. Who then is willing to consecrate himself this day to the Lord?" Then the rulers of the fathers' households, and the princes of the tribes of Israel, and the commanders of thousands and of hundreds, with the overseers over the king's work, offered willingly; and for the service for the house of God they gave 5,000 talents and 10,000 darics of gold, and 10,000 talents of silver, and 18,000 talents of brass, and 100,000 talents of iron. And whoever possessed precious stones gave them to the treasury of the house of the Lord, in care of Jehiel the Gershonite. Then the people rejoiced because they had offered so willingly, for they made their offering to the Lord with a whole heart, and King David also rejoiced greatly. So David blessed the Lord in the sight of all the assembly; and David said, "Blessed art Thou, O Lord God of Israel our father, forever and ever. Thine, O Lord, is the greatness and the power and the glory and the victory and the majesty, indeed everything that is in the heavens and the earth; Thine is the dominion, O Lord, and Thou dost exalt Thyself as head over all. Both riches and honor come from Thee, and Thou dost rule over all, and in Thy hand is power and might; and it lies in Thy hand to make great, and to strengthen everyone. Now therefore, our God, we thank Thee, and praise Thy glorious name. But who am I and who are my people that we should be able to offer as generously as this? For all things come from Thee, and from Thy hand we have given Thee. For we are sojourners before Thee, and tenants, as all our fathers were; our days on the earth are like a shadow, and there is no hope. O Lord our God, all this abundance that we have provided to build Thee a house for Thy holy name, it is from Thy hand, and all is Thine. Since I know, O my God, that Thou triest the heart and delightest in uprightness, I, in the integrity of my heart, have willingly offered all these things; so now with joy I have seen Thy people, who are present here, make their offerings willingly to Thee."

The final phrase states that the duty of the rich is to be **ready to share.** *Koinōnikos* (**ready to share**) derives from the common New Testament word for fellowship, *koinōnia,* and means "beneficent." Giving to others is not to be done in a cold, detached manner. Rather, there must be mutual care and concern arising from the common life believers share.

The Development to Consider

storing up for themselves the treasure of a good foundation for the future, so that they may take hold of that which is life indeed. (6:19)

Paul urges the rich to consider the end result of properly handling treasure. By sharing their earthly treasures with others, they are **storing up for themselves the treasure of a good foundation for the future.** *Apothēsaurizō* (**storing up**) could be translated "amassing a treasure," while *themelios* (**foundation**) can refer to a fund. The rich are not to be concerned with getting a return on their investment in this life. Those who lay up treasure in heaven will be content to wait to receive their dividends in the **future** when they reach heaven.

Those who invest in eternity show that they have taken **hold of that which is life indeed.** Real life, **life indeed,** is eternal life. Believers must live their lives in light of eternity. That is why the Lord Jesus Christ said in Luke 16:9, "Make friends for yourselves by means of the mammon of unrighteousness; that when it fails, they may receive you into the eternal dwellings." Christians should invest their money in the souls of men and women, who will be there to greet them and thank them when they arrive in heaven.

Handling Truth

26

O Timothy, guard what has been entrusted to you, avoiding worldly and empty chatter and the opposing arguments of what is falsely called "knowledge"—which some have professed and thus gone astray from the faith. Grace be with you. (6:20–21)

In 1 Timothy 3:15, Paul describes the church as "the pillar and support of the truth." Throughout history the true church has clung to the truth amid the swirling storms of persecution from without, and the insidious attacks of false teaching from within. Countless thousands of martyrs have paid the ultimate price rather than abandon or compromise the precious truth of God's Word. The church today has received that legacy of truth from those who have gone before. It is our responsibility to guard the truth, proclaim it, and hand it down unadulterated to those who will come after us.

That is a formidable challenge in our day. The cynical despair of Pilate, who demanded, "What is truth?" (John 18:38) permeates our culture. Dr. Mark M. Hanna notes that

> we are facing the following pernicious but widely held assumptions today:

> (1) It is doubtful that there is such a thing as truth; but if there is, it cannot be known.
>
> (2) If there is such a thing as truth, it is very unlikely that there is any *religious* truth. (*Crucial Questions in Apologetics* [Grand Rapids: Baker, 1981], 21; italics in original)

Unfortunately, it is a challenge the church today is often ill-prepared to meet. Called to be salt and light in the world, the church instead readily compromises with it. Secular psychology, based on pagan views of man, and an atheistic view of origins (evolution) are warmly embraced by many calling themselves evangelical Christians. They then proceed to reinterpret Scripture to accommodate those antibiblical views. Pragmatism is in; commitment to biblical truth is denigrated as poor marketing strategy. (For a further discussion of those points, see my book *Ashamed of the Gospel* [Wheaton, Ill.: Crossway, 1993].)

The most important yardstick by which a church can be measured is not how large it is, how good its fellowship is, or how interesting the pastor is. It is not how good the music is, how well the grounds are kept up, or how respected it is in the community. The most important measure of any church is how it handles the Word of God. Whether or not they teach and live out divine truth is the key issue, because the church's responsibility before God is to guard and proclaim the truths of Scripture. Consequently, the most severe crime against God is to mishandle His revelation, thus portraying a false, idolatrous image of Him to the world.

Scripture *must* be treated with reverence and care because it is the self-revelation of God. The psalmist writes, "Thou hast magnified Thy word according to all Thy name" (Ps. 138:2). Psalm 119:161 adds, "My heart stands in awe of Thy words," while in Isaiah 66:2 God declares, "To this one I will look, to him who is humble and contrite of spirit, and who trembles at My word." To fail to take God's Word seriously, whether by careless interpretation or by careless living, is to fail to take God Himself seriously. And if the church fails to take God seriously, why should the world?

Scripture is replete with warnings against perverting God's Word, as well as exhortations to guard it. Deuteronomy 4:2 cautions, "You shall not add to the word which I am commanding you, nor take away from it, that you may keep the commandments of the Lord your God which I command you"—a warning echoed by the apostle John in Revelation 22:18–19:

> I testify to everyone who hears the words of the prophecy of this book: if anyone adds to them, God shall add to him the plagues which are

> written in this book; and if anyone takes away from the words of the book of this prophecy, God shall take away his part from the tree of life and from the holy city, which are written in this book.

Paul, defending his ministry to the Corinthians, wrote, "We are not like many, peddling the word of God, but as from sincerity, but as from God, we speak in Christ in the sight of God" (2 Cor. 2:17). The apostle distanced himself from those hucksters who twisted Scripture to their own evil ends. Jude appealed to his readers to "contend earnestly for the faith which was once for all delivered to the saints" (Jude 3), while Paul exhorted his beloved son in the faith Timothy to "retain the standard of sound words which you have heard from me, in the faith and love which are in Christ Jesus. Guard, through the Holy Spirit who dwells in us, the treasure which has been entrusted to you" (2 Tim. 1:13–14).

Like today's church, the believers in first-century Ephesus also faced the temptation to compromise the truth of God's Word. Ephesus was a fervently pagan city, site of the temple of the goddess Diana (Artemis), one of the Seven Wonders of the Ancient World. Having ministered there himself for three years (Acts 20:31), Paul was well aware of the pressures and temptations to compromise or abandon the truth facing the Ephesian church. Not surprisingly, then, his two letters to their pastor (Timothy) are filled with exhortations to live, proclaim, and guard the truth. Indeed, those exhortations form a fitting summary of the two epistles:

> As I urged you upon my departure for Macedonia, remain on at Ephesus, in order that you may instruct certain men not to teach strange doctrines, nor to pay attention to myths and endless genealogies, which give rise to mere speculation rather than furthering the administration of God which is by faith. But the goal of our instruction is love from a pure heart and a good conscience and a sincere faith. For some men, straying from these things, have turned aside to fruitless discussion, wanting to be teachers of the Law, even though they do not understand either what they are saying or the matters about which they make confident assertions. (1 Tim. 1:3–7)
>
> This command I entrust to you, Timothy, my son, in accordance with the prophecies previously made concerning you, that by them you may fight the good fight, keeping faith and a good conscience, which some have rejected and suffered shipwreck in regard to their faith. (1:18–19)
>
> An overseer, then, must be . . . able to teach. (3:2)
>
> But the Spirit explicitly says that in later times some will fall away from the faith, paying attention to deceitful spirits and doctrines of demons, by means of the hypocrisy of liars seared in their own conscience as

with a branding iron, men who forbid marriage and advocate abstaining from foods, which God has created to be gratefully shared in by those who believe and know the truth. For everything created by God is good, and nothing is to be rejected, if it is received with gratitude; for it is sanctified by means of the word of God and prayer. In pointing out these things to the brethren, you will be a good servant of Christ Jesus, constantly nourished on the words of the faith and of the sound doctrine which you have been following. But have nothing to do with worldly fables fit only for old women. On the other hand, discipline yourself for the purpose of godliness. (4:1–7)

Until I come, give attention to the public reading of Scripture, to exhortation and teaching. (4:13)

Pay close attention to yourself and to your teaching; persevere in these things; for as you do this you will insure salvation both for yourself and for those who hear you. (4:16)

Let the elders who rule well be considered worthy of double honor, especially those who work hard at preaching and teaching. (5:17)

Teach and preach these principles. If anyone advocates a different doctrine, and does not agree with sound words, those of our Lord Jesus Christ, and with the doctrine conforming to godliness, he is conceited and understands nothing; but he has a morbid interest in controversial questions and disputes about words, out of which arise envy, strife, abusive language, evil suspicions, and constant friction between men of depraved mind and deprived of the truth, who suppose that godliness is a means of gain. (6:2b–5)

Fight the good fight of faith; take hold of the eternal life to which you were called, and you made the good confession in the presence of many witnesses. I charge you in the presence of God, who gives life to all things, and of Christ Jesus, who testified the good confession before Pontius Pilate, that you keep the commandment without stain or reproach until the appearing of our Lord Jesus Christ. (6:12–14)

Retain the standard of sound words which you have heard from me, in the faith and love which are in Christ Jesus. Guard, through the Holy Spirit who dwells in us, the treasure which has been entrusted to you. (2 Tim. 1:13–14)

The things which you have heard from me in the presence of many witnesses, these entrust to faithful men, who will be able to teach others also. (2:2)

Be diligent to present yourself approved to God as a workman who does not need to be ashamed, handling accurately the word of truth. But avoid worldly and empty chatter, for it will lead to further ungodliness. (2:15–16)

> Evil men and impostors will proceed from bad to worse, deceiving and being deceived. You, however, continue in the things you have learned and become convinced of, knowing from whom you have learned them; and that from childhood you have known the sacred writings which are able to give you the wisdom that leads to salvation through faith which is in Christ Jesus. All Scripture is inspired by God and profitable for teaching, for reproof, for correction, for training in righteousness; that the man of God may be adequate, equipped for every good work. (3:13–17)
>
> I solemnly charge you in the presence of God and of Christ Jesus, who is to judge the living and the dead, and by His appearing and His kingdom: preach the word; be ready in season and out of season; reprove, rebuke, exhort, with great patience and instruction. For the time will come when they will not endure sound doctrine; but wanting to have their ears tickled, they will accumulate for themselves teachers in accordance to their own desires; and will turn away their ears from the truth, and will turn aside to myths. But you, be sober in all things, endure hardship, do the work of an evangelist, fulfill your ministry. For I am already being poured out as a drink offering, and the time of my departure has come. I have fought the good fight, I have finished the course, I have kept the faith. (4:1–7)

The noble apostle's triumphant epitaph (2 Tim. 4:7) expresses the very heart of the ministry. Despite all the opposition and persecution he endured, Paul successfully guarded the truth entrusted him until the end of his life. And by his teaching and example he bids all Christians to do likewise.

As in his charge to the rich (1 Tim. 6:17–19), Paul gives Timothy three principles about handling truth: a duty to fulfill, a danger to avoid, and a development to consider.

The Duty to Fulfill

O Timothy, guard what has been entrusted to you, (6:20a)

O reflects Paul's emotional appeal to his beloved son in the faith. **Timothy** means "one who honors God," and the apostle calls upon him to live up to his name. **Guard** is from *phulassō,* a word used of keeping valuables in a safe place. **What has been entrusted to you** translates one word in the Greek, *parathēkē,* which means "deposit." The deposit Timothy was to guard is the truth. J. N. D. Kelly writes,

> The suggestion is that the Christian message . . . is not something which the church's minister works out for himself or is entitled to add to; it is a divine revelation which has been committed to his care, and which it is his bounden duty to pass on unimpaired to others. (*The Pastoral Epistles* [Peabody, Mass.: Hendrickson, 1987], 150)

Paul told the Thessalonians, "For our exhortation does not come from error or impurity or by way of deceit; but just as we have been approved by God to be entrusted with the gospel, so we speak, not as pleasing men but God, who examines our hearts" (1 Thess. 2:3–4). To the Corinthians he wrote, "Let a man regard us in this manner, as servants of Christ, and stewards of the mysteries of God" (1 Cor. 4:1). Every Christian, especially those in the ministry, has that sacred trust to guard.

The Danger to Avoid

avoiding worldly and empty chatter and the opposing arguments of what is falsely called "knowledge" (6:20b)

Ektrepō (**avoiding**) means "to turn away from." False doctrine must be avoided like the deadly plague it is. **Worldly** translates *bebēlos,* a word that originally referred to everything outside the sacred grounds of a Greek temple. It describes what is outside the realm of truth, and hence unholy and profane. Such **empty chatter** consists of useless, vain arguments that lead only to ungodliness (2 Tim. 2:16).

Opposing translates *antithesis,* a technical term used in rhetoric for a counter proposition in a debate. Timothy was to avoid the pseudo-intellectual **arguments** of those who merely wanted to attack Scripture. Such talk "will spread like gangrene" (2 Tim. 2:17).

The Development to Consider

which some have professed and thus gone astray from the faith. (6:21)

The danger of false teaching is obvious. Some **have professed** it **and thus gone astray from the faith.** The development to consider is apostasy, the abandoning of the truth which, sadly, is so common. Peter warns of false teachers who fall to the danger of error and lead many astray:

> But false prophets also arose among the people, just as there will also be false teachers among you, who will secretly introduce destructive heresies, even denying the Master who bought them, bringing swift destruction upon themselves. And many will follow their sensuality, and because of them the way of the truth will be maligned. (2 Peter 2:1–2)

Paul pleads with Timothy not to become like false teachers, but to guard the deposit of truth he had been entrusted to protect. What is involved in such protection? How can the treasure of truth be guarded?

First, by believing the Word of God. In John 5:24, Jesus said, "Truly, truly, I say to you, he who hears My word, and believes Him who sent Me, has eternal life, and does not come into judgment, but has passed out of death into life." John wrote in his first epistle, "I have written to you, fathers, because you know Him who has been from the beginning. I have written to you, young men, because you are strong, and the word of God abides in you, and you have overcome the evil one" (1 John 2:14).

Second, by honoring the Word. Job said, "I have not departed from the command of His lips; I have treasured the words of His mouth more than my necessary food" (Job 23:12).

Third, by loving the Word. In Psalm 119:97, the psalmist professes, "O how I love Thy law! It is my meditation all the day."

Fourth, by obeying the Word. In John 8:31, Jesus said to those who had professed belief in Him, "If you abide in My word, then you are truly disciples of Mine."

Fifth, by proclaiming the Word. Paul charged Timothy to "preach the word; be ready in season and out of season; reprove, rebuke, exhort, with great patience and instruction" (2 Tim. 4:2).

Sixth, by defending the Word. Jude 3 reads, "Beloved, while I was making every effort to write you about our common salvation, I felt the necessity to write to you appealing that you contend earnestly for the faith which was once for all delivered to the saints."

Seventh, by studying the Word. Paul commanded Timothy, "Be diligent to present yourself approved to God as a workman who does not need to be ashamed, handling accurately the word of truth" (2 Tim. 2:15).

Paul's closing salutation, **Grace be with you** (plural), goes beyond Timothy to embrace the entire congregation at Ephesus. All Christians are responsible to preserve and pass on to the next generation the precious heritage of truth they have received.

Bibliography

Barclay, William. *The Letters to Timothy, Titus and Philemon.* Philadelphia: Westminster, 1977.

Carson, D. A., Douglas J. Moo, and Leon Morris. *An Introduction to the New Testament.* Grand Rapids: Zondervan, 1992.

Dana, H. E., and Julius R. Mantey. *A Manual Grammar of the Greek New Testament.* Toronto: Macmillan, 1957.

Fairbairn, Patrick. *Pastoral Epistles.* Minneapolis: James & Klock, 1976.

Fee, Gordon D. *New International Biblical Commentary: 1 and 2 Timothy, Titus.* Peabody, Mass.: Hendrickson, 1988.

Gundry, Robert H. *A Survey of the New Testament.* Grand Rapids: Zondervan, 1970.

Guthrie Donald. *New Testament Introduction.* Downers Grove, Ill.: Inter-Varsity, 1990.

______. *The Pastoral Epistles.* Grand Rapids: Eerdmans, 1990.

Hendriksen, William. *New Testament Commentary: Exposition of the Pastoral Epistles.* Grand Rapids: Baker, 1981.

Hiebert, D. Edmond. *The Pauline Epistles*. Vol. 2 of *An Introduction to the New Testament.* Chicago: Moody, 1981.

———. *First Timothy.* Chicago: Moody, 1957.

Kelly, J. N. D. *The Pastoral Epistles*. Peabody, Mass.: Hendrickson, 1987.

Kent, Homer A., Jr., *The Pastoral Epistles*. Rev. ed. Winona Lake, Ind.: BMH, 1982.

Lenski, R. C. H. *The Interpretation of St. Paul's Epistles to the Colossians, to the Thessalonians, to Timothy, to Titus, and to Philemon.* Minneapolis: Augsburg, 1964.

Longenecker, R. N. "Paul, The Apostle." In Merrill C. Tenney, ed., *Zondervan Pictorial Encyclopedia of the Bible*, vol. 4. Grand Rapids: Zondervan, 1977.

Plummer, Alfred. *The Pastoral Epistles*. In W. Robertson Nicoll, ed., *The Expositor's Bible*. New York: A. C. Armstrong & Son, 1903.

Rienecker, Fritz, and Cleon L. Rodgers, Jr. *A Linguistic Key to the Greek New Testament.* Grand Rapids: Zondervan, 1982.

Robertson, A. T. *The Epistles of Paul.* Vol. 4 of *Word Pictures in the New Testament.* Nashville: Broadman, 1931.

Thayer, Joseph Henry. *Greek-English Lexicon of the New Testament.* Grand Rapids: Zondervan, 1970.

Trench, Richard C. *Synonyms of the New Testament.* Grand Rapids: Eerdmans, 1983.

Turner, Nigel. *Style.* Vol. 4 of James Hope Moulton, ed., *A Grammar of New Testament Greek.* Edinburgh: T. & T. Clark, 1980.

Vincent, Marvin R. *Word Studies in the New Testament*. Vol. 4. Grand Rapids: Eerdmans, 1946.

Wilson, Geoffery B. *The Pastoral Epistles*. Edinburgh: Banner of Truth, 1982.

Wuest, Kenneth S. *The Pastoral Epistles in the Greek New Testament.* Vol. 2 of *Word Studies from the Greek New Testament.* Grand Rapids: Eerdmans, 1978.

Indexes

Index of Greek Words

Index of Scripture

Index of Subjects

SINCE 1894, Moody Publishers has been dedicated to equip and motivate people to advance the cause of Christ by publishing evangelical Christian literature and other media for all ages, around the world. Because we are a ministry of the Moody Bible Institute of Chicago, a portion of the proceeds from the sale of this book go to train the next generation of Christian leaders.

If we may serve you in any way in your spiritual journey toward understanding Christ and the Christian life, please contact us at www.moodypublishers.com.

"All Scripture is God-breathed and is useful for teaching, rebuking, correcting and training in righteousness, so that the man of God may be thoroughly equipped for every good work."

—2 TIMOTHY 3:16, 17

THE NAME YOU CAN TRUST®